WITHDRAWN

NATIONALISM
AND THE
BREAKUP
OF AN EMPIRE

NATIONALISM AND THE BREAKUP OF AN EMPIRE

Russia and Its Periphery

Edited by
MIRON REZUN

PRAEGER

Westport, Connecticut
London

Library of Congress Cataloging-in-Publication Data

Nationalism and the breakup of an empire : Russia and its periphery /
   edited by Miron Rezun.
         p.   cm.
   Includes bibliographical references and index.
   ISBN 0-275-94320-8 (alk. paper)
      1. Soviet Union—Ethnic relations.   2. Minorities—Soviet Union.
   3. Nationalism—Soviet Union.   I. Rezun, Miron.
   DK33.I48   1992
   305.8'00947—dc20   92-4219

British Library Cataloguing in Publication Data is available.

Library of Congress Catalog Card Number: 92-4219
ISBN: 0-275-94320-8

First published in 1992

Praeger Publishers, 88 Post Road West, Westport, CT 06881
An imprint of Greenwood Publishing Group, Inc.

Printed in the United States of America

The paper used in this book complies with the
Permanent Paper Standard issued by the National
Information Standards Organization (Z39.48-1984).

10 9 8 7 6 5 4 3 2 1

For Simon and Anaïs

Contents

Preface

Nineteen ninety-two opened with the most astounding event in recent history. The Soviet state was officially dead, and 74 years of its history came to a close. Each of the 15 former Soviet republics had either declared or obtained their independence. It was a sad Soviet President Mikhail Gorbachev who agreed to transfer to the Russian federation a number of key agencies, including the State Bank (the country's central bank) and the Kremlin (federal government) itself. Other Soviet central agencies, such as the highly centralized Soviet economic and trade ministries, were being abolished. The empire had crumbled. All the republics were planning to move swiftly to a market economy.

The theme of this book portrays the long struggle of this empire with its seat of government at the Center, and analyzes both the disintegration of that Center and the collapse of its periphery.

Readers will be happy to learn that the chapters in this volume are based on sources in Russian, Latvian, Ukrainian, Georgian, Azeri, Uzbek, Turkish, and Chinese, not to mention French, German, and English. This testifies to the need for scholarly collaboration in a work of this scope. I wish to thank all the contributors to this volume for their excellent efforts and patience. I also wish to thank Wendy Boone and Angela Williams for their assistance with both the copyediting and the typing, and I am wholeheartedly indebted to the Canadian Social Sciences and Humanities Research Council (SSHRC) and to the Canadian Institute for International Peace and Security (CIIPS) for their support in subsidizing this project.

Finally, I wish to thank both colleagues and friends for their unstinting encouragement during the months it took to bring all the chapters together, making sure that the materials presented here have kept pace with the events that have shaken the Union of Soviet Socialist Republics. I am particularly indebted to historian Anthony Rhinelander of

St. Thomas University for the many hours of debating the future of Russia. I sincerely hope that this effort has been worthwhile and that the readers-- laypersons, students, academic experts, policy analysts, and others--will find our undertaking to be a worthwhile commentary on a transitional period of Russian and Soviet history.

Introduction

There was nothing new in prognosticating the collapse of the Soviet Empire. Soviet dissident Andrei Amalrik once wrote a pamphlet called *Will the Soviet Union Survive until 1984?* (1970). The prolific French Sovietologist Hélène Carrère d'Encausse had been one of the first experts to raise the same question in her *Empire Eclaté*, which came to English readers in 1979 as *The Decline of an Empire*.

Now, however, whatever remains of the former Soviet polity is going through its most difficult transition ever. Another critical *smutnoe vremya* (Time of Troubles) is in store for Russia. This time the changes will be so momentous as to have a lasting impact not only on the many non-Russians in the territory of the former USSR but on the rest of the world as well. It is clearly difficult to predict the implications of the disintegration of this once mighty polity. That will be left to the authors who have collaborated with me in this book. No doubt because of the stockpiles of Soviet nuclear weapons, what was once the Soviet Union will continue to be a superpower with a military capability second only to that of the United States.

In the last few years, we have witnessed an attempted coup by the Soviet military, an overwhelming referendum supporting independence in the Ukraine, Mikhail Gorbachev's struggles to form a new union, and continuous civil war on the periphery. At one point the Slavic core of this federation disengaged itself from the Center and formed a new commonwealth, binding Byelorussia, Russia, and the Ukraine economically and militarily, while retaining the independence of each nation. Then the Central Asian and Caucasian peripheries joined this Slavic core to form the Commonwealth of Independent States--*Sodruzhestvo Nezavisimykh Gosudarstv* (SNG). While this general crisis slouches toward some economic and political solution, which hopefully will come about sometime in our generation, people worldwide will hold their breath.

From the point of view of the Russian Center, however, the crisis is still involves the issue of imperialism: the decline and fall of the old empire, the undoing of the *Pax Russica* (Russian-imposed peace), and the derangement of the Russian imperial consciousness. From the viewpoint of the former nations and territories of the empire, the issue is one of nationalism.

Since Gorbachev launched his reform program under the rubric of *perestroika* (restructuring) and *glasnost'* (openness), the most dramatic changes taking place in the USSR have occurred in the area of ethnic and minority nationalism. The problem of the Soviet nationalities has become a central concern to all the nations of the world and to all minority and national groups, most especially those belonging to federal states.

Predictions of the denouement of this imperial-cum-nationalities problem range from a far-left picture of chaos, anarchy, and civil war to a far-right warning of harsh military dictatorship and ruthlessly centralized authoritarian rule. These are but the extremes. Each prediction also has a more moderate position. The moderate left sees what is left of the USSR in a state of overdue and irreversible imperial disintegration and no longer as a contemporary power; it predicts a former USSR broken up through more or less peaceful negotiation into several pieces, with the largest piece (for the moment) being Russia (and the rest of the Russian Soviet Federated Socialist Republic) together with Central Asia and left-bank Ukraine (Orthodox, Moscow-influenced); and the remaining pieces being Armenia, Georgia, Moldavia, and probably right-bank Ukraine (influenced by the Roman Catholic Church) and Byelorussia. Latvia, Estonia and Lithuania have completely gone their own way.

These pieces may be expected to flounder about in a sharply competitive and often hostile world, gradually coming into orbit around more or less compatible larger bodies (for example: a Baltic or Scandinavian union, the European Community, a new Eastern Economic union, and perhaps a pan-Slavic federation or an Asian-Turanian alliance).

The moderate right posits a restructuring of the former federal USSR into a confederation of more or less sovereign states, with a common currency and a unified defense, but with separate political and economic structures. This whole would be supervised benignly by Russians in Moscow or, in the case of a durable Slavic commonwealth, by a new Center in Minsk, which is basically a compromise location situated between Moscow and Kiev. Moderation requires peace, however, and nationalism produces a charged and volatile atmosphere.

An understanding of the historical background to the present imperial-national crisis is crucial to our attempt at predicting the future. A comprehensive history of Russian imperialism has yet to be written, either in the West or in Russia. Evgenii Anisimov, a historian at the Historical Institute of the St. Petersburg Academy, recently argued that Russian national consciousness and Russian imperial consciousness have been one and the same from the time of Peter the Great.

The Communists inherited not only the Russian Empire but also many old tsarist attitudes about that empire. One such attitude was a refusal to recognize the legitimacy of nationalism among non-Russians. Before 1917, non-Russians were treated paternalistically; the time-worn method of ruling their affairs was to co-opt the elite members of native societies into the imperial service. The more civilized the society, the easier it was to employ its citizens' services in furthering Russian civilization. After 1917, Soviet leaders (even, ironically, the non-Russian Joseph Stalin) also practiced co-optation in a Russian-centered world. Non-Russian languages and nationalisms were slated to disappear since they were unnecessary, peripheral, and irrational.

However, the non-Russian languages did not disappear, neither before 1917 nor after. The program of reform instituted by the Russian leadership in the period from 1905 to 1915, which involved decentralizing political and economic decision making, unleashed the latent nationalism of many of the non-Russians. The fact that Finland and the Baltic and Caucasian states declared independence in 1918 was hardly fortuitous. Those rapidly modernizing societies had been simultaneously developing their sense of national identity.

The program of reform instituted by the Russian leadership in the period 1985-1990 also aimed at decentralizing political and economic decision making. Similarly, it encouraged regional, political, and economic power and consequently unleashed pent-up nationalism in the non-Russian regions. After 1988, the threat of secession suddenly became real. All the Supreme Soviets of the Union Republics (the Supreme Soviet was the basis for republican government) have, in this period, adopted declarations of sovereignty, claiming property rights to all natural resources. There were also declarations of sovereignty proclaiming the supremacy of republican legislation over All-Union legislation. At long last, all the republics unilaterally declared themselves independent, with Lithuania leading the way in March 1990. Latvia, Estonia, Armenia, Georgia, and Moldavia soon followed suit. Azerbaijan also called for independence when Baku was sealed off by Azeri nationalists during the confrontation with Armenia. The Russian Federation itself threatened to leave the Union in its declaration of sovereignty in June 1990. However, not all Russians or Russian political groups effectively feel this way. Many are committed to keeping the empire intact, or at least to creating a new federalist structure with Russia at the center.

Gorbachev, like Prime Minister Peter Stolypin before him, was naive in imagining that the old system could simply be made more efficient by tinkering at the top. *Perestroika* (restructuring) and *glasnost'* (openness) have opened a Pandora's box of nationalist aspirations. The Russian President Boris Yeltsin is equally naive if he forgets that the Russian Soviet

Federated Socialist Republic (RSFSR) is but another empire within the former empire. Russia cannot be made more efficient or more democratic without stirring up long-quiescent nationalisms.

As each contributor points out, the issue of nationalism has per-vaded--indeed saturated--the politics of the entire country. What is required to demonstrate this critical modern phenomenon is an in-depth investiga-tion that combines both topical and territorial factors. We begin with an investigation of the impact of nationalism at the Center, in terms of ideology, defense, and the Russian national consciousness. We proceed to an analysis of the growth of nationalism in regional politics in the Baltics, Ukraine, Caucasia, and Central Asia. Finally, we conclude with discussions of the international ramifications of the problem regarding China, Western responsiveness, and, something quite unique, with Canadian parallels.

On this last note, most of the contributors to this volume either have or have had some institutional affiliation with Canada. Canadians are themselves experiencing severe ethnic, national, and constitutional problems and are especially sensitive to the issues of central control, federal and confederal unions, and of course separatism. The current Canadian national issue involves the rights of French, English, and abor-iginal peoples within the Canadian federation.Like the Soviet Union, the Canadian federal entity has come to a critical crossroads in its history.

We hope the discussion proves useful to students and scholars wishing to gain a clearer perspective on the imperial-national crisis that has destroyed the USSR and may be threatening the stability of Europe and the world.

Part 1

THE CENTER

What do we mean when we say "the Center" in Soviet politics?

The Center of the Soviet state and of the Tsarist Empire has always been Russia, or the Russian Republic. The Soviet state was essentially a Russian state, and the words "*Soviet*" and "*Russia*" have been used interchangeably. When we speak of the disintegration of the empire, the implication is that many of the non-Russian peoples in the other constituent republics are demanding not just autonomy or sovereignty within a larger Russian state but full independence. Russia occupies more than 80 percent of the state's total area and is the home of the Russian Orthodox faith.

Russian nationalism has been an important force in Soviet politics since the October Revolution of 1917. Vladimir Lenin, the founder of the Soviet state, believed that Russian nationalism had to be suppressed in order to secure the cooperation of non-Russians in the building of socialism. However, his successor, Joseph Stalin, took the opposite view: He believed that the nationalisms of the other non-Russian Soviet minorities must be suppressed, and Stalinist Russia was to engage in a vigorous Russification program for all non-Russian republics. By the 1930s, Stalin had begun to institutionalize a nationalities policy that was based on national assimilation. Officially, only Russian nationalism was allowed to survive.

Traditionally, ethnic Russians did not have a republican party organization and were represented by All-Union delegates, thus cementing their leading role in Soviet politics. Russian nationalism began to build in strength during the mid-1960s. It was, and still is, a nationalism concerned with the spiritual well-being and physical survival of Russian people as a distinct ethnic group. Today there are over 100 political parties within the Russian Republic. With the election of Boris Yeltsin as the first popularly elected republican president in early 1991, the Russian Republic is at once the core of the Center and an independent political actor in its own right.

The politics of Yeltsin, which are liberal democratic, would extend autonomy to non-Russians within the RSFSR. Russian author Alexander Solzhenitsyn's conservative brand of Russian nationalism would include only the RSFSR, Ukraine, Byelorussia, and parts of Kazakhstan in a new Russian state. By and large, the Center as we knew it--the Central Soviet government, or at least strong elements within it--were opposed to a remaking of the USSR on a narrowly confederal basis. That would have amounted to nothing less than the USSR's breakup. One should not compare a Soviet confederation to, say, a Swiss confederation.

The Russian Orthodox church itself has begun to take an active role in the revival of Russian nationalism. The church has used society's need to seek out spiritual and moral roots to update its own policies. The rising crime rate, alcoholism, and low morale that characterize Russian society have led to the church reasserting its traditional role as Russia's conscience and moral center. Gorbachev himself realized the role that the church could play in helping to create a more stable environment for the government's reforms and he took steps to win the clergy over as allies.

The Soviet army, too, has constituted the epicenter of Russia and the Soviet state. Traditionally, the armed forces were meant to promote the "School of the [Soviet] Nation." The soldiers created by the Soviet system have, for the most part, been Russian or Russified. Over 95 percent of the top Soviet officers in the Red Army were Russians, including the supreme high command and its *stavka*, the general staff, the commands of theatres of military operations, and the ministry of defense. Russian was *lingua franca* in the armed forces. Although each military unit has been ethnically mixed, there is always a preponderance of ethnic Russians in the more important units. In recent years, there has been a renewed interest in imperial tsarist traditions within the army, just like in the Russian Orthodox church, both of which are anchored in Russian nationalism.

Thus, Russian nationalism and the Russian armed forces continue to play an important part in the life of what is still an empire, if a crippled one. The security apparatus consisting of the KGB (*Komitet Gosudarstvennoy Bezopasnosti*--the Committee for State Security) and the GRU (*Gosudarstvennoe Razveditel'skoe Upravlenie*--Military Intelligence) has been the first victim of the general disintegration of central decision-making. Fragmented, it has been absorbed by the respective republics.

Unemployment and homelessness is already a major problem for Russian officers and their families. The Balts do not want them. They are well-trained, have had access to weapons, and, by and large, the 3.4 million man army supports traditional, authoritarian values. Higher ranking officers and specialists will be encouraged to hire out their services to the armed forces of other nations or states on a mercenary basis. There were some 4,000 nuclear specialists in the Soviet military and some may have already gone to work for Iran.

The extreme right (Communist) wing in Russian politics watched with growing horror as Gorbachev liberalized the economy, lost control of Eastern Europe, and began to make concessions to the republics which clamored for outright independence. After the devastating defeat of Iraqi leader Saddam Hussein by a U.S.-led, multinational force in the Gulf War, the Russian military began to feel very uncomfortable. Gorbachev was on the verge of signing the U.S.-Soviet Strategic Arms Reduction Talks (START) Treaty, which was to severely cut the Soviet Union's nuclear arsenal. In an article appearing on 16 August 1991, in the armed forces newspaper *Krasnaya Zvezda* (Red Star), the armed forces were called on to take up arms in order to prevent the undermining of the Communist party and the splitting of the armed forces.

That same day, Alexander Yakovlev, Gorbachev's closest ally and advisor, resigned from his post on the Presidential Council in anticipation of his expulsion by the Communist party. In a news conference announcing his resignation, he warned that the Soviet Union's reform process was threatened by a Stalinist coup within the party leadership. His prophecy came true.

On 19 August 1991, Mikhail Gorbachev was forced into house arrest and a committee of eight calling itself the State Committee for the State of Emergency in the USSR declared itself the interim head of government. At the top of this organization was Gennady Yanayev, Gorbachev's vice-president, who became acting president. Other members of the committee were the most prominent and highest ranking politicians in the country: Vladimir Kryuchkov (head of the KGB), Dmitry Yazov (defense minister), Boris Pugo (interior minister), Valentin Pavlov (prime minister), Oleg Baklanov (first deputy chairman of Soviet Defense Councils), Vasily Starodubstev (chairman of the Soviet Farmer's Union), and Alexander Tizyakov (president of the Association of Transportation and Communications Enterprises). Between them, the eight men represented nearly every sector of Soviet society, and they claimed that they legitimately represented nearly every Soviet citizen. For a few days the committee wielded total power.

The right wing, which the committee seemed to represent, believed that the economy had not only deteriorated under Gorbachev, but that living standards had also plummeted. They could not accept the Union Treaty (a political and economic treaty which would bind the signatories in a federal union), for it was tantamount to the internal dissolution of the Soviet Union. In a news brief released on 20 August 1991, the committee stated that it was taking control of the Interior Ministry, the KGB, the Defense Ministry, law enforcement bodies, the armed forces, and the mass media. The eight putschists promised to continue the political and economic freedoms established by Gorbachev and to honor all his international treaties. They pledged to lower prices, raise wages and pensions, improve housing conditions, and restore stability. However, they censored all the newspapers in the country except for nine that were conservative and came under their direct control.

Armored vehicles soon took up positions in Moscow around the heavily barricaded Russian Federation Building. Fears quickly built up that the new government would order the arrest of Boris Yeltsin and that the entire episode would end in a bloodbath. Thousands of protesters took to the streets in Moscow and the occupied Baltic states, which were under the control of General Fyodor Kuzmin. In response, Yeltsin called for a general strike (in which only the coal miners participated) and mustered popular support by referring to the new rulers as criminals. Yeltsin also ordered all army and KGB units involved in the overthrow to withdraw their support and announced that he was assuming control of the territory of Russia--the Center.

Also on August 20, mutinies within the military began. Individual soldiers and entire units refused to take up their ordered positions. Local Russian police units of the Ministry of the Interior and the KGB professed loyalty to Yeltsin. The hard-liners, on the other hand, deployed tanks near the Russian Parliament and proceeded to impose an 11 p.m. to 5 a.m. curfew throughout all Russia. Meanwhile, Estonia declared full independence and the Patriarch of the Russian Orthodox church, Alexi II, demanded that Gorbachev be allowed to address the country. Yeltsin supporters fortified barricades in Moscow. President Nursultan Nazarbayev of the Republic of Kazakhstan also demanded to hear from Gorbachev. The Parliament of the Ukraine unilaterally declared that all orders made by the hard-liners were to be considered null and void on Ukrainian territory.

On August 21, it appeared that the coup had come to a halt and that the Communist party, which had not condemned it, had been irreversibly compromised. Gorbachev was formally reinstated and the Soviet military announced that it would withdraw from the Baltics. The KGB formally disassociated itself from Kryuchkov, who, as KGB chief, was one of the ringleaders. The coup was stillborn, the Soviet Ministry of Defense ordered all troops to withdraw from Moscow, and Yeltsin assumed control of the armed forces. At this point, some members of the group of eight flew to the Crimea to meet with Gorbachev. Committee member Boris Pugo committed suicide before he could be arrested.

On August 22, Yeltsin threatened to remove any official who had cooperated with the conspirators. He also ordered the dissolution of Communist cells in the armed forces on Russian territory and assumed control of all state property. At KGB headquarters in Moscow, demonstrators pulled down the statue of KGB founder Felix Dzerzhinsky. Latvia and Lithuania outlawed the Communist party on their soil. The Kazakh president quit the republican Politburo (collective leadership of the republican Communist Party), saying that it had supported the coup. He also prohibited the Party from maintaining groups in public organizations. The following week, Leonid Kravchuk, the president of the Ukraine, likewise quit the Communist party.

Gorbachev announced that he would not stand in the way of any republic that wished to secede. While Gorbachev's power and influence were obviously waning, Yeltsin asserted himself as the only viable alternative. After the failed coup, the armed forces were shaken up, with most of the 345 generals and half the 80,000 political officers being dismissed. The soldiers had their own grievances, which are primarily connected to the state of collapse of the civilian economy and the breakup of the country, which threatened the unity of the armed forces.

Why did the coup fail? There was always the temptation to say that the Soviet Union is "uncoupable." The dispersal of power from the Center to the republics and the breakdown of the state monopoly on communications left several independent power bases outside the Kremlin chain of command. The plotters themselves could not galvanize the population to take to the streets in protest, to march, or to strike. Moreover, the coup lacked three essential elements: assured support from the military; control of transportation, telecommunications, and electric power grids; and physical elimination of the resistance leaders.

1

Continuity within Soviet Nationality Policy: Prospects for Change in the Post-Soviet Era

KURT NESBY HANSEN

The contest between the Center and the periphery is a common theme throughout the history of Russia, both during its imperial past and during the Soviet era. The interplay between sources of political power held by the dominant Great Russians and by their Slavic and non-Slavic neighbors provides a clouded lens through which the future possibilities for the nationalities' relations may be viewed. Considering these trends, the most likely of the future possibilities for the region known lately as the USSR is a reassertion of central authority over a significant portion of the traditionally nonethnic Russian territory.

The experience of the Soviet nationalities' relations, despite--or perhaps because of--distortions imposed by Leninism and Stalinism provides the observer with the best indications of future trends. For this reason it is valuable to review the late-tsarist and Soviet historical records concerning the perpetually vexing nationalities' question.

Politics and government in tsarist Russia were the preserve of the elite; political control was exercised by employing state instruments of coercion. This situation was also true for the Soviet state, wherein the power monopoly was maintained by the Communist Party of the Soviet Union (CPSU) through its army, secret police, and bureaucracy. Thus, there was much continuity with the tsarist past in the Soviet era. This continuity was apparent in the pattern of parallels between the tsarist and Soviet states in the treatment of their subject minority nationalities.

The nationalities problems found today within the borders of the federal state lately known to us as the USSR are by no means a Soviet creation. Rather, they are an inheritance from the Tsarist Empire and have defined historical roots within the multiplicity of ethnic groups that have comprised the Russian state since the time of Kievan Rus (the first Russian state which existed between the 9th century and 1169) and that continue to the post-Soviet present. More specifically, many of the current problems are rooted in Russian chauvinism during the Soviet era, especially the imposition of partial genocides and forced migrations of minority nations under Stalin's rule. For the Soviet leaders, the nationalities problem was an ideological embarrassment.[1]

Most nations within the Tsarist Empire were subject to direct political rule from Moscow yet still possessed a certain amount of cultural and economic autonomy. The tsarist state was mostly concerned with obedience and national revenue. The Soviet state was also concerned with direct rule, political obedience, and revenue, but its constituent nations had considerably less real cultural, and little or no economic, autonomy. The difference between these two situations lay within the realm of ideology. The similarity between them may be attributed to the centralization of state power and the inviolability in their states' retention of conquered territories and nations. This ingathering of "Russian" lands has been a consistent aim of Russian rulers since the rise of Muscovy, and its historical power was not lost on Soviet leaders.

The nationalities problem has been the burning question in the USSR throughout its history. While governmental forms and leadership styles altered vastly from Stalin to Gorbachev, it is clear that there was no substantive alteration in the basic nationalities policies of the Soviet leadership.

LENINIST NORMS

There are two main factors to be considered here: nationalism and Soviet communism. Both are variable in form, content, and direction, and both interconnect with the human elements that give them life. To gain an understanding of the Soviet Communist outlook on the nationalities question, it is necessary to examine the source of their ideology--the Leninist norms established during and immediately after the October Revolution of 1917. An understanding of these norms regarding the treatment of Soviet ethnic minorities is essential to a proper understanding of the entire nationalities question within the Soviet era.

Lenin stated, "No Marxist . . . can deny that the interests of socialism must override the rights of nations to self-determination."[2] His core policy was the direct subordination of all constituent nations to the central government. Like the tsarist regime, Lenin considered that a unitary state was the best possible system of government for the development of stability. However, he saw that overt centralization would create immediate difficulties with the restive, newly independent nations of the former Tsarist Empire. As a temporary measure Lenin was prepared to accept the achievable compromise of pseudo-federalism as long as the right to self-determination by the proletariat retained absolute precedence over the right to self-determination by nations. This concept is fundamental to understanding that the right of secession included within each succeeding Soviet constitution was merely a tag-end slogan that was never intended to have legal effect.[3] The Leninist corollary of this policy was the subordination of minority nations to an internationalist and centralist political structure which was eventually to guide all constituent nations of the Soviet Union toward realizing the meta-ethnicity envisaged within Marx's dictum, "Working men have no country . . . [and] must [themselves] constitute the nation."[4]

While Lenin was an advocate of extreme centralization, which included the subordination of all formerly Russian lands to the Moscow government, he was committed to this integrationist program on purely ideological grounds--Great Russian chauvinism had little to do with it. Lenin's own formula on the national question--as opposed to the unitary state--provided for the establishment of a federation of constituent nations. His famous slogan, "national in form, socialist in content," was intended to guide all relations between Soviet nations. Lenin believed that the right of self-determination by nations "was no more than a brief moment of independence, leading rapidly to social revolution and . . . [the] reestablishment of a unitary, revolutionary, workers' state."[5]

STALINIST DISTORTIONS

Successive Soviet leaders from Stalin to Gorbachev have claimed allegiance to Lenin's ideological norms and repeatedly returned to them for support and legitimacy as they sought to impose various reform measures. Active application of the full range of Leninist norms was short-lived, however. With Stalin's accession to power, the integrationist aims of the Soviet state were altered to overt assimilation of minorities into a strongly Russified Soviet nation. The primary visible manifestations of this program were the isolation or suppression of minority national cultures and the raising of Great Russian culture to a position of unquestioned dominance throughout the USSR. Russia's personality was etched quite visibly on the entire Soviet Union.

This was most apparent under Stalin. Stalin was both an economic revolutionary and a political reactionary. He created an ultra-centralized, Russocentric, coercive, and bureaucratic party-state in which the minority nations were entirely subordinate. This political program was a reaction to the centrifugal forces of minority nationalism and a reimposition of autocratic modes of government to a degree more extreme than those found within tsarist Russia. Stalin viewed nationalism as a manifestation of bourgeois culture which must be eliminated for the good of proletarian internationalism.

Stalin and Lenin had confrontations regarding nationality policies and the former reluctantly agreed to the creation of a federal state. Stalin believed in the necessity of accelerating the historical process that would cause the constituent nations to draw together and eventually to fuse into a single Soviet people. Once he had achieved undisputed power, he directed his policies toward implementing this process. In this program, Great Russian culture became a paradigm to which the smaller, "backward" nations should aspire. Centralist policies allowed nations the continuation of "harmless folk traditions" while pressing forward a program of Russification through the educational, cultural, and political instruments controlled by the central government. Integral to this program were the Party and class purges and forced migrations of whole nations from their ancestral lands.[6]

The aim of Stalin's policies was the creation of the Russo-assimilated, new Soviet man: the "*homo sovieticus*," whose primary loyalties would go to the Soviet state and to the ethics of Marxist-Leninism. Though Lenin's internationalism and horror of Russian chauvinism led him to prefer "integration" over assimilation, in the creation of the new Soviet man, he and Stalin were in agreement. However, in the instrumentalities employed by Stalin to achieve his aim, Lenin's full agreement cannot be assumed.

AFTER STALINISM

The post-Stalin era has had a variety of approaches to the nationalities question. Under First Secretary Nikita Khrushchev, the Leninist goals and limited forms of Stalinist methods were continued. Khrushchev was a firm believer in the eventual fusion of Soviet peoples and in the efficacy of Russification as a means of accelerating this achievement. His emphasis on such matters in his improvised program of reform was one of the many instabilities that led to his ouster in 1964 and the beginning of the period of Leonid Brezhnev's rule, which ended in economic stagnation. Khrushchev's tenure produced no lasting initiatives in the field of nationality relations.

Under Brezhnev, however, a substantial change in Soviet nationality practice took place. The minority elites' responses to Khrushchev's emphasis on accelerating the eventual fusion of the Soviet peoples were coupled with Brezhnev's early commitment to the "Leninist norms" of collective leadership to bring about a program of limited decentralization of power within the elite strata of the CPSU. Among these strata were the indigenous elites of the Union republics. Brezhnev distributed various portions of All-Union political and economic decision-making authority to these elites. In effect, he made them the semi-independent clients of the Moscow government. Within both the central government and the Union republic governments, programs for affirmative action or "positive discrimination" were set up to increase the representation of the minority nationalities within the highest levels of government.[7] These seemingly democratic and equitable programs combined with the glacial progress of central decision making to produce conditions that, in part, brought about the economic and political stagnation that were typical of the latter half of the Brezhnev era. A primary cause of this stagnation was the system of patronage inherent in the affirmative action programs which, in turn, led to the rise of regionally and/or ethnically based criminal networks that operated at the expense of the official economy.

GORBACHEV AND REFORM

As noted by Daniel Matuszewski, "Regime allegiances . . . remain at a high level as long as relative material prosperity is good and career mobility is available and attractive."[8] Unfortunately for the economic health of the USSR, the entrenched patronage system was antithetical to the maintenance of material prosperity--a fact that had become inescapable by the end of the Brezhnev era. The systemic dysfunctions within the Soviet economy and society were hopelessly intertwined with problems of economic stagnation, high-level corruption, and minority national elites.[9] Of necessity, the economic reform programs of President Gorbachev had to deal as well with the Soviets' burning question of how to deal with the minority nationalities.

Despite Gorbachev's pronouncements on *glasnost'*, *perestroika*, *demokratizatsia* (democratization), and *uskorenie* (acceleration) and the erratic, unplanned courses that these ideas followed, there can be little doubt about Gorbachev's quest for Leninist legitimacy. Nor, until the aftermath of the failed coup in August 1991, could there be an alternative for Gorbachev. For such a man, raised and schooled in the Stalinist and immediate post-Stalinist eras, the power of Lenin's authority and the ideals of Soviet communism are deeply ingrained. Gorbachev was a committed Soviet Communist until after the coup attempt. The Soviet Communist state was founded on Marxism-Leninism, and Gorbachev sought its reform and perpetuation. Gorbachev's agenda was thus to preserve Leninist ideology and use its norms to confirm the legitimacy of the present regime.[10]

However, the chief problem for Gorbachev and the former Soviet Union was, and still remains, one of economics. The need to improve economic indicators, to modernize all sectors of the economy, to redistribute investment into the consumer sector, and to stop the hemorrhage of the official economy into the endemic criminal second economy were the main drives within Gorbachev's reform program.[11]

It would be misleading to depict Gorbachev as having been anything other than a Communist reformer. His real goal did not lie in the transformation of the Soviet system into liberal-democratic, or capitalist, modes of organization. Rather, Gorbachev was anxious to make the existing system function rationally and efficiently, while preserving both Leninist democratic-centralism within a strongly centralized federal union and a Soviet socialist economy. The public relations campaigns that invariably accompanied *perestroika* and *glasnost'* distracted many Western observers from these very basic features of Gorbachev's program.

Although an ethnic Russian, Gorbachev can be regarded as the *homo sovieticus* that Lenin hoped would result from socialist education. A trained lawyer and Marxist-Leninist, Gorbachev's worldview evolved from the norms of socialist legality and internationalism. His approach to solving the problems that confronted the USSR was formulated along these lines. A minimization of inefficiency within the labor force, labor discipline, and a return to socialist puritanism formed the foci of Yuri Andropov's brief reform program (1982-1984) and became the first manifestations of Gorbachev's own reform efforts. To deal with criminality and economic diversion, Gorbachev relied on socialist legality and obedience to the central authorities. This second phase of Gorbachev's program was marked by alterations to the political power structures at the federal and Union Republic levels and brought him into direct confrontation with the national minority elites. The resurgence of minority nationalism within Soviet territory was thus, in part, a direct result of *perestroika* and *glasnost'*.

In order to combat the deleterious effects of patronage, rampant criminality, and the tyranny of a second economy within the Union Republics, Gorbachev conceived of removing republican leaders and replacing them with competent appointees from the center. One such replacement took place in Kazakhstan on 16 December 1986, when, after 25 years of patronage and corruption as first secretary, Dinmukhamed Kunaev was removed from power and replaced by the Russian Gennadii Kolbin. Kunaev, a native Kazakh, had established a regime marked by institutionalized inefficiency, nepotism, mismanagement, and crime on a grand scale. Kolbin, who was subsequently replaced by an ethnic Kazakh, was a rational, puritan, Communist technocrat appointed by Moscow in order to restore Soviet efficiency, power, and prestige and was a complete outsider to Kazakh politics.[12]

Kazakh public reaction to this imposition by Moscow immediately took a nationalist form as rioting, directed not in support of the corrupt Kunaev but against the installation of an ethnic Russian, swept Alma Ata on 17-18 December. Agitation against Kolbin's appointment seems to have originated from the corrupt cadres, who had everything to lose from his accession to power. It immediately found fertile ground among native Kazakhs, however, who resented and feared cultural envelopment and career truncation at the hands of the Russians. Thus, the needs of *perestroika* brought Kazakhstan's nationality problems to a flashpoint and, through the mechanism of *glasnost'*, allowed them to reverberate across the USSR, where a sympathetic audience was found among the nationalists of many other minority nations.

Situations in which nationalists and national elites co-opt each group to the other's aims became endemic throughout the USSR. The ramifications of the Alma Ata riots and unrealistic minority expectations of Gorbachev's reform program also led to a variety of nationalist expressions,[13] not least of which were the numerous referenda concerning questions of sovereignty or independence. Nations deported by Stalin once again demand to be returned to their ancestral lands. Territorial disputes and armed border clashes occur between Union republics. Of all such interethnic issues and disputes, the most public and most serious took place between the Armenians and the Azeris. The resultant deployment of Soviet troops to defuse the crisis was widely reported under *glasnost'* and provided further impetus to the centrifugal forces operating among the minority nations of the USSR.

The difficulty for the new leadership in the matter of minority nationalism had at least two diverging, albeit connected, themes. First, there was the matter of genuine nationalism, which has long been subject to repression by a central government that officially denied its existence. This undercurrent within Soviet society was sustained by nationalists' hopeful interpretations of Gorbachev's reforms and continues to be sustained by the newly recognized independence of the Baltic republics. Second, there was the self-serving identification by parochial elites with a genuine nationalist cause. Such elites, operating at or beyond the fringes of criminality, recognized that they have everything to lose from a strengthening of discipline and the maintenance of the federal Union.

These two themes have operated in tandem. The application of Soviet power for the elimination of inefficiency needed to eliminate criminality. The means employed to achieve this aim had the effect of threatening legitimate nationalist movements that have widespread support throughout many of the Union republics. This effect strengthened the position of the national elite, including its criminal elements. The constant interaction of aim, means, and effect accelerated the centrifugal forces that eventually destroyed the integrity of the Soviet state.

GORBACHEV'S NATIONALITIES POLICY

Gorbachev's record of policy development regarding the nationalities question was a reflection of the fluid situation within which he had to operate. Gorbachev saw his role in part as a leader in the "resolute struggle against national narrow-mindedness, nationalism, and chauvinism."[14] The Soviet leader faced what amounted to a widespread states' rights movement. Not all the nationalities sought the same ends, and Gorbachev carefully weighed his responses in order to keep to the middle ground: to maintain flexibility of response and avoid the alienation of his opponents and his supporters.

For every legislative move toward independence, the Soviet leadership provided a superficially constitutional countermove. Faced with nationalist grievances, Gorbachev repeatedly expressed sympathy for the principle of greater autonomy but also maintained that it must occur within the bounds of Soviet constitutionality. Confronted with declarations of independence by republican legislatures, he criticized their lack of popular support from referenda. Presented with pro-independence referenda, he declared them invalid under Soviet law. In this way Gorbachev maintained an outward semblance of legality and constitutional rule and sought to preserve a power base within the traditional centers of Soviet power: the CPSU, the KGB, and the armed forces.

As each active nationalist expression became evident, Gorbachev tailored his response to the particular situation. Moves by the Soviet central government were made in accordance with Gorbachev's evaluation of the severity of each situation and an appreciation for the amount of Western media attention likely to result. His economic blockade of Lithuania in 1990 offered an example of the nonmilitary responses available for pressuring nationalist groups. His overt military intervention in the Caucasus throughout 1988 to 1990 contrasted with his much less violent response (until January 1991) to provocations within the Baltic republics, indicating his measured tactics. Gorbachev pragmatically chose his responses to nationalist challenges, varying them from appropriate demonstrations of reformist restraint to centralist resolve. In doing so, Gorbachev was able to protect his constituency for *perestroika* within the minority nations, the institutions of Soviet state coercion, and the West.

For Gorbachev's program to succeed, the eventual cooperation of all of the aforementioned groups was necessary. His precarious balancing act led to obvious failures, such as the Karabakh dispute, wherein Gorbachev inadvertently transformed an Armenian revanchist threat to Azerbaijan into an anti-Soviet independence movement. There were also examples of successes emanating from Gorbachev's program, with an obvious case provided by popular agitation within the Tatar Autonomous Socialist Soviet Republic (ASSR) for full republican status within a refurbished Soviet federation.[15]

Gorbachev's program aimed for a renewed Soviet federation. Contrary to *Economist* writer John Parker's view of events within the Soviet Union, Gorbachev's record was not that of a liberal reformer but rather of a committed Communist, seeking to reform the Soviet socialist system and make it function efficiently.[16] To this end he made the drafting of a new Union Treaty his immediate priority and did everything possible to delay or deny moves toward independence by minority nations until an acceptable treaty could be prepared. As nationalist pressures grew, Gorbachev responded by drawing closer to the conservative elements within the Soviet Union and by making increasing use of the instruments of state coercion. These trends were apparent in the increasing presence of federal security forces in the streets of the USSR. From January 1989 until March 1991, troops were used to enforce 13 separate states of emergency.[17] This instrumental use of the security forces was reflected organizationally by Gorbachev's choice of conservative leaders from those forces to replace more liberal elements within the Presidential Council.[18] It is ironic that President Gorbachev, the dedicated Marxist-Leninist who sought to preserve and improve the Soviet system, facilitated the Communist coup through his choice of conservative leaders. The August 1991 coup destroyed both Soviet power and the CPSU and placed the Russian Federation firmly in control in the post-Soviet era.

CONCLUDING THE SOVIET ERA?

It is not hard to draw clear conclusions from the records of Stalin and Gorbachev. In essence, neither had a nationalities' policy *per se*. Much to the contrary, their policies regarding such matters were strongly antinational and were directed toward the development and maintenance of Soviet power within a highly centralized, pseudo-federal state. Stalin's policies were explicitly assimilationist and were enacted by means of overt coercion. President Gorbachev's policies were directed toward the same aim but were infinitely more liberal in nature and maintained a careful distance from Stalinist excess.

The results of Gorbachev's policies were made clear to the world during the Communist coup and in the weeks following its failure. Obviously, Gorbachev had pleased neither the Communist hardliners nor the national elites. The coup's failure brought with it the downfall of the instruments of state coercion, and the entire fabric of the USSR began to unravel. Daily declarations of sovereignty or independence by most of the Union republics pressed the federal structure to the brink of destruction. However, once at the brink, most nationalist leaders could see the economic collapse implicit in the complete destruction of the Union. Not all the leaders felt that they could chance such ruin by following the Baltic republics' path toward full economic and political independence. Practical considerations led these same leaders to negotiate seriously on alternative courses. During September 1991, ten republics agreed in principle to a new system of quasi-federalism. The other five republics agreed to consider taking some part in an as-yet undefined common market structure. While these forms and the numbers of their participants remain in a state of evolution, the Russian Republic, by virtue of the sheer size of its resource base, industrial capacity, and market could be assured of being the dominant actor in both these structures.

Despite these seemingly amicable arrangements, much--nearly everything--remains to be done to regularize the political and economic relations existing between the former Soviet republics. The old divisions of ethnicity within and between these republics have not faded away; if anything, they have become more sharply defined. These divisions will provide the backdrop against which all continuing and future negotiations must be conducted: a backdrop providing the dry tinder in which the sparks of interrepublican disputes may easily kindle flames.

YELTSIN'S NEW RUSSIA AND OLD ETHNIC PROBLEMS

Democracy and freedom have not yet arrived in Russia. Following the failed coup, there was a second--and this time successful--attempt to seize control of the Soviet central government. The second coup was led by none other than Boris Yeltsin, president of the Russian Federated Republic; it received little or no recognition in the West. While there is small doubt that most of the old Soviet executives were at least tainted by the coup and had to be removed from power, it is clear that the Russian president possessed no constitutional right to choose or dismiss their replacements. Nonetheless, this is exactly what transpired.

Bereft of any real power base, Soviet president Gorbachev was forced to acquiesce to direction received from the leader of one of his constituent republics. The Russian prime minister, Ivan Silaev, became Soviet prime minister, while the new KGB chief and the new defense minister were also ethnic Russians who were handpicked by Boris Yeltsin.[19] The fact of Russians occupying such high places came as no surprise to anyone; however, the concurrent fact that their appointments were made by the Russian president and merely confirmed by Gorbachev serves to underscore the redistribution of real political power likely to obtain within the USSR's successor state or in the post-Soviet republics.

Within the Russian Federation itself, the prospects for real democracy seem dim. Considering the necessarily low state of democratic political culture there, this is understandable. President Yeltsin's predilection for centralism is manifest in the governmental organization that he is creating. With a strong central administration in Moscow, he intends to rule the vast expanse of the federation by means of governors-general who will, at least in the first instance and then probably whenever it is deemed necessary, be appointed by Moscow.[20]

At the same time as this structural reform is being implemented, the only really organized political party--the Russian Communists--has been banned and its assets have been seized by the government. Although there is understandable rough justice in such moves, there is small evidence of democracy. Neither is democracy apparent in Yeltsin's dealings with his own constituent republics and autonomous regions. The Russian tricolor and double eagle have returned, bringing with them imperial ways of dealing with captive nations: Tatarstan is an object case.

In August 1990, the Parliament of the Tatar ASSR declared the republic's independence from the Russian Federation and then applied to become the newest full member of the Soviet Union. At that time, Boris Yeltsin publicly approved of these declarations. Then, however, he was at odds with a still powerful Soviet central government; as a consequence, he was walking softly and talking loudly about democracy. These situations have now been altered dramatically and Yeltsin is reasserting firm Russian central authority over the Communist-controlled Tatar ASSR. Tatarstan, with 43 percent of its population composed of ethnic Russians, is the first test of Russian ingathering instincts versus Russian democratic rhetoric, and democracy has not made a strong showing.[21]

This first case bodes poorly for peace between nationalities in the post-Soviet era in what, it seems, will be known as the Confederation of Independent States (CIS). There are 25 million Great Russians living outside the borders of the Russian Federation. In three former republics of the USSR (Kazakhstan, Latvia, and Estonia), Russians comprise approximately one-third of the population; in two more republics (Ukraine and Kirgizia), about one-quarter of the people are Russian; in another seven republics (not including Armenia), Russians make up from 13 percent down to as little as 6 percent of the population totals.[22] When the question of the ingathering of Russians and their lands arises--as it already has, the lands occupied by these Russian minorities, which are contiguous with the borders of the Russian Federation, become objects of bitter contention.

President Yeltsin has spoken openly about the question of border adjustments in the post-Soviet era. Considering that 20 of the 23 interrepublic boundaries are in dispute already, this question concerns the eventual disposition of large amounts of territory. No republic wants to cede territory to another, regardless of the ethnic origins of the population. No ethnic majority wants to abandon its kinspeople to foreign control. As long as questions concerning borders and national minorities can be asked between willing constituents of a federated state, they are less likely to be answered with outright violence. Although the Karabakh dispute provides a pointed case to the contrary, the fact remains that Moscow has, by means of the authoritative allocation of territory and by firm rule, largely contained widespread interethnic violence during the last 40 years of Soviet rule. The fall of Soviet power, the diminution of central authority, and the rise of Russian dominance severely threaten the continuation of the *Pax Sovieticus* into a *Pax Russica*.

THE ONCE AND FUTURE EMPIRE

The future holds a variety of real possibilities for friction between the constituent republics of the new CIS. Most of these revolve around the methods whereby issues inherited from the Soviet era can be settled. Foremost among the issues are the persistent problems of ethnicity and territory which, exacerbated by 70 years of Soviet-directed resettlement, comprise the current nationalities question. No matter what other question arises, it seems that the answer is divided along planes of cleavage that are firmly marked by nationality.

Solutions to the nationalities question are neither readily apparent nor, when formulated, easily administered. Almost any solution beyond a negotiated settlement is sure to involve bloodshed on a significant scale; solutions of this nature will not be accepted gladly by any of the republics. A workable alternative that is already in its formative stages is the preservation of some variety of federal center that will allow negotiation and can authoritatively police the resultant agreements. By virtue of its sheer size, its potential strength, and its actual strength in comparison to the other republics, the Russian Federation is the only practical candidate for such a role. Indeed, Russia is already well on the way to a new position of central power among the ruins of the Soviet Union. Its history is one of centralization, and current events have demonstrated renewed centralist tendencies. In all likelihood, the CIS will evolve into a Russian-dominated, quasi-federal state, kept together by the new versions of the old instruments of state coercion.

NOTES

1.   Bohdan Nahaylo, "Nationalities," in *The Soviet Union under Gorbachev*, ed. Martin McCauly (New York: St. Martin's Press, 1987), p. 86.

2.   Francoise Thom, *The Gorbachev Phenomenon--A History of Perestroika*, trans. Jenny Marshall (London: Printer, 1989), p. 87.

3.   Richard Pipes, *The Formation of the Soviet Union*, rev. ed., Russian Research Centre Studies no. 13, (Cambridge, MA: Harvard University Press, 1964), pp. 44-48, 276.

4.   Karl Marx and Friedrich Engels, *The Communist Manifesto*, trans. Samuel Moore, intro. A. J. P. Taylor (Harmondsworth, U.K.: Penguin, 1986), p. 102.

5.   Hélène Carrère d'Encausse, "Determinants and Parameters of Soviet Nationality Policy," in *Soviet Nationality Policies and Practices*, ed. Jeremy R. Azrael (New York: Praeger, 1978), p. 40.

6.   John B. Dunlop, *The Faces of Contemporary Russian Nationalism* (Princeton, NJ: Princeton University Press, 1983), pp. 134-136.

7.   Alexander J. Motyl, "The Sobering of Gorbachev: Nationality, Restructuring and the West," in *Politics, Society, and Nationality inside Gorbachev's Russia*, ed. Seweryn Bialer (Boulder, CO: Westview Press, 1989), pp. 152-153; Nahaylo, pp. 80-87; Amir Taheri, *Crescent in a Red Sky: The Future of Islam in the Soviet Union* (London: Hutchinson and Co., 1989), p. xvii.

8.   Daniel C. Matuszewski, "Nationalities in the Soviet Future: Trends under Gorbachev," in *Gorbachev and the Soviet Future*, ed. L. W. Lerner and D. W. Threadgold (Boulder, CO: Westview Press, 1989), p. 96.

9.   Thom, p. 21.

10.   Mikhail Gorbachev, *Speeches and Writings*, vols. 1 and 2, in

Leaders of the World Series, gen. ed. Robert Maxwell (Oxford: Pergamon Press, 1986, 1987).

11.   Nahaylo, p. 86.

12.   Matuszewski, pp. 100-106.

13.   Jeremy R. Azrael, Restructuring and the Polarization of Soviet Politics, RAND Publication N-3142-A (Santa Monica, CA: RAND Corporation, June 1990), pp. 5-6.

14.   Gorbachev, 2: 59.

15.   *Newsweek*, 12 November 1990, pp. 40-41.

16.   John Parker and colleagues, "A Survey of the Soviet Union--Now What?" *The Economist*, 20-26 October 1990, pp. 4-5.

17.   *The Economist*, 9 March 1990, p. 45.

18.   Theodore Karasik and Brenda Horrigan, Gorbachev's Presidential Council, RAND Publication P-7665 (Santa Monica, CA: RAND Corporation, August 1990).

19.   *Economist*, 31 August 1991, pp. 38-40.

20.   *Economist*, 17 August 1991, p. 44.

21.   *Economist*, 7 September 1991, p. 46.

22.   *Economist*, 31 August 1991, p. 38.

2

The Army and the National Question

DAVID JONES

Students of the Soviet Union have been amazed by the speed at which events have unfolded. Nothing holds firm. Yesterday's leaders, once lauded as people of genius, are today discarded as senile fools. As Mikhail Gorbachev pursued the elusive dream of economic plenty through some sort of *perestroika*, his hopes were threatened with disintegration from the long-suppressed national and ethnic grievances that were unleashed by the parallel policies of democratization and *glasnost'*.

Until recently, most Western analysts focused on the strengths and weaknesses of the Soviet Armed Forces as potential opponents in a future conflict. True, they frequently noted (and occasionally evaluated) both the problems of national diversity within the ranks and the dangers posed by a decreasing number of Slavs (Great Russians, Byelorussians, and Ukrainians) in the pool of available draftees. On occasion, they even chronicled the problems of non-Russian conscripts. Nonetheless, they normally dealt with such issues from the narrow point of view of the Soviet army's immediate combat potential and capabilities. As a result, few gave serious consideration to the possible impact of the national issue on the future of that force's structural forms or organization or on its ability to support the empire's internal cohesion.[1]

Western analysts justified ignoring these last questions in part by pointing to the seeming lack of concern over these issues displayed by most Soviet writers. Discussing the "internal and external" functions of traditional armies, for example, minister of defense Marshal A. A. Grechko noted (1975) that these merely reflected "the internal weakness and the essential contradictions rending capitalist society." These factors explained the frequent use made of the troops as a support of the civil authority. However, Grechko insisted, "since the inception of the Soviet Armed Forces, the content and social trend of these two functions have been radically different from those of bourgeois armies." For once the revolution had emerged victorious from the flames of civil strife, both class and national antagonisms would disappear in the process of "building socialism." Thus, "there is no call for the Soviet Armed Forces to exercise their internal function," even though its servicemen did not "stand aloof from the mainstream of social life" and were fully "involved in political, social and cultural life."[2]

In less than two decades the marshal's confident words were belied by events in Tbilisi, Baku, and elsewhere, including the attempted coup of 1991. In pursuing his goal of political and economic *perestroika*, Mikhail Gorbachev appeared to have opened yet one more of the periods of *smuta* ("troubles") that have punctuated the history of what became the Russian Empire. Further, the displays of nationalist turbulence of the past few years offer vivid proof that the former Soviet Union was not only heir to the Tsarist Empire but was in itself "an empire in the classical sense that it covers a territory of considerable extent embracing a vast diversity of ethnically dissimilar peoples who are ruled by a single sovereign authority, Russia."[3]

Indeed, despite Moscow's claims to the contrary, the Soviet Union was the last of the great multinational empires of the nineteenth century. Moreover, like other such empires, the USSR contained forces that promoted unity as well as those which favored disintegration. Prominent among the former in tsarist times were a number of transnational institutions that helped bind the empire together under a strong central government. Among these we might include the central government's ramified administrative system with its numerous bureaucracy, a multinational aristocracy (*dvoriane*) that remained open to newcomers of talent, a developing mercantile and industrial elite, and, to some extent, the Orthodox church. Despite its alleged revolutionary heritage, the Soviet Union developed analogous institutions in its own extensive state and industrial bureaucracies and in the Communist party, which replaced both the church as the source of the ideological inspiration for imperial unity and the aristocracy by means of the *nomenklatura* (bureaucracy appointed by the party). In both these Great Russian imperiums, the final bulwark of the state's order and unity was its powerful internal security establishments, which were backed by its even more powerful armed forces.

That the Tsarist and Soviet regimes developed parallel institutions to fulfil similar and necessary functions was only natural. More surprising, however, was the fact that when the Tsarist and Soviet structures are viewed side by side, they appear remarkably similar in both form and behavior. This was particularly true with regard to the organization and operation of the national security and military establishments. Thus, Russian armies, both before and after 1917, were regarded as important instruments of national indoctrination and integration as well as the means of last resort in cases of civil unrest. For this reason, it was not unreasonable to compare the Red Army's performance in these regards with that of its predecessor before turning to the impact that growing ethnic and nationalist turbulence had on the future forms and roles of the military and security forces. It has become increasingly apparent that these concerns interact with each other. Thus, the ability of the regime to depend on the armed forces as a means of preserving order and combating attempts at secession may have demanded that the latter assume new organizational forms: forms that simultaneously defused some and exacerbated other ethnic problems. Whatever the form chosen, not only does it alter the ethos of the military profession, it also has a major impact on the military's future relationship with the empire's Slav and non-Slav subjects, and indeed on the ultimate fate of the Soviet Empire as a whole.

THE ARMY OF A "NEW TYPE"

The place of national and ethnic minorities within the Red Army has changed with each military reorganization since 1917. The various national contingents that were raised to fight for Soviet power between 1918 and 1921 were replaced by national territorial units which, in 1930, comprised some 10 percent of the total of this category of divisions.[4] However, the return to a centrally controlled, regular cadre/reservist model was completed by the law on national formations which was adopted on 7 March 1938. This ordered the conscription on the *kadrovyi printsip* or *esprit de corps* of all draft-age males, regardless of national or cultural background, into the ethnically composite, Russian-language units that formed a unified and multinational military and naval establishment. As a result, all national formations and units, along with ethnically based military schools, were to be transformed into All-Union units staffed in an extraterritorial manner. This step was justified by the assertion that overall cultural progress and the universal knowledge of the Russian language had made national units obsolete: All ethnics could now serve in regular units, as demanded by mechanization and the demands of modern warfare.[5]

During the crisis of 1941-1945, Stalin again was forced to allow national formations of Latvians, Estonians, Kazakhs, Georgians, Azeris, Armenians, Tadzhiks, and other groups. Their contribution was recognized by a decree of 1 February 1944 which permitted the federal republics to establish their own foreign offices and armies, a move that Stalin claimed was justified by their record of wartime service.[6] While this provision remained formally in place until the Brezhnev constitution of 1977, after 1945 the national/ethnic units were disbanded as the Soviet Armed Forces returned in practice to the principles of 1938. The latter were reaffirmed by the conscription law of 12 October 1967, which remained in force despite the growing pressures for military reform.[7] By the early 1980s, some 75 to 80 percent of all Soviet military personnel were two- to three-year conscripts.[8] With regard to the population as a whole, some 80 percent of all adult males had seen military service, a figure that may have risen even more thanks to subsequent revisions to the conscription law of 1967.[9]

Indeed, the Soviet Armed Forces remained closer in form and style to the great conscript/reservist and cadre armies with which the Great Powers marched to war in 1914 than it did to most modern military establishments.[10] Filled by conscripts and commanded and administered by a centralized Defence Ministry and General Staff through a network of military districts, the Soviet Armed Forces retained most of the major traits introduced over a century ago by D. A. Miliutin and his fellow reformers.[11]

If the "reversion to type" was obvious here, it was equally evident in other areas as well. This was particularly true with regard to a shared belief in the educational utility of military service for the draftee. The military establishment was to serve as a sort of national university in which conscripts would learn the basics of literacy and a fundamental, Russian-focused patriotism. In this manner, the army was to serve as a positive force promoting both the modernization and the unity of the empire.[12]

RUSSIFICATION IN THE "NATIONAL UNIVERSITY": THE THEORY

In restoring a standing conscript army, the Soviet leaders, consciously or unconsciously, were resorting to an institution that their tsarist predecessors had adopted to meet similar problems. This shared view of the nature and purposes of military service had considerable significance for the national question in the armed forces.

The continued use of the armed forces as an instrument of imperial unity resulted, according to one Western analyst, from the fact that in practice, "Soviet nationality policy evolved as a device for justifying continuation of the Russian Empire while reducing the strains and contradictions inherent in a difficult history of nationality relations."[13] Indeed, the Soviet government's initial (1919-1922) concentration of control by the central command and administrative agencies in Moscow, over the forces raised by the future Union republics, roused the suspicions of the sensitive non-Russian troops.

To redress this situation, the Ukrainian delegates demanded that minority troops receive "political and cultural training in their own language" and that the Red Army be replaced by a national-territorial militia system.[14] In its response, the central leadership sought to appease the opposition while simultaneously avoiding the creation of local national armies. To this end, the Party Congress ordered the establishment of a relatively small regular cadre army staffed mainly with Great Russians and other Russianized Slavs and backed by a large reserve of the less expensive territorial-militia divisions. Meanwhile, ethnic concerns were to be met by creating, within the cadre divisions, ethnic companies and battalions and regiments for the smaller ethnic groups, and also by organizing a relatively small number of "national military divisions" within the larger national republics and autonomous regions. Finally, the military-educational system was to be expanded in order to prepare more ethnic troops for positions of command.[15]

In this manner, as M. V. Frunze noted, the regime avoided facing the specter of a number of national republican armies and instead created a federal army under a strong central military administration. Moreover, thanks to the national units, "no nationality [would] feel left out or victimized," while the army would emerge as a "single, strong entity."[16] While space does not permit a full investigation of the resulting system, its major advantages deserve mention. In the first place, national detachments were clearly a political necessity inasmuch as they were "a clear testimony to the securing of equal rights and obligations of all peoples of the USSR in defence of the socialist fatherland." Equally important, they served as essential halfway houses through which the obligation for military service could be extended to minorities who had earlier been exempt.[17] As Frunze pointed out, the result was that while Great Russians "constituted and will constitute the nucleus of the army and the basis of all its strength," the system did "not deprive all other nationalities . . . of the right and responsibility to defend the Soviet land, with weapons in hand."[18]

Although the numbers of non-Russians in the ranks increased considerably (for example, from 21 percent in 1922 to 39 percent in October 1925), this did not necessarily serve to diminish nationalist anxieties about the continuing process of Russification after 1924.[19] Despite the fact that ethnic formations contained 10 percent of the army's personnel, even these were not necessarily "ethnically pure" and free from the pressures of de facto Russification.[20]

The struggle with nationalist and ethnic currents within the armed forces well illustrates "the inherent problems of multinationalism for Soviet policy."[21] It is in this context that we should consider Defense Minister Grechko's injunction, given to a group of military graduates in 1974, for officers to aid the party and *Komsomol* (the official Soviet youth organization) in the work of inculcating in their troops "the high principles of Communism, the sense of Soviet patriotism and that of proletarian internationalism and [of the need to maintain] constant readiness to defend the achievements of socialism."[22] For the military's success or failure in converting its recruits into politically conscious citizens of the Russian-led Soviet state, in whom nationalist antagonisms had been muted by their common experience in the ranks, was an important indicator of the USSR's success in dealing with its ethnic problems. From another point of view, the army's ability--or inability--to fulfill this function may become a significant factor in future decisions concerning the utility of preserving, during conditions of financial stringency, this vast establishment of conscripts as a major weapon in the struggle with nationalist separatism.

ETHNIC CONSCRIPTS IN THE MILITARY: THE PRAXIS

Judgments of success or failure in this regard must consider not only the army's ability to absorb and utilize the regular, biannual influxes of conscripts but also its ability to attract minority candidates for long-term service as officers. Although I will treat them separately, the two issues are intimately connected since a cultural-ethnic gap between officers and conscripts will be reflected in the life and capability of the troops.

For all its defects--most of which have reappeared in its successor army--the Imperial Army was spared the problem of serious ethnic tensions. In part this resulted from the deliberate decision of those framing the law of 1874 to exempt from service members of some 45 national groups. Known as the *allogenic peoples*, they were deemed too socially and politically backward to make reliable soldiers.[23] However, as a result of the financial strain under which tsarist military planners had to operate, the army could only absorb a small proportion of the available Slavic conscripts.

The interaction of these factors permitted the tsar to retain an ethnically unified army until 1915. The Bolsheviks, on the other hand, found themselves committed to a multi-national force both by their theoretical program and by the political dynamics of the Civil War. As we have seen, their interest in preventing the rise of uncontrolled national armies led them to accept the existence of ethnic militia units until 1938, after which they had little choice but to merge non-Slavs with Slavs in mixed units. This having been accomplished, the leadership was left with little choice but to step up its attempts at Russification, if only in the interest of military efficiency. This increased the urgency with which the military had to pursue its educative function. Simultaneously, it complicated the problems of barracks life.

This problem was further exacerbated in the late 1980s and early 1990s. In the first place, the expansion of the Soviet Armed Forces--from 3 million in 1970 to 5 million in 1985, according to one authority--meant the drafting of ever greater proportions of the conscript pool.[24] This was paralleled by demographic patterns that reduced the number of Great Russians and other Slavs available. One Western analysis of Soviet census data estimated that in 1970 the draft pool were comprised of was 74 percent Slav, 13 percent Muslim, and 13 percent other groups, but that the equivalent figures for 1985 were 63 percent, 24 percent, and 13 percent (to give a net Slav loss of 11 percent for the 15-year period).[25] Although Soviet figures are rare, those available generally confirmed their Western counterparts. Y. I. Deriugin, the author of an article noting that conscripts from Transcaucasia made up 28 percent of the total in 1980 and 37 percent in 1988, cited a Western prediction that Muslims would provide over half of the armed forces in the year 2000.[26]

Given staffing policies that favored some services (for example, the navy, internal troops, air forces, and strategic rocket forces), it was difficult to sketch the ethnic composition of a typical Soviet unit. In the mid-1980s, however, one U.S. analyst suggested that ground force units normally would be "approximately 75 to 80% Slavs, 10% Central Asians, 5% Balts, and 5% Caucasians, with a scattering of other nationalities," but that its equivalent in the construction troops would have 80 to 90 percent non-Slavs in its ranks.[27] While these estimates only sketch a general picture, the potential for ethnic friction increased proportionately.

With the coming of *glasnost'*, the military lost its ability to disguise the true state of affairs.[28] Much to the annoyance of many senior commanders and military conservatives, a number of reformers, including officers, civilian critics, and curious reporters, fell on the military and exposed skeletons in the service closets. Among them was the grass-roots Committee of Soldiers' Mothers which charged that 15,000 members of the armed services perished in the ranks during peacetime service during the latter half of the 1980s. In particular, they insist that *dedovshchina* (hazing) was a major cause of such deaths and injuries, and their demands that steps be taken to halt the practice were supported by those military professionals advocating radical reform.[29]

If these revelations underscored the misfortunes of the average conscript, others made it evident that the ethnic soldier was a particular target of *dedovshchina* and other abuses. Reports indicating the violence suffered by many non-Russians first emerged in the early 1980s. At that time, perhaps thanks to the ethnocentric bias of Western analysts, they were interpreted as signs of radical tensions between light-skinned "Europeans" and dark-skinned "Asians" from the Caucasus and Central Asia.[30] Contributing factors to this friction were identified as insufficient command of Russian and a lack of technical education among minority conscripts, which led to them being hazed as punishment for failure to acquire military skills as rapidly as their Slavic fellows.[31] Even so, one prominent analyst cautioned that it was easy "to read too much into such anecdotes" since many "other ex-servicemen report that they could recall no ethnic problems in their units," argued that ethnic violence was less significant than that of "excessive hazing" in general, and believed that both difficulties could be largely avoided by "effective small-unit leadership and decent food."[32] Others took these reports more seriously and concluded that ethnic violence "is not a rare occurrence and may even be commonplace."[33]

Reports also surfaced to demonstrate that the problems went far beyond simple racism as defined by color. It was soon evident that Balts and Moldavians had been suffering along with Caucasians, Central Asians, and other "coloureds."[34] Rumors of numerous deaths among ethnic conscripts did much to fuel the flames of nationalist dissatisfaction. Meanwhile, official explanations of such deaths which sought to diminish the ethnic dimension ended instead by confirming its existence.[35]

ETHNICS IN THE OFFICER CORPS

If the tsarist regime saw advantages in closing the ranks of its army
to ethnic conscripts, matters were different when it came to command personnel. Following in the footsteps of Muscovy and Peter I, the authorities
of the late tsarist regime recognized fully the advantages to be gained by
co-opting members of other national or native elites into the Great Russian
civil and military service. An officer's career, therefore, was open to all
competent citizens of the empire with the exception of "Talmudic" Jews
and, with regard to the General Staff, Polish Catholics after 1863. This
caveat made, and even admitting that Great Russians comprised the majority, one can still say without exaggeration that many units, including the
prestigious Imperial Guards, were commanded by the truly multinational
ofitserstvo (officer corps).[36]

Overall, the imperial regime deserves high marks for its integration of
ethnic elites into its officer corps. All, of course, were Russified in the
process, and thus were alienated from their roots and native cultures. In
this manner, the tsarist regime created an image of equality in imperial
service that proved attractive to Russians and members of ethnic groups
alike, and so reduced the leadership left to the minorities. The Soviets
recognized the potency of this image and attempted to mimic it. They, too,
went to pains to demonstrate that minority soldiers could, and did, rise to
the top of the Soviet army. V. F. Samoilenko, in discussing the multinational essence of the Red Army, pointed out that the four fronts involved
in Operation Bagration in 1944 were commanded by a Russian, an Armenian, a Ukrainian, and the "Pole" General K. K. Rokossovskii. Elsewhere,
in listing illustrious commanders of the Great Patriotic War (1941-1945), he
included five Russians, four Ukrainians, two Belorussians, two Armenians,
three Georgians, three Ossetians, one Kalmyk, and one Tatar.[37]

Even so, there is good reason to suspect that the Soviets were much
less successful than their predecessors in using the officer corps as a
means of ethnic integration. True, the creation of national formations in the
period before World War II was paralleled during the so-called military
reform of 1924 by a decree establishing 13 schools for ethnic officers and
5 for ethnic political officers. As a result of these measures, as well as of
a deliberate policy aimed at increasing ethnic representation within the
command cadres, the proportion of non-Russian officers reportedly rose
from 18 percent in 1920 to 38 percent in 1926 and political officers increased from 26 to 35 percent.[38]

Although such figures are impressive, the abolition of ethnic formations triggered a phasing out of the special officers' schools. Figures
indicating the impact of these developments on the national composition
of the Soviet army's officer cadres were infrequent at best and often
incomplete. However, if we assume that the army and air forces contained
some 500,000 troops in 1943, figures provided for the non-Russian ele-

ment would suggest that at that time, ethnic Russians made up roughly 90 percent of the total, Ukrainians some 5 percent, and Belorussians just over 1 percent. The remainder comprised a mixture of Armenians, Tatars, Chuvashi, Mordovinians, and similar groups. Figures for artillery officers confirmed this pattern. The demands of war, and possibly Stalin's repressions as well, had worked to undercut the gains made in the prewar period, although enough prewar veterans remained to provide the Red Army's high command with a pleiad of non-Russians.[39]

Despite the loyal service of non-Russians and non-Slavs during World War II, since 1945 there seemed to have been a deliberate effort to create an *ofitserstvo* (officer corps) that was even more predominantly Russian, or at least Slavic. Again, the available data is fragmentary and, in some ways, contradictory. For example, Rand Corporation researchers were told by émigrés that rather than recruit ethnic officers, the authorities had instead attempted to "purify" the corps of non-Russian ethnics. The same sources also reported two specific (but unsubstantiated) cases of such "purification": that of Jewish officers in the early 1950s and of ethnics during Khrushchev's demobilizations.[40] Even so, a decade later, a *Red Star* sample of 1,000 lieutenants included representatives of 30 different nationalities, including all the major ones except the Turkomen.[41]

The majority of Western analysts have accepted the fact that since that time, entrance requirements and the traditions of service greatly favored the recruitment and advancement of Russians or of kindred ethnic groups (for example, other Slavs), who were assumed to be more easily Russianized and assimilated. As a result, the Soviet command cadres were some 80 percent Russian and 10 to 15 percent Ukrainian and Belorussian.[42] The accuracy of these figures was borne out by the data published on the origins of officers in the General Staff, the body from which the majority of generals was drawn. In late 1989 *Red Star* noted that this group was 85 percent Russian, 10 percent Ukrainian, 3 percent Belorussian, and 2 percent Tatar, Armenian and Chuvash.[43]

CONCLUSIONS

The recent Soviet army failed miserably in indoctrinating either its ethnic recruits or its officers into a force imbued with "proletarian internationalism" or "Soviet patriotism." This failure is all the more striking when compared to the successful policies implemented within the Imperial Army by D. A. Miliutin and his fellow reformers after 1874. Further, it also has obvious implications for the future of the army as a bulwark of internal order and for the decisions now being made for the reform of the existing military system. Both the growing weight of members of ethnic groups in the recruit pool and the apparent unwillingness of many national republics to permit their recruits to serve either in mixed units or outside their home territories have created major problems for the authorities who are charged with carrying out the draft. Moreover, in the future, these same factors could make some units unreliable when serving in the gendarme or policing role as well.[44]

Given the demands for cuts in defense spending, a cutback in troops seems inevitable, whatever form is adopted for the military establishment. Before the attempted coup of August 1991, Soviet military reformers were considering four possible organizational variants for the armed forces:

1.   A territorial militia with a core of professional cadres, which I call the Frunze model since it resembles the model em-ployed by the Red Army in the 1920s and, in some ways, that of the United States with its regular units, reservists, and the National Guard;
2.   A purely professional force comprised of long-service volunteers who serve in accord with a contract, along the lines of the British or Canadian armed forces;
3.   A reduced conscript-cadre force that, like the tsarist army before it, inducts only a portion of the recruits who become available each year; and
4.   A mix of a larger professional core with large numbers of short-term (perhaps six-month) conscripts, from which additional, long-service *profy* (professionals) could be recruited.[45]

While the first (the militia) system has the political advantage of satisfying growing ethnic and nationalistic pressures, it nonetheless increases chances that the army will cease to serve as an instrument of centralizers in Moscow and a factor in maintaining internal cohesion within the USSR. However, as the tsarist model indicates, the other three choices could avoid this drawback by avoiding the conscription of ethnic minorities altogether. Meanwhile, increased efforts to improve service within the ranks, and to induce non-Russians to enter a revamped officer corps could simultaneously provide a system that, if necessary, could again expand its recruitment base.

At present, it is still too early to discern exactly which model will provide a guide to reformers. For these reasons, it seems likely that the future form of the Russian military organization, or at least of the ground forces, will begin by resembling that maintained by the tsars: for example, a reduced conscript-cadre force. However, this may well be only a transition stage on the path to the fourth model with its increased core of long-service professionals on contract, drawn from a reduced intake of short-term conscripts. Then, if the empire stabilizes in terms of its national problems, this eventually could be buttressed in some regions by a territorial National Guard and/or reserve formations.

If, however, such stabilization does not occur, the same system would still provide the military authorities and their political masters with a force from which the causes of the worst national-ethnic friction have largely been eliminated. In addition, such an army would be more likely to serve as an instrument for preserving imperial unity and the repression of outbreaks of ethnic discontent and nationalist separatism within the Russian Republic per se. Here we would do well to recall that Russia has passed through other periods of *smut* (turmoil), only to reemerge once more as a power on the world stage. However, even if the predictions of pessimists become reality, an army organized in this manner would serve equally well for the defense of a new Great Russian state based--if need be--on the RSFSR alone. However, even in this case, it is obvious that the ethnic issue must remain at the forefront among the factors considered by Russian reformers, whatever the ultimate fate of any post-coup federation.

NOTES

1.   Exceptions to this generalization are the works of a small group of scholars such as Hélène Carrère d'Encausse, Teresa Rakowska-Harmstone, and a group centered in the Rand Corporation in the early 1980s, including S. Enders Wimbush and Alexander R. Alexiev.

2.   A. A. Grechko, *The Armed Forces of the Soviet Union* (Moscow: Progress, 1977), pp. 105-106.

3.   S. Enders Wimbush, "The Ethnic Costs of Empire," in *Soviet Nationalities in Strategic Perspective*, ed. S. Enders Wimbush (London: Croom Helm, 1985), p. xxi. Further, the USSR is a multinational empire which, according to the census of 1979, contains 104 distinct national groups. Of course, such groups vary considerably in size and importance from the 3 major Slav groups (Great Russians, White or Byelorussians, and Ukrainians or Little Russians) at one end of the spectrum to 22 "foreign" groups (Germans, Greeks, Koreans, Poles, and so forth) at the other. In between are 47 groups, whose written or vernacular languages mainly belong to the Christian Orthodox tradition, and 29 other "historic" nations with their own cultures, traditions, and religions. These last include the Balts (Estonians and Latvians), the Georgians and Armenians, and 24 Muslim nations; Wimbush, p. xxii. On the USSR as the last great empire, or an "empire restored," see, Daniel C. Matuszewski, "Empire, Nationalities, Borders: Soviet Assets and Liabilities," in *Soviet Nationalities in Strategic Perspective*, ed. S. Enders Wimbush (London: Croom Helm, 1985), p. 75; and Paul B. Henze, "The Spectre and Implications of Internal Nationalist Dissent: Historical and Functional Comparisons," in *Soviet Nationalities in Strategic Perspective*, ed. S. Enders Wimbush (London: Croom Helm, 1985), pp. 12-15.

4.   M. V. Zakharov, ed., *50 let Vooruzhennykh sil SSSR* (Moscow: Voenizdat, 1968), p. 173. On national formations in this period, see Susan L. Curran and Dmitry Ponomareff, *Managing the Ethnic Factor in the Russian and Soviet Armed Forces. An Historical Overview*, Rand

Publication R-2640/1 (Santa Monica, CA: Rand Corporation, July 1982), pp. 9-25; V. F. Samoilenko, *Druzhba narodov--Istochnik mogushchestva Sovetskikh Vooruzhennykh sil* (Moscow: Voenizdat, 1972), pp. 38-54; and Hélène Carrère d'Encausse, *Decline of an Empire: The Soviet Socialist Republics in Revolt* (New York: Newsweek, 1979), pp. 156-159.

5. The text of the law is reprinted in V. N. Malin and V. P. Moskovskii, eds., *KPSS o Vooruzhennykh Sil Sovetskogo Soiuza. Sbornik dokumentov, 1917-1958* (Moscow: Politizdat, 1958), p. 353. Also see P. Rtischev, *"Leninskaia natsional'naia politika i stroitel'stvo Sovetskikh Voorunzhennykh sil," Voenno-istoricheskii zhurnal,* no. 6 (1974), 6; I. Z. Zakharov, *"Sovetskie Vooruzhennye Sily na zashchite natsional'nykh i internatsionnal'nykh interesov narodov SSSR,"* in *Uchenye zapiski kafedr obshchestvennykh nauk vuzov Leningrada: Istoriia SSSR,* vol. 13, p. 115; and Teresa Rakowska-Harmstone, "The Soviet Army as the Instrument of National Integration," in *Soviet Military Power and Performance,* ed. John Erickson and E. J. Feuchtwanger (New York: Archon, 1979), pp. 134-135.

6. d'Encausse, p. 159; Rtischev, p. 8; Anna Louise Strong, *Peoples of the USSR* (New York: Macmillan, 1944), p. 246.

7. The law of 1967 is outlined in S. M. Shtemenko, *Novyi zakon i voinskaia sluzhba* (Moscow: Voenizdat, 1968); Harriet F. Scott and William F. Scott, *The Armed Forces of the USSR,* 3rd ed. (Boulder, CO: Westview Press, 1984), pp. 320-323, 335-340; S.A. Tiushkevich, ed., *Sovetskie Vooruzhenie sily Istoriia stroitel'stva* (Moscow: Voenizdat, 1978), pp. 449-450; Rakowska-Harmstone, pp. 135-139.

8. Christopher Donnelly, "The Soviet Armed Forces since 1945," in *The Cambridge Encyclopedia of Russia and the Soviet Union* (Cambridge: Cambridge University Press, 1982), p. 439.

9. Ibid., p. 439; International Institute for Strategic Studies, *The Military Balance, 1985-1986* (London: IISS, 1985), pp. 21-22, 24. For a brief account of the life of a contemporary Soviet recruit, see Mikhail Tsypkin, "The Conscripts," in *The Soviet Union Today: An Interpretive Guide,* ed. James Cracraft (Chicago: Bulletin of the Atomic Scientists, 1983), pp. 113-122. However, if there are indications that the percentage of conscripts accepted has increased, other factors (especially the growing availability of statistics on health and crime) suggest that the figure of those actually drafted could scarcely have exceeded 70 percent.

10. See Mark Galeotti, "The Military's New Battlefields," *Detente,* no. 16 (1989): 12.

11. The Miliutin army is described in detail in P. A. Zaionchkovskii, *Voennye reformy 1860-70 godov v Rossii* (Moscow: 1952).

12. On the Miliutin law and its intentions, see Jacob W. Kipp and W. Bruce, "Autocracy and Reform: Bureaucratic Absolutism and Political Modernization in Nineteenth Century Russia," *Russian History,* 1, no. 2 (1979): 1-21, and David Jones, "Imperial Russia's Forces at War," in *The First World War,* vol. 1 of *Military Effectiveness,* ed. A. R. Millett and W.

Murray (London: Allen and Unwin, 1988), pp. 272-277.

13.   Wimbush, "Ethnic Costs," pp. xxi-xxii. Also see Alain Besancon, "Nationalism and Bolshevism in the USSR," in *The Last Empire: Nationality and the Soviet Future*, ed. Robert Conquest (Stanford, CA: 1986), pp. 5-6.

14.   d'Encausse, pp. 157-158; Rakowska-Harmstone, pp. 131-133.

15.   *KPSS v rezoliutsiiakh s'ezdov, konferentsii i Plenumov*, 8th ed. (Moscow: Politizdat, 1970), 2: 441; Christopher D. Jones, "Historical Precedents: Ethnic Units and the Soviet Armed Forces," *The Greater Socialist Army: Integration and Reliability*, vol. 1, part i of *Warsaw Pact: The Question of Cohesion*, ed. Teresa Rakowska-Harmstone (Ottawa: Operational Research and Analysis Establishment, Department of National Defense, 1983-1986), pp. 93-97.

16.   M. V. Frunze, *Izbrannye proizvedeniia* (Moscow: Voenizdat, 1977), p. 238; d'Encausse, p. 158.

17.   N. Makarov, "*Stroitel'stvo mnogonatsional'nykh Vooruzhennykh Sil SSSR v 1920-1939 gg.*," *Voenno-istoricheskii zhurnal*, no. 10 (1982): 43.

18.   Frunze, p. 191.

19.   Ellen Jones, *Red Army and Society: A Sociology of the Soviet Military* (Boston: Allen and Unwin), p. 184.

20.   *Ibid.*, pp. 183-186; Christopher Jones, pp. 93-101; Makarov, pp. 40-42.

21.   S. Enders Wimbush, "Nationalities in the Soviet Armed Forces," in *Soviet Nationalities in Strategic Perspective*, ed. S. Enders Wimbush (London: Croom Helm, 1985), p. 227.

22.   "*Priem v Kremle v cheste vypushnikov voennykh akademii*," *Krasnaia zvezda*, 2 July 1974, p. 2.

23.   d'Encausse, p. 156; Curran and Ponomareff, pp. 5-8; Robert F. Baumann, "Universal Service Reform and Russia's Imperial Dilemma" in *War and Society*, no. 2, September 1986.

24.   David R. Jones, "The Two Faces of Soviet Military Power," *Current History* (October 1987): 337. Figures from International Institute for Strategic Studies.

25.   Ellen Jones, p. 188.

26.   Yu. I. Deriugin, *Psichologicheskii zhurnal*, no. 1 (1990): 114, as cited by Suzanne Crow, "Inter-Ethnic Conflict in the Soviet Military," *Jane's Soviet Intelligence Review*, no. 5 (1990): 223.

27.   Wimbush, pp. 232-233.

28.   See, for example, the interviews and reports cited in Alexander Alexiev, *Inside the Soviet Army in Afghanistan*, Rand Publication R-3627-A (Santa Monica, CA: Rand Corporation, May 1988), pp. 35-55.

29.   On the anger of the military establishment, see Mark Galeotti, "The Troubled Army," *Jane's Soviet Intelligence Review*, no. 2 (1990): 62. The appeal of the Committee of Soldiers' Mothers appeared as "We'll Not Let Our Sons Be Killed," in *Moscow News*, no. 22 (1990): 5. For the

committee's charges and the reformers' attack on hazing, see G. Zhav-
oronkov, "Save and Protect," *Moscow News*, no. 30 (1990): 11; and Major
V. Semashko, "Army Must Be Law-Governed," *Moscow News*, no. 16
(1989): 12.

30.   For the racial interpretation of violence in the ranks, see
Wimbush, "Nationalities," pp. 238-239; and E. S. Williams, *The Soviet
Military: Political Education, Training and Morale* (London: MacMillan,
1987), pp. 82-84.

31.   Donnelly, p. 110.

32.   Ellen Jones, p. 193.

33.   Wimbush, p. 239.

34.   Suzanne Crow, "Inter-Ethnic Conflict in the Soviet Military,"
Jane's Soviet Intelligence Review, no. 5 (1990): 224; Suzanne Crow,
"Soviet Conscripts Fall Victim to Ethnic Violence," *Radio Liberty Report on
the USSR* (Munich) (13 October 1989): 8-9.

35.   "A Nationalist Threat to Soviet Military," *Current Digest of the
Soviet Press* (13 December 1989): 1-8.

36.   E. Messner, ed., *Rossiiskie ofitsery* (Buenos Aires, 1959), pp. 15-
18; on Jewish and Polish officers, see Peter Kenez, "A Profile of the
Prerevolutionary Officer Corps," *California Slavic Studies*, vol. 10, no. 7
(1973): 137; A. I. Denikin, "*Natsional'nyi vopros v staroi Russkoi armii*,"
Pereklichka: Voenno-politicheskii zhurnal, no. 56 (1956): 7; M. Grulev,
Zapiski generalaevreia (Paris, 1930); and Reuben Ainsztein, *Jewish
Resistance in Nazi-Occupied Eastern Europe* (London: Weidenfeld and
Nicolson, 1964), pp. 144-157.

37.   Samoilenko, pp. 138, 81.

38.   Makarov, pp. 41-42. Although he gave no figures, he claimed that
subsequently the numbers of non-Russians increased still further. For the
history of one such school, see A. A. Ammosov, "*O Yakutskoi natsional'noi
shkole i ee vupusknikakh*," *Voenno-istoricheskii zhurnal*, no. 1 (1986): 76-
79.

39.   Samoilenko, p. 80; Rakowska-Harmstone, pp. 142-143;
Rtishchev, p. 7.

40.   S. Enders Wimbush and Alex Alexiev, *The Ethnic Factor in the
Soviet Armed Forces*, Rand Publication N-1486-NA (Santa Monica, CA:
RAND Corporation, May 1980), pp. 27-28.

41.   *Krasnaia zvezda*, 5 April 1969, as reported in F. Khaturin and A.
Shchelokov, "Lieutenants: Sociological Portrait," *Soviet Military Review*, vol.
7, no. 55 (1969): 2-8.

42.   Wimbush and Alexiev, p. 28; Rakowska-Harmstone, pp. 143-144.

43.   "*Ofitzer general'nogo shtaba*," *Krasnaia zvezda*, 29 October
1989, p. 2.

44.   Murray Feshbach, "The Soviet Military's Recruitment Nightmare,"
Washington Post, 19 August 1990, p. C4. On the demands of various
ethnic and national groups *vis-à-vis* the draft see Robert Arnett and Mary

C. Fitzgerald, "Restructuring the Armed Forces: The Current Soviet Debate," *The Journal of Soviet Military Studies* (June 1990): 198-199.

45.   Arnett and Fitzgerald, pp. 196-205; Kerry L. Hines and Susan E. Springer, "The Soviet Army to the Year 2000," *The Journal of Soviet Military Studies* (June 1990): 234-243.

Part 2

THE EUROPEAN PERIPHERY

The European periphery of the defunct USSR was always an area with separatist aspirations. In the weeks that followed the aborted August 1991 hard-line coup, thirteen of the Soviet Union's fifteen republics declared their independence. The Union President, Mikhail Gorbachev, finally conceded the independence of the three Baltic states. These Baltic states, or republics, Estonia, Latvia, and Lithuania were among the youngest and smallest of all the Soviet republics, and had been independent between the two World Wars. The Molotov-Ribbentrop Pact of 23 August 1939 (signed by Nazi Germany and the Soviet Union under Stalin) gave control of these republics to the Soviet Union. These states each have their own language, culture, and religion. They are the most urbanized and Western-oriented of all the republics. Estonia and Latvia are multiethnic, while Lithuania's population is 80 percent Lithuanian. In recent years they have captured the West's attention in their struggle for independence.

The Southwestern republics of Byelorussia, Moldova, and Ukraine are also part of the European periphery. The Ukraine is the best known of these republics, especially in Canada, which has the world's largest population of Ukrainians outside the Ukraine. One-eighth of the population of the Union (37 million) were Ukrainians (the population of the Ukrainian republic itself was 52 million); and this Republic produced one-fourth of the entire country's wealth. Eastern Ukrainians, who are Orthodox like their Russian brethren, are the most Russified of all non-Russians, and the present territory of the Ukraine possesses a large number of Russians living primarily in the Crimea, which is basically Russian-speaking and always (except since the 1950s in the Soviet period) belonged to Russia. But like the Baltic states, Ukraine became independent by referendum vote in December of 1991.

The Moldovians are linguistically and culturally related to their neighbors, the Romanians. The original republic of Moldavia was created in 1924 from the partition of the Ukrainian Republic. The rest of what would become modern Moldova was given to the Soviet Union by the 1939 Molotov-Ribbentrop Pact.

Discussed in this part of the book are chiefly the Balts and Ukrainians.

These Westernmost republics have had historical links with their neighbors in Eastern Europe (Poland, Germany, Austria, and Hungary) and Scandinavia for centuries. This cultural linkage is the single most important factor in their desire to secede from the Center. It has been extremely problematic for the Center to allow the Balts and the Ukrainians to go, and wrangling over ownership of land and territory will continue for many years into the future. Russia will be cut off from Russian territory west of the Baltic states, which the Soviet Union seized from Nazi Germany's East Prussia. Russia is also expected to bicker with Ukraine over the Crimean peninsula and over all the Russians (11 million in all) who still live in Ukraine and still consider Russia their spiritual homeland. A sizeable proportion of the Soviet nuclear arsenal will be left on Ukrainian soil and the new state is endowed with its own armed forces, and, who knows?-- one day its own currency.

Finally, all the republics of the Soviet west, including Russia itself, have vocal diasporas in Western Europe, the United States, and Canada. They also have a close historical legacy with Slavic and/or Scandinavian cousins in the rest of Eastern Europe. With the separation of these re- publics and their subsequent recognition by Western states, future devel- opments in the post-Soviet republics will have an enormous impact on the stability and security of the entire region, on Western Europe, and on the United States.

One is reminded of the proverbial Emperor whose realm is about to disintegrate. The Emperor might wish to salvage or retrieve at a later date whatever is retrievable, or he might reassert his honour and authority by military expansion--expansion into the Baltic states and the Ukraine once again. In this day and age nothing is conceivably beyond a realistic pos- sibility.

3

Latvia: Chronicle of an Independence Movement
JURIS DREIFELDS

The Baltic countries of Estonia, Latvia, and Lithuania, each with its own unique mix of historical developments, began to experience a common fate after their incorporation into the Russian Empire during the 1700s. The subjection of the three distinct ethnic groups was accomplished within the span of one century. This process began with Peter the Great. In his quest for a window on Europe, he succeeded in wresting Estonia and northern Latvia (including Riga) from Sweden in 1721. In 1772, the Southeastern part of Latvia was appropriated by Russia, along with Belorussia and parts of Poland. The western part of Latvia--the semiautonomous Duchy of Courland, which had been under Polish-Lithuanian sovereignty--was ceded to Russia in 1795 in conjunction with the third partition of Poland. Lithuania was attached to Russia during the three partitions of Poland (1772-1795).

All three peoples experienced the heavy hand of Russification, although Lithuania had to bear a much greater burden because of its Catholicism and its association with Poland. Especially after the Lithuanian insurrection of 1863, the Latin alphabet was outlawed for publication and Russian became the language of schools, and Lithuanians were no longer allowed to teach. In Estonia and Latvia, Russification policies began in a serious way after the 1880s, but these did not attain the dimensions found in Lithuania. Russification in the two northern republics was checked to some extent by the Baltic German nobility who were able to retain their right to property and land even after becoming subjects of the tsar.

Both countries experienced the end of serfdom in the period 1816 to 1819, half a century before the rest of Imperial Russia (including Lithuania). The efforts of the Baltic Lutheran clergy spurred the spread of elementary education so that these two countries attained the highest rates of literacy in the empire. This, in turn, created a broad local market for newspapers, journals, and books and allowed Estonians and Latvians to come into contact with new ideas in politics, economics, and lifestyles. Their modernization was further speeded up by the very rapid growth of industry. Their geopolitical location and access to ice-free ports caused a boom in business and trade and rapid rates of urbanization. Riga, the capital city of Latvia, became one of the thriving centers of the empire and radicalism began to flourish there, attaining levels comparable to those of St. Petersburg and Moscow. By the end of the nineteenth century, the population of both countries had become severely split along ideological lines. In Latvia, however, the forces of socialism experienced a far greater boom than in Estonia. By 1900, a majority of workers in Latvia had adopted a Marxist orientation and by the end of 1905, the Latvian Social Democratic party had more members in absolute terms than the Mensheviks and Bolsheviks together in the rest of the empire.

The dramatic events of 1905 in Latvia radicalized not just the workers but the peasantry as well. The killing of 70 peaceful demonstrators by Russian troops in Riga on 13 January 1905 was followed by massive strikes and eventually by arson against hundreds of manor houses and the execution of Baltic German nobles. In retaliation, the Imperial Army shot about 3,000 revolutionaries and sent many to Siberia. Close to 5,000 were forced to flee abroad (including the later president of independent Latvia, Karlis Ulmanis).

The 1905 experience and its aftermath set the stage for radical action in 1917 and, in the words of a U.S. historian, forced a large part of the Latvian intelligentsia to "seriously question Latvian membership in the empire."[1] The Latvian rifle regiments in the tsarist army joined the ranks of the Bolsheviks and eventually became the foundation of the Red Guards and Lenin's principal troubleshooters. The first commander-in-chief of the Red Army, J. Vacietis, came from Latvia, as did many of the top generals, Cheka (Extraordinary Commission for the Struggle with Counterrevolution and Sabotage--the first secret police organization of the USSR) organizers and Bolshevik political luminaries (J. Rudzutaka, I. Smilga, P. Stuchka, R. Eiche, K. Baumanis, I. Mezhlauks, and V. Mezhlauks). Their efforts were pivotal in the dissolution of the empire, and this dissolution was a key to the emergence of the independence of Baltic republics. Vacietis explicitly noted the connection in his memoirs, which were published in 1922-1924:

> Many still do not appreciate just how significant the slogan "Free Latvia" was for the Latvian Riflemen. The Latvian *strelnieki* as a group were, and continued to be, nationalist in the best sense of the word. . . . The Latvian *strelnieki* understood well that if reaction were to return to Russia, all power in the Baltic region would likewise return to the reactionaries. Thus, in struggling

against Russian reaction, the Latvians gained freedom for the Balts, providing the foundation of a free Latvia.[2]

Latvian independence was declared on 18 November 1918 but foreign troops were driven from its soil only by 1920. In that year, the Soviet Union signed separate peace treaties with Estonia, Latvia, and Lithuania, by which it recognized "forever" the sovereignty and independence of the Baltic republics.

Until 1939, the Baltic republics prospered as independent actors in the world community and were full members in good standing of the League of Nations, having diplomatic relations with most countries of the world. They had their own currency, governments, armed forces, and free market economies. The end of their independence was sealed with the secret protocols of the Molotov-Ribbentrop Pact. According to former Politburo member and the chairman of the commission investigating the Molotov-Ribbentrop Pact, Aleksandr Yakovlev, the secret protocols "reflected precisely the inner essence of Stalinism." He called it "one of the most dangerous delayed-action mines from the minefield we have inherited."[3] As a result of the protocols, the Baltic republics fell to the USSR, which sent in its occupation troops in June 1940. This occupation was followed by single-slate elections and incorporation into the USSR in August of that year. Within a year, Soviet power was replaced by that of Nazi Germany. However, by May 1945, the Red Army was once again in control.

The occupation of the Baltic republics in the aftermath of the Molotov-Ribbentrop Pact did indeed turn out to set "delayed-action mines" for the new empire. The Baltic republics became trailblazers of national consciousness and republican sovereignty, and indeed were catalysts and examples for national movements in other republics, including Moldova and the Ukraine.[4]

It is noteworthy that within the Baltic, Latvia was the first to demonstrate its opposition to Soviet rule, on 14 June 1987. The impetus for this initiative appears to have been the sense of frustration and hopelessness induced by a decreasing Latvian demographic proportion, the marginalization of Latvian language in everyday life, and the rebirth of a new environmentalism, all of which, under *glasnost'* precipitated a negative view of Soviet developments in Latvia.

Military occupation by two bloody regimes resulted in demographic scars to the Latvian population. Latvia lost an estimated 600,000 people--30 percent of its population--as the direct result of wartime casualties, executions, deportations, and the exodus of refugees. A large part of its intelligentsia and political leadership died in Siberia or fled in terror to the West.[5] Conditions promoting stark terror lasted until the mid-1950s. They were replaced by a brief period of political and cultural thaw that ended abruptly in July 1959.

For a quarter century since 1959, political repression in Latvia and systematic Sovietization and Russification of its citizens were severe. Heavy-handed repression began as a reaction to the enlightened programs initiated during the mid-1950s by a Latvian-oriented Communist elite under the leadership of the deputy chairman of the Council of Ministers, Eduards Berklavs. These "National Communists," as they were called, introduced a series of regulations that required increased used of the Latvian language in the public service, a limit on immigration from other republics, expansion of the percentage of native Latvians in leadership positions, and restrictions on the uncontrolled growth of heavy industry in view of the dearth of local labor and natural resources.[6] Moscow choreographed a purge of these Latvian-oriented individuals after July 1959. The leadership of Secretary Arvids Pelse (1959-1966) ushered in a harsh period of reaction, which was continued by his protégé Augusts Voss (1966-1984). It was a period of assertive mediocrity and narrow-minded repression.

The psychosocial Sovietization of the Latvian consciousness was coordinated with a planned demographic and linguistic dilution. The proportion of Latvians within their own republic decreased from 83 percent at the end of World War II to 52 percent in 1989, mostly as a result of the constant pressure from immigration from Russia, Belorussia, and Ukraine. According to the 1989 census, since 1935 the Russians have increased by 737,000, or more than 500 percent; the Belorussians by 450 percent; and the Ukrainians by 4600 percent, to 92,000. These three Slavic groups now account for 44.9 percent of the total population; they comprised only 10.2 percent in 1935. The absolute total of Latvians remains below the 1935 level. By 1989, Latvians had become a minority in the seven largest cities and a minority in the 19-to-22 age group.[7]

At the same time the leadership launched a powerful linguistic and cultural assault. By 1989, 66 percent of Latvians had become fluent in Russian, whereas 21 percent or fewer of Ukrainians, Belorussians, and Russians spoke Latvian.[8] Public social intercourse, which was conducted mainly in the cities, operated within the framework of the language understood by the majority: Russian. Latvian culture and media have thus remained largely inaccessible to three-quarters of non-Latvians, whereas Russian culture and media have become an obligatory aspect of life for most urban Latvians.

The dramatic changes now under way in Latvia began with the three Calendar (the public commemorations of significant historic events) demonstrations, which were initiated by working-class youths in Riga in 1987. Young people from the Helsinki '86 group challenged the "organs of repression" by publicly reviving the memory of significant events from the Latvian past. These demonstrations were not mere exercises in historical recall. Three events in particular were seen to have been twisted, excluded from discussion, or simply denied by the Soviet leadership, and their restitution served as a symbolic battering ram against the very legitimacy of Soviet rule in Latvia.

The Calendar demonstrations focused on the following events: the 14 June 1940 deportations of tens of thousands of civilians to starvation and death in Siberia, the 23 August 1939 collusion between Stalinist Russia and Nazi Germany to carve up Eastern Europe and the Baltic under the secret protocols of the Molotov-Ribbentrop Pact; and the 18 November 1918 declaration of Latvian independence.[9]

These demonstrations were a powerful catalyst for a wide circle of Latvians, especially the intelligentsia, some of whom were initially opposed to the iconoclastic tendencies of ill-informed youths.[10] The impact of these demonstrations was enhanced by several other factors. News about the planned actions by Helsinki '86 in Latvia received a wide audience through the medium of Radio Free Europe in Munich.[11] It became the relay point for news and analysis among activists and the wider Latvian public and broke the monopoly of news that had been hitherto enjoyed by the Soviet establishment.

In response to this unsanctioned media incursion, the Soviet media was compelled to provide its own version of the actions, which had been perpetrated, in their view, by small groups of "hooligans."[12] Such attention, in turn, galvanized the world media. Latvia and the Baltic became a new "hot spot." Reporting by foreign broadcasts had a further mobilizing effect on the Latvians. After so many decades of being ignored, they finally saw a glimmer of hope in their quest for independence.

An important contributing factor to the growth of opposition appears to have been the ineffective use of force by central and republican institutions. An immediate, full-scale, Stalinist-style assault with wholesale arrests of participants might temporarily have slowed the progress of the national movement. Massive repressions were expected. Consequently, their delay was crucial, for it encouraged the participation of less daring individuals. The authorities were certainly opposed to the demonstrations, but they believed that only a small handful of people was involved and that this group could be checked by traditional forms of harassment.[13] The need to maintain the credibility of the policy of *glasnost'* and the belief that these nationalist-led forces of change could eventually be harnessed to economic and political reform led to contradictory ad hoc actions, which in turn helped to inflame the situation further.

By March 1988, however, the initiative had passed from the radical Helsinki '86 group and other informal protest organizations into the hands of the established intelligentsia. Janis Peters, who was head of the Latvian Writers' Union, a renowned poet, and a full member of the Central Committee of the Latvian Communist party, began to organize commissions to investigate and rehabilitate victims of Stalinism. On 25 March, Peters and the Writers' Union organized a commemoration of the deportations of 1949, when over 43,000 Latvians were sent to Siberia. For this occasion they chose the Cemetery of the Brethren in Riga. On this same day, Helsinki '86 organized demonstrations at the groups traditional meeting place, the Freedom Monument. The media focused on the official event in the cemetery, ignoring for the most part the activities at the monument.[14]

The Latvian Writers' Union plenum, held on 1-2 June 1988, became a watershed in the airing of other critical Latvian issues: history, demography, pollution, and language. It also established the credibility and legitimacy of the official, state-supported intelligentsia.[15] When, on 21 June, a small group from Helsinki '86, together with reformist clergy and other radical reformers, signed a petition for the creation of a popular front, the petition was not published by the media.[16] In its place, another, similar document with signatures of other, more "acceptable" individuals was broadly publicized. Thereafter, the organization of the first congress of the Latvian Popular Front was undertaken by a collective "brain trust" under Peters's direction.[17]

It became increasingly evident that it was the enlightened members of the establishment, the "bright forces" (gaisie speki), who initiated the preemptive moves by the Writers' Union. Once they saw the wide resonance of support for the policies supported by Helsinki '86 and other informal groups, they took the lead in the popular front, hoping to channel and guide developments without disrupting Gorbachev's grand strategy.

Among Latvian nationalists, the debate continues concerning exactly when these "bright forces" lost their ability to control the development of events within the front. Whatever the case, the resultant Latvian awakening and the actions of the Kremlin and its local supporters brought about major changes in the political environment of Latvia. It focused the attention of Latvians on the illegitimacy of Soviet rule and the forced character of Latvia's incorporation into the USSR in 1940. The Latvian Popular Front movement provided for the growth of legitimacy of a new nationally oriented elite which eventually replaced Moscow's nomenklatura, or selected appointees. When this elite was threatened militarily, it received the unstinting loyalty of an overwhelming majority of the population from all classes and ethnic components of society. The pressures of the new Latvian prise de conscience brought long-repressed issues out into the open, such as demography, language, and environment, all of which were seen to be of critical importance to Latvian survival.

For decades the only officially acceptable political body in Latvia was the Communist party. Suddenly, the Latvian political spectrum widened dramatically, extending from groups who wanted to return to the old ways (namely, a single-party Soviet Communist rule) to groups wanting a democratic, independent, and free market Latvia, some of whom supported granting citizenship only to those who were themselves, or whose parents were, citizens of Latvia prior to 1940. Among the former was the International Front, or Interfront, which was created in reaction to the Latvian People's Front. It officially opposed the primacy of the Latvian language in the republic as well as the introduction of a market economy. It tailored its appeal to the Russian-speaking part of the population, especially to those associated with the military. Its support has dwindled, however, as a result of extremist positions. The various strikes it has called have received little tangible solidarity from the working class, and the demonstrations it has organized have been poorly attended. Interfront's geographical base of operation is Daugavpils, the second largest city in Latvia. Daugavpils lies close to the Byelorussian border and contains an ethnically diverse population. In 1989, only 13 percent of its population was Latvian. Despite Interfront's dwindling public support, it still publishes its own newspaper and has been able to maintain ties with the Latvian Communist Party (LCP).[18]

Before its split in April 1990, the membership of the LCP was only 39 percent Latvian. However, its leadership which was headed by a Latvian agriculturist named Janis Vagris, was mostly Latvian. Prodded by the growing influence of the popular front, the LCP oriented itself in favor of relative openness, reconstruction, and responsiveness to Latvian cultural, linguistic, and demographic demands. Its stance on issues such as immigration regulation and Latvian language expansion created discontent within the Party. Finally, on 6 April 1990, the reform-wing delegates, who were almost all Latvians, walked out of the 25th Latvian Party Congress and never returned to the LCP fold. The remaining delegates elected as first secretary Alfred Rubiks, a hard-liner and a Latvian of Polish origin. Rubiks had previously been mayor of Riga, but his staunch opposition to nationalistic reforms made him a darling of the reactionary Russian speakers.

Many supporters of Interfront were elected to the new Central Committee, and the LCP and Interfront developed mutually advantageous forms of cooperation. The vast resources of the Party were appropriated by Rubiks and his supporters. Their claims to many public enterprises as private property of the Party led to confrontations with the new Latvian government which was elected in May 1990.

A major source of tension was the occupation by the armed Black Berets of the main printing and publishing complex in Riga, which was responsible for the publication of the bulk of the printed media in Latvia. The Latvian government had decreed that in view of the original investment in this plant of government rather than Party money, only a small share of the property belonged to the Party. The Party felt otherwise and, with the help of its Black Beret mercenaries, on 2 January 1991 it abruptly evicted all news staff without even allowing them to remove private computers, manuscripts, or personal effects.[19] Armed guards prevented the further publication in "their" facilities of reformist Latvian newspapers and journals. The latter were forced to scale down their circulation and depend on small district printing process scattered throughout the republic and even beyond, in Estonia and Lithuania.

The LCP and Interfront also provided the leadership for the shadowy All Latvia Public Salvation Committee. Under Rubiks's leadership, it was expected to replace the elected Supreme Council after the institution of presidential rule in January 1991. World reaction, however, forced Gorbachev's hand and, according to one of the reactionary members of the LCP, Colonel Viktors Alksnis, Moscow abandoned its loyal Salvation Committee.[20]

The reformist wing of the LCP, which had walked out from the April 1990 Party Congress, formed its own political organization. Its membership was almost exclusively Latvian and was comprised of most of the "bright forces" that had helped to form the vanguard of the LPF. Under the leadership of the former ideological secretary of the LCP, Ivars Kezbers, the breakaway group adopted a new name, the Latvian Democratic Work party, and a new social-democratic platform.

The most important single organization in the political arena is the Latvian Popular Front. It has the support of the majority of Latvians as well as most non-Latvians. It won the majority of seats in the election to the Latvian Supreme Council in May 1990, and the government leader, Ivars Godmanis, as well as many cabinet members, comes from its ranks.

The election of the Latvian Supreme Council was a turning point in Latvian political life. Beginning on 17 March 1990 and continuing through several rounds of elections until the end of April, the LPF mobilized every activist voter and tried its utmost to obtain over two-thirds of the seats in the council. On 16 March the front page headline of *Atmoda*, the LPF weekly newspaper, expressed the concern and tension felt by most Latvians with its headline: "Now or Never!" On 4 May 1990, Latvians listened with bated breath during the roll call on the declaration of independence, which was broadcast throughout the republic. The magic number for victory was 134; which was calculated on a basis of a total of 201 seats. The resolution on independence obtained 138 votes.

Only 15 of the deputies analyzed by the Electoral Commission had previously served in the Supreme Soviet of Latvia. The "old guard" had been trounced and replaced.[21] A palpable mood of burnout and lack of interest in politics permeated the Latvian population in the summer and fall of 1990.[22] The empty store shelves, the growth of criminality, the skirmishing with Moscow, the gasoline shortages, and, most important, the sense of pessimism about the advent of real Latvian independence that began to take hold three months after the May declaration created a depressing pall. This depression was enforced by disturbing signals from Rubiks and Moscow: The elected council and government of Latvia would be replaced under presidential rule by a Committee of Public Salvation made up of reactionary members of the local Communist party.[23]

Bloody events did occur when Moscow authorized the storming of the Latvian Interior Ministry by Soviet Black Beret troops in January 1991. Five people lost their lives in a shootout, and Riga was shaken. The fear of a coup led by the armed forces and the Black Berets rallied tens of thousands of Latvians to the defense of the Parliament building and television tower. Barricades were erected in the narrow streets of the inner city and groups of volunteer guards sat by their fires round the clock to resist unwelcome Soviet tanks and supporters. Young and old, Latvians and non-Latvians, radicals and conservatives, all came together during these heady days. Farmers even rolled in their heavy machinery to block the passage of enemy tanks.

The resistance had great psychological significance. It cemented a stronger cohesion among many political and ethnic groups that had earlier begun to fall apart under the stress of a disintegrating economy. Even in the middle of the war in the Middle East, world public opinion rallied in defense of Baltic democracy. The European Community cancelled billions of dollars of credits designed to aid Soviet economic recovery.[24] The army retreated to its barracks, Riga's street barricades were slowly dismantled, and life there returned to normal.

By mid-February the Latvian Supreme Council had begun to debate strategies to deal with another serious challenge: the Gorbachev referendum on the union, which was set for March 17. The Latvian Council (in parallel with the Estonian Council) decided to hold its own, nonbinding, consultation vote to test popular support for a democratic and independent Latvia.

Voting took place on 3 March and 73.7 percent of voters indicated their preference for independence. Furthermore, 87.6 percent of all those eligible had voted, thus sending a clear message to the Kremlin and the world that Latvian independence was desired by more than two-thirds of the inhabitants and that a plurality of non-Latvians was opposed to the continued existence of Latvia as a federal unit of the USSR.[25] The council decided not to support Gorbachev's referendum.

Monumental changes have occurred in Latvia, as they have in most other Soviet republics. Freedom of expression and debate, freedom of assembly and association, and political pluralism and electoral democracy now permeate the daily experience of Latvian citizens. The Latvian national awakening was able to induce changes in policy in areas that were considered important by most Latvians. Many of these changes were introduced even before the advent of the new council and government in May 1990. Latvia's historical symbols, such as the flag of independence, the national anthem, and the coat of arms, have been reestablished as the official emblems of the Latvian state. Holidays for Christmas, Easter, and the traditional midsummer folk festival of *Jani* have replaced revolutionary memorial days. Traditions of the 1930s, such as fraternities, formal dances, and what might be termed bourgeois sophistication, have returned to Latvian social life.

A more objective review of Latvian history has also been initiated. The three Baltic republics together were able to pressure the Kremlin to investigate the way in which they, along with Moldavia, had been handed to Stalin in the secret protocol of the Molotov-Ribbentrop Pact of 23 August 1939. A special commission of the USSR Congress of People's Deputies, under the chairmanship of Aleksandr Yakovlev, reported and denounced the collusion between the Nazis and Stalinist Bolsheviks.[26] Revelations about the 1940 takeover of Latvia, the 1941 and 1949 deportations, the 1959 purges of National Communists, and other such events have become the daily fare in the Latvian media.

Demographic problems are still acute, yet a regulation limiting immigration, together with the actual emigration of nervous Russians and others upset by the changes in the republic, have slowed, if not halted, the increase of non-Latvians. By the end of 1990, there was actually a net decrease in the population of Latvians as a result of emigration.[27]

In the area of language, a law promulgated on 5 May 1989 required secondary school and university graduates to pass a Latvian language examination. It also required all persons working in areas of frequent contact with the public to become bilingual in Latvian and Russian by 1992. In the realm of ethnic relations, a law was passed establishing a Nationalities Council to advise the Supreme Council on issues and participate in the formation of laws relating to nationality interests and rights.[28]

However, many non-Latvians have adopted some of the cardinal concerns of the native population. Many voted for LPF candidates, which ensured support for independence and reform in the Latvian Supreme Council. When forced to choose between remaining a part of the USSR or supporting a democratic and independent Latvia, a large proportion opted for the latter in the plebiscite of 3 March 1991. Such signs of solidarity have helped allay Latvian fears about demographic vulnerability.

This increasing solidarity and the practical need for the support of the non-Latvian population has accounted for the lack of support for Latvian nationalist absolutism. On the other hand, hard-line Communists also realize that their political salvation lies in exacerbating the differences between Latvians and non-Latvians, and in creating polarization and ethnic strife. The claim of ethnic disorder and discrimination was precisely the rallying cry of the Public Salvation Committee when it attempted to oust the elected government under direct presidential rule from Moscow.

The changes in Latvia have been fundamental. Even if all the policy changes and democratic processes achieved since 1987 were to be reversed, the psychological reconstruction of the Latvian collective consciousness and the strengthening of Latvian cohesion and solidarity have created a new foundation for Latvian survival. By itself, Latvia could not change the Soviet world. However, Latvia is no longer alone. The Russian democratic movement (with tens of thousands of educated, rights-oriented individuals) the leadership of the RSFSR under Boris Yeltsin, and other republics which also sought independence were all sympathetic to Latvian survival and independence.

The example of Latvia and the other Baltic republics and their organizational talent played an important role in undermining the legitimacy of the central Soviet empire. It is interesting that Soviet empire-savers displayed particular animosity toward the Baltic. The excesses of the hard-liners and the bridge building with Russian and other democrats no doubt will speed the development of full democracy in all parts of the former Soviet empire, leading to new forms of cooperation between sovereign and independent state units.

NOTES

1. Andrejs Plakans, "The Latvians," in *Russification in the Baltic Provinces and Finland, 1855-1914*, ed. Edward C. Thaden (Princeton, NJ: Princeton University Press, 1981), p. 267. For the development of the Baltic within the Russian Empire and after, see Andrew Ezergailis, *The Latvian Impact on the Bolshevik Revolution* (New York: Columbia University Press, 1983); Stanley W. Page, *The Formation of the Baltic States* (New York: Howard Fertig, 1970); and Georg von Rauch, *The Baltic States: The Years of Independence, 1917-1940.* (Berkeley, CA: University of California Press, 1974).

2. Jukums Vacietis, *Latviesu Strelnieku Vesturiska Nozime* (PSKOV, USSR: Spartaks, 1922), 1: 101, as quoted in Uldis Germanis, "The Rise and Fall of the Latvian Bolsheviks," *Baltic Forum* (New York) 5, no. 1 (Spring 1988): 11.

3. Aleksandr Yakovlev, speech to the Second Congress of the USSR People's Deputies on 23 December 1989, verbatim translation published in *Foreign Broadcast Information Service--Soviet Union*, (hereafter FBIS-SOV) 89-248, 28 December 1989.

4. See Bohdan Nahaylo, "Baltic Echoes in Ukraine," in *Toward Independence: The Baltic Popular Movements*, ed. Jan Arveds Trapans (Boulder, CO: Westview Press, 1991); and Kathleen Mihalisko, "The Popular Movement in Belorussia and Baltic Influences," in *Toward Independence: The Baltic Popular Movements*, ed. Jan Arveds Trapans (Boulder, CO: Westview Press, 1991).

5. R. Misiunas and R. Taagepera, *The Baltic States: Years of Dependence, 1940-1980* (Berkeley: University of California Press, 1983), pp. 274-275.

6. For the policies of the "national Communists" and the reaction to these policies, see Juris Dreifelds, "Latvian National Demands and Group Consciousness since 1959" in *Nationalism in the USSR and Eastern Europe in the Era of Brezhnev and Kosygin*, ed. George W. Simmonds (Detroit, MI: University of Detroit Press, 1977).

7. Latvijas PSR Valsts Statistikas Komiteja, *1989 Gada Vissavienibas Tautas Skaitisanas Rezultati Latvijas PSR* (Riga, Latvia, 1990) and Latvijas PSR Valsts Statistikas Komiteja, *Latvija Sodien* (Riga, Latvia, 1990) p. 13, age profile by ethnicity from computer printout of Soviet census results in Latvia.

8.   Ibid., pp. 18-19.

9.   Dzintra Bungs, "One-and-a-Half Years of Helsinki-86," *Radio Free Europe Research*, 16 February 1988, Jan Arveds Trapans, "The Sources of Latvia's Popular Movement," in *Toward Independence: The Baltic Popular Movements*, ed. Jan Arveds Trapans (Boulder, CO: Westview Press, 1991), Juris Dreifelds, "The Latvian National Rebirth," *Problems of Communism* 38, no. 4 (July-August 1989).

10.   For example, a director of a high school wrote in *Skolotaju Avize* (20 June 1987) that the weak instruction in local history in schools had led to the negative activity around the Statue of Liberty. Maris Caklais, the editor of the cultural weekly *Literatura un Maksla*, also indirectly blamed the lack of Latvian history books for the demonstrations of 14 June.

11.   One of the leaders of the 14 June demonstrations, Rolands Sila-raups, described in an interview the process of communications involved:

We informed the authorities of our plans for the demonstration about one week before 14 June. We also advised Latvian organizations in the West and requested help from Munich radio stations to help spread the word about the demonstration, as we had little opportunity of doing so ourselves. In Latvia we had no access to the press, radio of television. We informed people by word of mouth as best we could, but a lot people found out from Radio Free Europe or the Voice of America. (*Baltic Forum* 4, no. 2 (Fall 1987): 22)

12.   Dzintra Bungs, "Soviet Press on the Demonstration: Searching for an Explanation" in *Radio Free Europe Research*, 29 August 1987. See also translations in *Current Digest of Soviet Press*, 14, no. 34 (23 September 1987): 1-8.

13.   Ibid.

14.   *Baltic Bulletin* (Los Angeles) 7, nos. 2 and 3 (1988).

15.   The official theme of this plenum was "The Actual Problems of Soviet Latvian Culture on the Eve of the 19th CPSU Conference." The various speeches of this plenum were published in the 10 June, 17 June and 1 July and 8 July 1988, editions of *Literatura un Maksla*.

16.   Dzintra Bungs, "People's Front Planned," *Radio Free Europe Research*, 12 July, 1988. *Jurmala*, 20 October 1988. Dainis Ivans, the first president of the Latvian Popular Front, noted that the first memorandum was given to *Padomju Jaunatne* (Soviet Youth) and *Skolotaju Avize* (Teachers' Newspaper) for publication:

As a result of this memorandum, for the first time in history of the Soviet Union *Skolotaju Avize* came out with a white spot [censored area]. I was invited in turn by the Editor of "P.J." Andrejs Cirulis, to be enlightened as to why the document that was signed by "such" people could not be published. (*Armoda*, 2 October

1990)

17.   *Jurmala*, 20 October 1988.

18.   The International Front received support from 6 percent of Latvians, 48 percent of Russians and 45 percent of other nationalities in a poll taken in November 1988 by the Center for Research on Social Thought and Prognosis (affiliated with the LCP Central Committee), but obtained only 2 percent from Latvians and 17 percent from others in July 1989 when polled by the same organization, *Padomju Jaunatne*, 7 December 1988 and 27 July 1989.

19.   *Atmoda*, 8 January 1991. Radio Free Europe, *This Week in the Baltic States*, 2 January 1991.

20.   *Argumenty i fakty*, no. 1 (1991), Radio Free Europe, *This Week in the Baltic States*, 31 January 1991, p. 1.

21.   The report by the electoral commission analyzed only 197 delegates because 4 others were still under review for possible breaches of electoral laws. In line with trends in the 1989 March election, and even with worldwide parliamentary representation trends, this was preponderantly a body of highly educated, middle-aged men. Among the deputies there were only 11 women, but 180 deputies had a higher education (plus 3 with an incomplete higher and 14 with a secondary education), and only 6 were under the age of 30. The most popular age groups were 30-40 (54), 40-50 (59), and 50-60 (68). The most popular profession were engineering (23), law (16), economics (13), journalism (12), and medicine (9).

22.   The first president of the Latvian People's Front, Dainis Ivans, noted the "tiredness" of the front in October 1990: "We can count on the fingers of one hand, the people who can realistically work at the Latvia-wide level," *Atmoda*, 2 October 1990, p. 8. A deputy of the Latvian Supreme Council, Andrejs Pentelejvs, claimed "There is widespread apathy and lethargy among the people. It may seem quite surprising, but wherever one looks, there appears to be a chronic shortage of active hands and thinking minds," *Awakening* (Riga), 28 February 1991. I observed this myself during a four-month visit to Riga and other Latvian cities at the time.

23.   Alfreds Rubiks, the first secretary of the Communist party in Latvia and also head of the All-Latvia Public Salvation Committee, declared that the party had taken over the reins of power on 15 January 1991. By 29 January he had announced that his committee was discontinuing its claim to executive power in Latvia. The chairman of the Latvian Supreme Council has divulged the information that Rubiks had sent a letter to Gorbachev requesting the right for his committee to take over power, Radio Free Europe, *This Week in the Baltic States*, 31 January 1991, pp. 6, 7.

24.   Radio Free Europe, *This Week in the Baltic States*, 7 February 1991, p. 3.

25.   *Neatkariga Cina*, 9 March 1991.

26.   Aleksandr Yakovlev's report on the Molotov-Ribbentrop Pact was

officially presented to the second session of the USSR Congress of People's Deputies in December 1989, but newspaper briefings appeared earlier in the Summer. *Latvian News Digest*, August 1989, Radio Free Europe, *This Week in the Baltic States*, 31 January 1991.

27.   The net increase in 1990 was only 516, but this included a sharp increase in non-Latvian military and Ministry of Interior personnel, *Latvijas Jaunatne*, 7 March 1991, and 9 March 1991.

28.   *Diena (pielikums)*, 21 February 1991.

4

Ukrainian Nationalism and the Future

BOHDAN HARASYMIW

In 1987, Alexander Motyl published a book entitled *Will the Non-Russians Rebel?*[1] His answer to that question was that the non-Russians will not rebel because they cannot. The gist of his theoretically refined, closely reasoned, and, at the same time, witty, argument can be summed up as follows: A state's stability is a matter of its control over society. More specifically, it is essentially the relationship between the state and groups that oppose it. This involves a political struggle, the most important feature of which is the state's survival. Instability means loss of control. Challenges to this stability, however, require a culmination of several key factors, including collective action. "Stability, or the effective pursuit of survival," therefore, "consists of a state's prevention and containment of antistate collective actions by antistate forces."[2] Since there are "political, class, and ethnic authority patterns," stability is therefore also tripartite, and thus "*antistate* refers to opposition to a state's political, class, and ethnic patterns of authority."[3] Effective collective action, according to Motyl, requires ideas of rebellion against the state, the deprivatization of such ideas, organized opposition, and leadership, all of which are relatively undeveloped among the non-Russians of the USSR.

Since the USSR is multiethnic and the Soviet state is Russian, argued Motyl, the initiative for rebellion, for the destabilization of the state, and for effective challenge to its survival had to come from the largest non-Russian group, the Ukrainians. The Ukrainians, however, are unlikely to initiate and mount any such effective challenge to the state's survival because of their relative economic well-being, their acceptance of the Marxist-Leninist ideology that legitimize Russian dominance; their acquiescence in Soviet

I am grateful to Professors Robert Henderson and John Jaworsky for their helpful critical comments on the first draft of this chapter.

language policy, which subordinated Ukrainian to Russian; their enjoyment of Unionwide career opportunities as well as local political hegemony; and, finally, the effectiveness of the KGB in coercing compliance and docility. The combination of these inhibit rebellion, primarily among the Ukrainians, and ensures the survival of the Soviet Union as a multiethnic empire. Motyl's conclusion is almost categorical:

> If economic decline and ideological erosion set in and outside interference continues, behavioral reasons for rebellion may accumulate. . . . But . . . as long as the public sphere is occupied and . . . the KGB remains intact, the deprivatization of anti-state attitudes will be problematic, antistate collectivities . . . will be unlikely to mobilize, alliances . . . will not materialize, and rebellion . . . will be well-nigh impossible.[4]

Paradoxically, Motyl's thesis that the non-Russians will not rebel because they cannot is both wrong and right. It is wrong because things have changed dramatically in the past few years in ways that cannot have been anticipated on the very threshold of the Gorbachev era. The non-Russians are obviously rebelling against the Soviet Russian state, as are, indeed, the Russians themselves. They are rebelling against both the Russian and the Soviet character of that state, for it is one in which the Communist Party of the Soviet Union (CPSU) permeates the government, the Russians dominate the state, and the state controls the society. Motyl's thesis is right because his theoretical framework helps explain this unexpected rebellion.

According to Motyl, actions by the state itself are critical in determining the effectiveness of challenges to its stability.[5] The policies of openness (*glasnost*) and democratization (*demokratizatsiia*), including the introduction of relatively free elections, have, it could easily be argued, transformed conditions so fundamentally that non-Russians and Russians alike *are able* to rebel against the Soviet system as we have known it. The only factor inhibiting full-scale rebellion, in Motyl's scheme, is the continued presence of the KGB, but even this is being eroded.[6] Consequently, those of us who appreciate both liberty and good political science should be glad to see Motyl's thesis disproven, while his analysis, with its emphasis on ethnicity as the key to the stability of the Soviet state, is vindicated.

Ukrainians are today included among the non-Russian rebels, and their rebellion is tinged by nationalism, but will this lead to a nationalist revolution? Are events moving in the direction of the nationalist revolution, where this means a violent overthrow of the existing order borne on an uncompromising ideology of national self-determination and self-assertion, or is it a democratic revolution that is liable to espouse ethnic equality? In short, what sort of state is now being formed in Ukraine?

In their search for alternatives to Soviet communism as a fundamental principle of political organization, and in common with other non-Russians, the Ukrainians have not much choice but to reach for some combination of nationalism, liberalism, and democracy. Anathematized by Marxism-Leninism, which endorsed a combination of authoritarian centralism, Russian dominance, and working-class leadership, these alternatives are decentralization, autonomy, and leadership by some other class or classes (such as the intelligentsia). It boils down to a decidedly bourgeois nationalism.

Is the situation in Ukraine a rebellion or revolution in more than a figurative sense? It may, after all, simply result in an adjustment of the relationship between Moscow and Kiev and between state and society within Ukraine, and not in a fundamental change, that is, a transformation of the state and the political system. To determine the answer we must perform the analysis in terms of specified set of determinants of change. Simply put, the determinants of change can be said to include ideas for change, organizations of collectivities working for change, the leadership of these organizations; and the responses (both in ideology and action) of the established authorities. Ideas for change have been present in Ukraine in the dissident movement since the 1960's, but their proponents were atomized and their ideas privatized; it is the public expression of ideas for change--their deprivatization--that is needed.[7]

Violent, revolutionary change has, according to Chalmers Johnson, all these components in extreme form plus a power deflation (so that anyone's power is as legitimate as anyone else's), an intransigent regime, and, finally, the collapse of the army.[8] The process of change, whether evolutionary or revolutionary, operates in contingent rather than causal fashion. The end point of the process--transformation or adaptation--is not predetermined by the mere presence of any one of the variables but rather depends on the operation of other factors that may or may not come into play. What happens at each stage of the process may delay or accelerate change.

Let us examine the state of play in the Ukrainian SSR in the autumn of 1990. Was there a trend toward fundamental change of the Ukrainian state from Soviet and Communist to something else? Clearly, the situation had changed in certain basic respects from the point at which Alexander Motyl drew his conclusions just three years earlier.[9] *Glasnost'* allowed the public expression of previously forbidden ideas throughout the USSR.

Participants and observers alike were astonished by the explicit anti-Sovietism which swept the country. *Perestroika*, Gorbachev's ideology of modernization, sanctioned the sidelining of Marxism-Leninism and its replacement by liberalism, of which Gorbachev himself was the leading exponent.[10] The acknowledgment of the failure of Soviet socialism resulted in the discrediting of communism and in opening the way for one of its only available alternatives, nationalism. Antistate ideas were no longer privatized, thanks to the modern means of communication--television, telephone, videotape, radio, cassette players, xerox, and facsimile.

The retreat by the Communist party from its monopoly position opened up public space to other entities. The elections of 1989 and 1990
facilitated the formation of alternative political organizations (parties and
proto-parties). The resulting legislatures, with their lively, well-publicized
sessions and important committee hearings, served as incubators for still
more political parties.[11] The KGB remained active in disrupting antistate
activity but was unable to block it altogether. The abolition of the Fifth
Chief Directorate in the KGB for the prosecution of dissidents and the
creation of a Department for the Preservation of the Constitutional Order
could be seen not so much as a liberalization as an adaptive move to keep
up with the deprivatization of antistate ideas.[12] The government and the
Communist party became unstuck; the state no longer controlled society.

IDEAS AND THEIR DEPRIVATIZATION

In the realm of publicly expressed ideas, Marxism-Leninism in Ukraine
was under siege and nationalism was on the way up. Practically everyone
who is active in politics, including the Communist Party of Ukraine (CPU),
was a nationalist in the sense of being an advocate of the primacy of the
republic's rights over those of the Center. Practically everyone was in favor
of a Ukrainian cultural rebirth.

The CPU was against separatism, for the equality of all languages,
and for sovereignty within the framework of a restructured Union. It warned
of the economic costs of separation, although its opponents countered with
convincing data about the cost of continued union.

No comprehensive surveys of people's attitudes had appeared, but it
was not unreasonable to assume that the old political symbols lost their
meaning.[13] Reports spoke increasingly of the "desecration" of statues of
Lenin.[14] The public display of the blue-and-yellow flag also indicated a
basic shift in public opinion from acquiescence to some sort of nationalist
opposition.[15] Further evidence of the development of nationalist ideas could
be seen in the evolution of the opposition umbrella movement, the Popular
Movement for Reconstruction or Rukh. At its formation in 1989, it aimed
to accelerate the Gorbachevian reconstruction policy within the existing
state structure, while a year later, it advocated outright independence.[16]

ORGANIZED COLLECTIVITIES WORKING FOR CHANGE

The formation of political parties and other organizations in Ukraine
added to the evidence of unforeseen fundamental change. These "organized collectivities" made the uncoupling of Kiev from Moscow and the
Communist party from the government, as well as the control of the state
by the society in Ukraine, more likely.

Among the notable developments were:

1. The transformation of the Ukrainian Helsinki Union into the Ukrainian Republican party;
2. The registration of the Popular Movement for Reconstruction as a political party during the elections of 1990; it formed the core of the opposition in the elected assemblies;
3. The formation of a radical splinter from the CPU united around the Democratic Platform, whose deputies joined the opposition in the national assembly;
4. The creation of the Democratic Party of Ukraine (DPU) out of *Rukh*;
5. The organization of the parliamentary opposition in Kiev into the People's Council (*Narodna rada*), which comprised about 25 percent of the deputies;
6. The changeover to Kiev time (one hour behind Moscow but one hour closer to Europe);
7. The formation of a republic-wide Coordinating Council of Democratic Associations and Democratic Blocs (namely, of opposition groupings, parliamentary and extraparliamentary alike);
8. The organization of a Liberal-Democratic Party of Ukraine;
9. The creation of a Green Party of Ukraine;
10. The formation within the national assembly of numerous groupings, such as Accord, Rebirth, Independence, For Human Rights, and Free Democrats; and
11. The establishment of the right-wing youth movement SNUM, which is associated with the Ukrainian Republican party.

All this activity indicated the breakdown of the Soviet one-party state in Ukraine. The degree of popular support for the ideas of change of these various parties will have to be assessed at the next elections, or whenever serious public opinion polling is eventually undertaken.

On the crucial question of independence, the organized formations in Ukraine could be ranged along a continuum from the CPU's conservative position at one end to the URP's unequivocally nationalist stance at the other. It would entail a longer process of differentiation, clarification, and coalition building than has been indicated in the Communist-controlled press. For its own political purposes, the CPU was attempting to emphasize the polarization of political forces on the stage today. By exaggerating the differences between itself and the nationalists, it presented itself as the only alternative to Hitler.

Examining the different stands on independence, the preservation of Soviet institutions, pluralism, and nationalism revealed differing shades of opinion rather than stark contrast. None of them, however--not even the CPU--accepted the pre-*perestroika* status quo.

For its part, the CPU was attempting to repair rather than replace its ideology and structure. Its platform promised greater economic independence for Ukraine from the central ministries in Moscow, state sovereignty for the republic within the proposed Union Treaty, retention of the welfare state with its guarantee of work, equality of all languages and ethnic groups, a regulated market economy, revival of the countryside, and a renewed CPU somehow independent of the CPSU but still a vanguard within it.[17] It was specifically opposed to separatism and did not foresee the dismemberment of the USSR. This rather conservative platform, which offers to improve socialism, was not likely to sustain the party's popularity at a time of a widespread shift toward nationalism.

The CPU, furthermore, was no longer monolithic. According to one survey, its left wing was said to comprise about 20 percent of the membership; the center, a majority of 52 percent, and the right wing, 22.5 percent. These groupings were, in turn, fragmented into various attitudinal and opinion clusters.[18] The clearest evidence of the fragmentation of the CPU was the formation of the splinter group based on the Democratic Platform of the CPSU. Those of its followers who were deputies in the national assembly joined the official opposition and were contemplating forming a distinct political party.[19] The Democratic Platform was distinct from the CPU in rejecting the party's centralism and insisted on its becoming a democratic socialist party.[20] While the Democratic Platform did not make a point of incorporating nationalism into its program, it did speak of turning the CPSU into a true union of republic parties seeking an honest mandate from the public. The emergence of the Democratic Platform was part of the process of the unraveling of the Soviet state, accepting as it did the idea that the Party had to discard its authoritarianism, both internally and externally.

Rukh began as an auxiliary to the Communist party rather than an opposition to it.[21] It appeared to offer to help the CPU by mobilizing popular support for democratization, economic renewal, restoration of the environment, and cultural survival. By the time of its founding congress in September 1989, however, its program, while still supporting the CPSU's proclamation principles of "radical social renewal," had moved more definitely in the direction of bourgeois liberalism and nationalism and away from Soviet socialism.[22] This amounts to a moderate and constructive movement for reform with a nod in the direction of all the chief concerns of the day: ecological, economic, libertarian, socialist, and nationalist.

While there is not much besides its explicit elaboration to distinguish *Rukh*'s emphasis on the individual and the rule of law from Gorbachev's liberal-democratic position, its stand on the national question is uncompromising. Its program states that, among other things, "every nation must have the following rights:

--the right to existence; . . .
--the right to political self-determination; the right to choose its own economic and social system; . . .

--the right to dominion over territory it has settled from time immemorial; . . .

--the right to its natural resources; . . .

--the right to a democratic order which serves the interests of the entire population; . . .

--the right . . . as an entire community to self-preservation on territory which has belonged to it from time immemorial, by securing the primacy of its language, national traditions, customs--everything which composes the culture of the *ethnos*."[23]

In the section of its program dealing specifically with the national question, *Rukh* states unequivocally its position that:

--"nations are basic units of human civilization, human communities with a historical future; . . .

--a higher level of maturity of a nation is national statehood. Only under conditions of political, economic and cultural sovereignty is the free development of nations possible; . . .

--the Ukrainian nation holds the status of the historical master in the republic. Ukraine is the only territory in the world where the full-valued existence and development of the Ukrainian *ethnos* are possible;

--an important integrating factor in ethnic communities is language and national consciousness. A national language is the foundation and the primary source of a culture. . . . When a national language dies, the people perish as a nation."[24]

Rukh espouses a belief in the equality of peoples. It "favors the development of the national cultures of all nationalities residing in Ukraine."[25] At the same time, it gives priority to the Ukrainian people and language because these are imperiled in the present circumstances. Even though its membership is open to Communists, this espousal of nationalism has put *Rukh* at odds with official communism.

The Democratic Party of Ukraine (DPU) is somewhat less Bolshevik and more nationalist than either the CPU or its Democratic Platform members. It is a social-democratic party that rejects the totalitarian impulses of the Communists and claims to embrace the ideals of freedom, justice, and popular power.[26] The DPU favors a confederal, rather than federal, link between Kiev and Moscow, as this would accord with the idea of full state sovereignty on the model of Western Europe. This would mean Ukraine's exit from the USSR. "An independent Ukrainian state is one of life's historical needs, an objective need both of the Ukrainian nation as well as of the entire population of Ukraine," says the party's manifesto. Its position on the nationalities question, however, is not as ethnocentric as that of the republicans. It promises the harmonizing of interethnic relations and the satisfaction of the national-cultural needs of all groups in Ukraine.

At the furthest end of the spectrum is the Ukrainian Republic party (URP). It rejects altogether the Gorbachevian idea of a new Union Treaty and advocates not only Ukraine's exit from the USSR but also the dissolution and abolition of the Communist party, to the alarm of the Communists. The URP has been extremely effective in resurrecting traditional Ukrainian nationalist symbols and heroes, not least among them the wartime guerrilla leader, Stepan Bandera.[27] The Communist press depicts the URP as plotting the violent overthrow of the state.

Not only are virtually all organized Ukrainian political groups in favor of some degree of independence, but the opposition has appropriated the term *democratic* to differentiate itself from the Communists. Some of these democrats called for the removal of Communist representatives from the assemblies, despite their proper election. The Communists view the idea of being removed without due process as destabilizing. They have not yet decoupled in their minds the concepts of government and the Communist party. For them, a challenge to the Communist party is a challenge to the state. For their opponents, while removing Communists from power would not mean the end of the state, it still had a revolutionary flavor.

The fate of these organizations and groupings depended on the leaders' control over their followers, the incentives they could offer, their ability to build lasting coalitions, and their competence as perceived by the public. The factor of leadership was already working to the disadvantage of the Communists, as their mounting difficulties in attaining and retaining positions of leadership in the assemblies, especially the republic Supreme Soviet, attested to.[28] Even the Communist press expressed reservations about the abilities of CPU leaders.

OTHER FACTORS PROMOTING FUNDAMENTAL CHANGE

Spurred by the opposition, within the Parliament as well as on the street, the Soviet Ukrainian government enacted a number of laws attempting to respond to the nationalistic concerns of the public and thereby forestall loss of control: laws on the ecological situation, a law which made Ukrainian the state language, a law on economic sovereignty, and a law on sovereignty itself.[29]

The declaration on state sovereignty was the most important document for present purposes. It went beyond the RSFSR's earlier example and beyond the CPU program, and yet it was approved in the Supreme Soviet by an overwhelming vote of 355 to 4 in spite of the fact that the opposition held only one-quarter of the seats.[30] It declared, according to one commentary, that "the people of Ukraine, as masters of the land, airspace, mineral wealth, and waterways of the republic, enjoy the exclusive right to make use of its natural resources."[31] It also provided for the republic to have its own citizenship and its own financial arrangements, including banking, taxation, budget, and currency. The declaration differed from its Russian counterpart in that it did not concede powers to the center in Moscow. Instead, it "proclaims the right of Ukraine to have its own army and security forces, and it asserts the republic's intention to become a neutral and military non-aligned state."[32] Although the document was a statement of intention rather than a declaration of independence--it dealt with "state" rather than "national" sovereignty--it was just as clearly a step toward the end of the Soviet state, the entity calling itself a federation that we knew.

Local governments went further. They set up their own militia, curtailed the activities of the Communist party and press, suspended the drafting of conscripts into the Soviet army, and switched flags and symbols long before this was done in the capital.[33] Particularly in western Ukraine, where *Rukh* had preponderant support, to the chagrin of Communists everywhere, assemblies went beyond statements of intent and began to carry out the de-Sovietization and de-Partification of the state.

These measures did not met the opposition's demands, but they went considerably farther than the CPU on its own would have gone. More important, they indicated a movement away from stability, Russian hegemony, Communist Party dominance, and state control of society. The Ukrainian Supreme Soviet amended the constitution so that its laws had primacy on its own territory, and popularly elected Soviets were taking control of some outlets of the mass media away from the Communist party.[34] Moves were made to have international recognition by and diplomatic relations with other independent states.[35] Nothing significant happened, however, in the crucial area of the old links that the CPU maintained with the CPSU, the KGB, and the *nomenklatura*.

The CPU fought this all the way. If it dug in its heels, if there was a power deflation, or if the army proves unreliable, then there could be a revolutionary change. However, as of the end of 1990, this scenario looked doubtful, not least because the regime was not an intransigent one and the army was known to be unreliable. Unless the new representative institutions and their participating political parties lost legitimacy, the transition from the Soviet order to independent statehood was likely to be stormy but nonviolent.

OUTLOOK

There is no doubt that the non-Russians are rebelling, and even though Motyl's prediction on the face of it was wrong, we may understand better, thanks to him, why they are rebelling. The future of the nationalist rebellion that we are witnessing in Ukraine will depend on several variables. These are:

1.   Whose definition of nationalism is likely to win out in the parlia-

mentary and electoral struggle yet to come? Will it be democratic
or authoritarian, centralist or decentralizing? Will it be integral,
conservative, and intolerant (as nationalist movements in Ukraine
in the past have been), or political, liberal, and tolerant (as the
Rukh is trying to be)?

2.   Who will control the KGB, Moscow, and Kiev? Will it be the
Communists, some other governing party or coalition, the legislature, or the government?[36]

3.   Will Ukraine itself be destabilized by ethnic and regional conflicts? Will the issue be settled by secession? When will the last
nation-state have been formed? The answer, of course, is that
there is no finite end to this process and to the pursuit of the
principle of national self-determination. The principle must
ultimately be displaced by some other principle.

In any case, beyond the resolution of these key considerations lies the
fact that nationalism--whatever its program--cannot address all political
issues facing the republic or soon to confront it as the result of communism's collapse. For the moment, until the ethnic inequalities between Russians and Ukrainians are perceived to have been righted, nationalism will
remain at the top of the Ukrainians' political agenda.

NOTES

1.   Alexander J. Motyl, *Will the Non-Russians Rebel? State, Ethnicity, and Stability in the USSR* (Ithaca, NY: Cornell University Press, 1987).

2.   Ibid., p. 7.

3.   Ibid., p. 14, emphasis in the original.

4.   Ibid., p. 170.

5.   As he said, "State policies . . . directly permit anti-state attitudes,
collectivities, and elites to arise and antistate collective action to threaten
state stability" (p. 18).

6.   This is a distillation from Motyl, pp. 14-17; and Andrew C. Janos,
*Politics and Paradigms: Changing Theories of Change in the Social Sci-
ences* (Stanford, CA: Stanford University Press, 1986).

7.   Ludmilla Alexeyeva, *Soviet Dissent: Contemporary Movements
for National, Religious, and Human Rights*, trans. Carol Pearce and John
Glad (Middletown, CT: Wesleyan University Press, 1987), ch. 1, "The
Ukrainian National Movement."

8.   Chalmers Johnson, *Revolutionary Change*, 2nd ed. (Stanford,
CA: Stanford University Press, 1982). "Revolutionary change," he said, "is
a special kind of social change, one that involves the intrusion of violence
into civil relations" (p. 1). Further on, he wrote: "True revolution is neither
lunacy nor crime. It is the acceptance of violence to cause the system to

change when all else has failed, and the very idea of revolution is contingent on this perception of social failure" (p. 13).

9.   Motyl.

10.   See M. Gorbachev, "*Sotsialisticheskaia ideia i revolutsionnaia perestroika*," *Pravda*, 26 November 1989, pp. 1-3.

11.   See, for instance, "Unofficial Parties, Clubs Burgeon," *Current Digest of the Soviet Press*, 17, no. 13 (28 March 1990): 5-8, 28 (hereafter *CDSP*); and "Legislative Factionalism in Russia, Ukraine," *CDSP*, 17, no. 25 (20 June 1990): pp. 10-13.

12.   "*Sovetskomu konstitutsionnomu stroiu--nadezhnuiu zashchitu,*" *Pravda*, 2 November 1989, p. 3; Viktor Yasmann, "The KGB," *Report on the USSR*, 2, no. 52 (29 December 1989): 8-10; and Alexander J. Motyl, "Policing Perestroika: The Indispensable KGB," *Harriman Institute Forum*, August 1989.

13.   A public opinion poll of uncertain validity was reported by the North American service of Radio Kiev as showing "the critical mood of the Ukrainian population in the country's current situation." It said that "82% of those polled believe the restructuring has only partially met their expectations. Among the young the percentage is even higher: 90. Only 33% of those polled believe economic problems can be solved positively. As to the nationality question, almost 40% expressed great doubt that it can be solved by directives." The report concluded, "The young are especially pessimistic. Over 40% of this group believes the situation in the country is not changing at all." *Foreign Broadcast Information Service-Soviet Union* 90-037 (23 February 1990): 64 (hereafter *FBIS-SOV*). While this indicates some general pessimism about *perestroika*, it says nothing about antistate attitudes.

14.   "Kiev Procuracy Denies Wrongdoing in Demonstrators' Arrests," *JPRS-UPA* 90-050 (27 August 1990): 60; "Nationalist Tensions on Rise in Poltava," *JPRS-UPA* 90-050 (27 August 1990): pp.60-61; "Ukraine CP Protests Dismantling of Lenin Statues," *FBIS-SOV* 90-155 (10 August 1990): 64; "Ukrainian Ralliers Denounce Union Treaty," *FBIS-SOV* 90-157 (14 August 1990): 75; "Removal of Lenin, Marx Statues Protested," *JPRS-UPA* 90-052 (3 September 1990): 51-52; "Lvov Deserters' Situation Examined," *FBIS-SOV* 90-178 (13 September 1990): 97-98; "Donetsk Protesters Decry Monuments' Destruction," *FBIS-SOV* 90-185 (24 September 1990: 97; and "Explosion Occurs at Lenin Monument in Feodosiya," *FBIS-SOV* 90-193 (4 October 1990): 99. See also, for instance, I. Dmytrenko, "Demokraty' poriadkuiut," *Radians'ka Ukraina*, 3 August 1990, p. 1; and V. Desiatnykov, "*Tak khtozh my ye? Z pryvodu deiakykh politychnykh aktsii novykh 'demokrativ',*" *Radians'ka Ukraina*, 29 August 1990, p. 3; and "Kiev Rally Protests Destruction of Lenin Monuments," *JPRS-UPA* 90-056 (24 September 1990): 45. For the official viewpoint, see CPSU Central Committee declaration, "*O faktakh politicheskogo vandalizma i protivopravnykh deistviiakh v otnoshenii pamiatnikov V. I. Leninu,* 14 avgusta 1990 g.," *Izvestiia TsK*

KPSS, no. 9 (1990): 11-12.

15.   Note the contrast between "*Gorispolkom narushil zakon*," *Pravda Ukrainy*, 30 March 1990, p. 3, and "Kiev Sanctions Use of Prerevolutionary Symbols," *FBIS-SOV* 90-184 (21 September 1990): 65. See also "Ukrainian National Flag Raised in Kiev," *JPRS-UPA* 90-056 (24 September 1990): 43-44.

16.   Roman Solchanyk, "Beginnings of the Ukrainian Popular Front: An Interview with Pavlo Movchan," *Report on the USSR* (28 July 1989): 21-25; "Ukrainian Popular Front to Seek More Autonomy," *Ottawa Citizen*, 9 September 1989, p. A7; "*Dva pohiady na Rukh'*," *Literaturna Ukraina*, 1 February 1990, p. 5; "Rukh, Ukraine Party Official Express Views," *JPRS-UPA* 90-006 (7 February 1990): 19-21; "Kravchuk Reviews Rukh's Program, Perestroyka," *FBIS-SOV* 90-198-A (12 October 1990): 11-14; and "Ukrainian People's Movement Meets, Seeks Independence," *Foreign Broadcast Information Service--Soviet Union* (26 October 1990), citing *Izvestiia*, 26 October 1990, p. 2. Even more remarkable is the fact that, as Roman Solchanyk said, "In the short space of several months, the top leadership of Ukraine has begun to defend positions formulated by the Popular Movement of Ukraine for *Perestroika*, "Rukh," and for which the latter had been roundly criticized by the very same Party and government leadership," "Ukrainian Party Congress Supports State Sovereignty," *Report on the USSR*, 20 July 1990, p. 22.

17.   "*Programmnye printsipy dejatel'nosti Kompartii Ukrainy*," *Pravda Ukrainy*, 30 June 1990, pp. 1-2; available in English in "Principles of Ukrainian Party Program Stated," *FBIS-SOV* 90-159 (16 August 1990): 72-81.

18.   "Discontent with Party Leadership in Eastern Ukrainian Oblasts Viewed," *JPRS-UPA* 90-050 (27 August 1990): 54.

19.   *Izvestiia*, 13 June 1990, p. 4, translated in *CDSP*, 14, no. 25 (18 June 1990): 25; "USSR: Ukrainian Deputies Explain Resignation from CPSU," citing Moscow Television Service in Russian, 2101 GMT 26 July 1990 in *Federal Broadcast Information Service--Soviet Union*, 083 (26 July 1990).

20.   *Ob'yednavcha demokratycha platforma do XXVIII z'yizdu KRPS (Demokratychnu platforma u Kompartii Ukrayiny): Proekt*," *Radians'ka Ukraina*, 3 June 1990, p. 2.

21.   See the draft of its original program, "*Prohrama Narodnoho Rukhu Ukranyiny za Perebudovu*," *Literaturna Ukraina*, 16 February 1989, p. 3.

22.   *The Popular Movement of Ukraine for Restructuring, RUKH: Program and Charter*, ed. by George Sajewych and Andrew Sorokowski, trans. Martha D. Oliynyk (Kiev: Smoloskyp Publishers, 1989).

23.   Ibid., pp. 15-16.

24.   Ibid., p. 28.

25.   Ibid., p. 29.

26. "*Manifest Demokratychnoi partii Ukrainy*," *Literaturna Ukraina*, 31 May 1990, pp. 4-5.

27. "*Pid 'Respublikans'km' kamufliazhem, abo Chomu ia vyishov z Ukrains'koi respublikans'koi partii*," *Radians'ka Ukraina*, 16 August 1990, p. 3; "Ukrainian Republican Party Rally Opposes Treaty," *FBIS-SOV* 90-173 (6 September 1990): 97-98; "Ukrainian Party Chief Opposes Union Treaty," *FBIS-SOV* 90-183 (20 September 1990): 89; *Pravda*, 30 September 1990, p. 2.

28. The stormy elections of Volodymyr Ivashko and Vitalii Masol and their subsequent resignations are illustrative of this problem. See, for instance, "*ChP v parliamente Ukrainy*," *Izvestiia*, 28 June 1990, p. 2 (Moscow evening edition); "Party Chief Elected President of Ukraine," *Globe and Mail*, 5 June 1990; "*Izbran Predsedatel'*," *Pravda*, 5 June 1990, p. 2; "Dead Souls' Vote in Ukrainian Supreme Soviet," *FBIS-SOV* 90-137 (17 July 1990): 80-81; "Kiev Fails to Elect New Leadership," *FBIS-SOV* 90-136 (16 July 1990): 87 and "USSR: Ukraine Council of Ministers Head Resigns, Denies Charges," *FBIS-SOV* 071OCT23, citing Moscow TASS International Service in Russian, 1640 GMT 23 October 1990.

29. For the language law, see *Pravda* Ukrainy, 3 November 1989; for the ecology law, see "*Pro ekolohichu obstanovku v respublitsi ta zakhody po yiyi dokorinnomu polipshenniu*," *Radians'ka Ukraina*, 1 March 1990, p. 2, and the commentary of David Marples, "Decree on Ecology Adopted in Ukraine," *Report on the USSR*, 6 April 1990, pp. 15-16; on economic sovereignty, see "*Ob ekonomicheskoi samostoiatel'nosti Ukrainskoi SSR*," *Pravda Ukrainy*, 8 August 1990, pp. 1-2, available in English as "Ukrainian Law on Economic Independence Published," *FBIS-SOV* 90-166 (27 August 1990): 99-102. The declaration of sovereignty is outlined in "Ukraine, Belorussia Declare Sovereignty," *CDSP*, 14, no. 35 (29 August 1990): 8, and "Ukraine Declares Sovereign Rights," *Globe and Mail*, 17 July 1990.

30. Kathleen Mihalisko, "Ukraine's Declaration of Sovereignty," *Report on the USSR*, 27 July 1990, pp. 17-19.

31. Ibid., p.18.

32. Ibid., p.17.

33. Nick Worrall, "Ukrainian City Spurns Communism," *Christian Science Monitor*, 21 May 1990; Linda Feldman, "Democrats Take Over in Lvov," *Christian Science Monitor*, 28 August 1990; "Lvov Forms Municipal Militia," *JPRS-UPA* 90-048 (16 August 1990): 54; "Lvov Oblast Suspends Military Conscription, *FBIS-SOV* 90-177 (12 September 1990): 99, "Lvov Deserters' Situation Examined," *FBIS-SOV* 90-178 (13 September 1990): 97-98; "Army Conscription Commission in Lvov Suspended," *FBIS-SOV* 90-182 (19 September 1990): 83; "Proceedings of Lvov Soviet of People's Deputies Meeting Viewed," *JPRS-UPA* 90-055, (19 September 1990): 26-29; "Lvov Oblast Sets Up Own Customs Center," *JPRS-UPA* 90-056 (24 September 1990): 42-43; "Lvov Area Streets to Be Renamed," *JPRS-UPA* 90-056 (24 September 1990): 43; and "Ternopol Nationalizes Party

Property," *FBIS-SOV* 90-197 (11 October 1990): 111.

34.   "Ukrainian Supsov Declares Supremacy of Ukrainian Laws," *Foreign Broadcast Information Service* 123 Oct 26, citing *Izvestiia* (Union edition) (27 October 1990): 2 "*Holos Ukrayiny'--Gazeta Sovetov,*" *Pravda Ukrainy*, 2 September 1990, p. 3, "*Redaktory ob"ediniaiutsia,*" *Izvestiia*, 25 September 1990, p. 2 (Moscow evening edition).

35."USSR: Ukraine, Hungary Establish Consular Links," *Foreign Broadcast Information Service* 117 Sep 27, citing Budapest Domestic Service in Hungarian, 1600 GMT (27 September 1990); and "Poland to Establish Consular Relations with Ukraine," *FBIS-SOV* 143 OCT 13, citing Warsaw PAP in English, 1901 GMT (13 October 1990).

36.   The demonstration at the Lublianka off Dzerzhinsky Square in the autumn of 1989 and the more recent picketing of the republic KGB headquarters in Kiev on 30 August 1990 might be indicative in this regard. Francis X. Clines, "Protesters March to K.G.B. Headquarters," *New York Times*, 31 October 1989; "*Piketirovanie zdaniia KGB USSR,*" *Pravda Ukrainy*, 1 September 1990, p. 2; "Protest Picket Held at Ukrainian KGB Offices," *FBIS-SOV* 90-172 (5 September 1990): 121. Although the initials of the Committee for State Security in Ukraine are KDB (*Komitet Derzhavnoi Bezpeky*), I use the more familiar abbreviation, KGB.

Part 3

THE CAUCASIAN PERIPHERY

The Caucasian periphery of the Soviet Union was chiefly composed of three republics: Armenia, Azerbaijan, and Georgia. These republics are relatively small but densely populated. Soon after the October Revolution of 1917, this area was united under the Transcaucasian Socialist Federative Soviet Republic, a political entity that existed until 1936. Each of the republics have their own language. The Armenians and Georgians are Christians, while the Azeris are Shi'i Muslims. This area is located on the main routes from Asia to Europe and has thus come under the influence of Persian, Turkish, and Russian rule. The three republics are also the homelands of a significant number of other nationalities. In fact, the Abkhazians, South Ossetians, and Adzharians have had their own territorial status, as does the Nakhichevan Autonomous Socialist Soviet Republic in Armenia and the Nagorno-Karabakh Autonomous Socialist Soviet Republic in Azerbaijan.

The Armenians are an ancient people who were first conquered by the Turks and the Iranians. In 1915, the Turks slaughtered more than 1.5 million Armenians in one of the worst cases of genocide in this century. The Armenians and the Azeris have been involved in major ethnic disputes virtually since the inception of their republics. The Nakhichevan ASSR in Armenia is populated mainly by Azeris, while the Nagorno-Karabakh ASSR in Azerbaijan is mainly populated by Armenians. Ethnic violence between the two republics came to a head in February 1988, resulting in many deaths. Georgia has also been the site of ethnic violence, especially in the Abkhazia, South Ossetia, and Marneuli areas. The Abkhazians and South Ossetians have long desired their own republics, something the Georgians are loath to give them.

The Caucasian periphery had been in the Western media for the past few years due to natural disasters and ethnic violence. Like other Soviet republics, these republics were seeking independence and separation from the Center. Armenia, with an active diaspora abroad, supported strong confederal ties but was more reluctant to secede from Moscow than are the Georgians, primarily because of a perceived (Turkic) Muslim threat to their security. The Azeris, on the other hand, rediscovered their links with the Turks of Turkey and with their co-religionist and ethnically kin Azeris of Iran. Indeed, most Azeri nationalists would prefer to set up an independent state of Azerbaijan and be reunited with ethnic kinsmen in Iranian Azerbaijan. Recently, Ebulfez Elcibey was elected president of Azerbaijan, and he and his nationalist party have revived the age-old Azeri dream of a greater Azerbaijan, in which Armenia has no place.

The chapters that follow will concentrate primarily on Christian Armenia and Georgia. A more in-depth analysis of Azerbaijan is contained in the section on the Muslim periphery, where the Azeris are examined against the general background of Islamic Central Asia.

5

Georgia: The Long Battle for Independence

STEPHEN JONES

Georgia, like other nations in the USSR, has rejoined the 'nationalist' track of independent statehood. Until 1921, when Georgia was annexed by the Soviet state, it had followed a pattern of nation-building that was familiar to Europeans. The modernizing Russian Empire, which incorporated the small Georgian kingdoms at the beginning of the nineteenth century, helped create the conditions for Georgian national development: a native intelligentsia, an increasingly literate Georgian public, urbanization, improved communications between town and village, and contacts with Europe. If we were to follow Miroslav Hroch's schema of nationalist development, phase A (the period of scholarly interest in the native language and tradition) had been reached by the 1830s; phase B (the period of patriotic agitation by the intelligentsia), by the 1860s; and phase C (the rise of a mass national movement), by 1918.[1] Under Moscow's guidance, Georgian national consolidation continued in the 1920s with the institutionalization of Georgian state structures and the "ethnicization" of the republic's political elites.[2] However, under Stalin and his successors, the Soviet state, by a mixture of suppression, assimilation, and accommodation, effectively put the quest for independence into abeyance.

This did not lead to the loss of Georgian national identity. The underlying structures and policies laid down by Lenin and Stalin (republican parliaments, the ascription of nationality in passports, the promotion of native elites, mass education, and urban development) ensured the opposite. Socialism did not deliberately help each Soviet "nation to spread its wings," as Gorbachev implied in his *Perestroika: New Thinking for Our Country and the World*, but his view that "the growth of national self-consciousness and the growth of a nation's natural interest in its historical roots" were indirectly promoted by Soviet policies of educational, cultural, and economic growth is accurate.[3]

National identity can, to some extent, be measured by demographic patterns, native language loyalty, émigré surveys, public opposition, and the rate of endogamy. The ideology of nationalism, however, which Antony Smith, in one of the best definitions, describes an "ideological movement for the attainment and maintenance of self-government and independence, some of whose members conceive it to constitute an actual or potential 'nation' like others," is harder to pinpoint in the pre-Gorbachev period.[4] The public expression of Georgian nationalism was prevented by a totalitarian state and its all-encompassing ideology. Marxism-Leninism, which in its more dynamic phase before the war, had a powerful attraction for many non-Russian social groups, displaced nationalism. However, because the aspiration for independence and the advocacy of a Georgian nation-state went unheard in the West, except from Georgians abroad, it cannot be assumed that nationalist sentiment ceased to exist. Core nationalist ideas, such as the stress on cultural and collective individuality, the idealization of an independent past, and comparison of one's own nation with others, continued to be expressed by Georgians, particularly outside the period of Stalinism. Such ideas were tolerated, even promoted by republican elites as a means of legitimacy and social control.

After reviewing the background to the rise of the Georgian national movement in the 1980s, we shall deal with the emergence of the "new nationalism" in Georgia since Gorbachev.

GEORGIAN ETHNIC CONSOLIDATION

The 1989 census shows that Georgians continue to increase their weight in the republic. They now make up 70.1 percent of the republican population, the highest figure since 1897.[5] This is due to the net outflow of Russians and Armenians, to the assimilation of some of the smaller minorities (notably the Ossetians), and to low Georgian geographical mobility, but not to differing fertility patterns.

In 1989, Georgians were second only to Lithuania in terms of native residential concentration, with over 95 percent of Georgians in the USSR living within the Georgian republic.[6] The emigration of non-Georgians and the immigration of Georgians into the republic is likely to increase as legislation throughout the Union republics promotes separate ethnic interests. Ethnicity in the USSR was being transformed from an "implied" claim to privilege to a legally guaranteed claim.[7] The corollary is that minorities within the Union republics were becoming increasingly anxious about their status as protected minorities.

Other indications of the continuing strength of Georgian national identity in the Soviet period are the Georgians' attachment to their language (in 1989, 98.2 percent of Georgians considered Georgian their native tongue), the lack of intermarriage with representatives of other Soviet nations, and the constant glorification, at both unofficial and official levels, of Georgian national traditions.[8] This strong attachment to "Georgianness," combined with Soviet policies of *indigenization* and the devolution of powers to the republics since the middle 1950s, led to Georgian hegemony of the republic's political and cultural life. The highly personalized nature of Georgian society, with its traditional kinship and peer group networks, reinforced by the ethnic solidarity that is often characteristic of small nations, favors Georgian monopolization of strategic and managerial positions.[9] The exception to this is in the Abkhazian and South Ossetian administrative areas, where policies of affirmative action have favored the minorities, restricting Georgian domination.[10]

In 1985, Georgians made up 79.1 percent of the Communist party of Georgia, 9 percent more than their total number in the republic. The percentage was even higher in the upper levels of the party hierarchy.[11] In 1970, 82.6 percent of all students in higher education in the republic were Georgian; in 1987, 94 percent of students at Tbilisi University were also Georgian.[12] In 1985, 91 percent of all republican book production was in the Georgian language, as were 86 percent of all newspaper titles and 83 percent of total newspaper circulation.[13] Two Georgian television channels and eleven radio stations dominate the airwaves, although allocations are made for minority language programs. There are some indications, too, that Georgian economic control has led to the relative neglect of non-Georgian regions although this trend was reversed somewhat in the 1970s when Eduard Shevardnadze became party boss in Georgia.[14]

In short, Georgians in the pre-*glasnost'* era consolidated their position in the republic politically, culturally, and demographically. The social and political basis for a strong Georgian nationalist movement has long been present.

GEORGIAN NATIONALISM IN THE PRE-GLASNOST' PERIOD

For Soviet leaders, the difference between healthy "national self-consciousness" and unhealthy "narrow, nationalist views" has always been blurred. Under the ideologically lax leadership of Georgian first party secretary Vasilii Mzhavanadze (1953-1972), the expression of what Teresa Rakowska-Harmstone has called "official nationalism" (the articulation of national-cultural sentiment) became widespread.[15] At Moscow's behest, Mzhavanadze's successor, Eduard Shevardnadze (1972-1985), led the campaign against this "half-baked nationalism." The church, traditional Georgian festivals, excessive "Georgian-centrism," the second economy, nepotism, and ethnic favoritism were all targets. The campaign was unsuccessful, however, and the 1970s were characterized by an actual increase in the overt expression of nationalist sentiment. This was reflected in an unceasing stream of stories in the press and television on the glories of

Georgian history, literature, and language and by popular historical novels idealizing traditional Georgian rural life or resistance to foreign enemies.[16] Petitions and demonstrations defending the Georgian language multiplied, the most famous being the demonstrations in April 1978, when thousands publicly protested an attempted constitutional reduction in the status of the Georgian language.[17] There was a revival in the Church which, according to Georgian opinion polls, was a result of national rather than religious feelings and a surge of interest in the preservation of national monuments. The biological well-being of the Georgian people became a popular concern. This was reflected by publicizing the high rate of abortions, the low birth and high mortality rates, and the problems of perceived demographic decline. Football matches boiled over into riots against rival national teams. Human rights and ecology became inextricably linked with the national question.[18]

This "ethnic revival" in Georgia was the result of both transnational factors (the European ecology and human rights movements, the breakdown of informational isolation, and the example of other national struggles) and domestic factors (the growth of a powerful middle class, the decline of Marxism-Leninism's ideological *élan*, and the slowdown in economic growth). However, a national movement with a coherent nationalist ideology did not emerge. Dissident nationalists and their parties, while soliciting widespread sympathy, remained isolated. Only after Gorbachev's *glasnost'* and democratization campaigns did organized parties with public manifestos seek mass support and resume the struggle to regain the independence that was lost in 1921.

NATIONALISM REGAINED: THE FIRST STAGE

The reasons for the nationalist revival in Georgia under Gorbachev were much the same as elsewhere in the Union. They included economic decline, which led to increased job competition among ethnic groups; political insecurity among former national elites, which attempted to mobilize mass support around national programs; new opportunities for political organization; the realistic possibility of independence; the collapse of the center and its ideology; and the public revival of old national disputes and resentments by a (relatively) free and patriotic press. However, the cultural and political conditions in each republic led to wide differences in the pace, focus, and success of nationalist movements.

In Georgia, despite the creation of "informal" groups and the greater outspokenness of cultural elites, mass support for nationalist ideas did not emerge until 1988. Part of the explanation for this tardiness was the resistance of the new first party secretary, Jumbar Patiashvili (who succeeded Shevardnadze in July 1985) and the general skepticism regarding Gorbachev's chances of success.

As in neighboring Armenia, it was an environmental campaign that led to the first popular challenge to the Party's authority. After a six-month campaign of public meetings and newspaper articles conducted by an alliance of the intelligentsia and informal groups, in August 1988 the Georgian Party postponed the construction of the Caucasian Mountain Railway, which would have seriously damaged the environment of northern Georgia.[19] This was followed by massive demonstrations in October 1988 over the much more volatile issue of interethnic relations. In this case the casus belli was the rape of a Georgian girl by an Azeri from Marneuli, an Azerbaijani district in southern Georgia. In November, the issue was political sovereignty. Popular demonstrations protested the new constitutional changes proposed by Gorbachev, which were seen as an attack on republican rights.[20] The Georgian demonstrators' demands, and those of other non-Russian republics, were quickly accepted by Moscow. The Georgians interpreted this as a sign of the Center's vulnerability to pressure.

Between November 1988 and April 1989, when Georgian politics entered a new, radical nationalist stage following the brutal suppression of a popular demonstration for independence by Ministry of Internal Affairs (MVD) and army troops, the party fought a losing battle to retain its authority against the growing power in the streets. It attempted conciliation with the publication of three state programs on the Georgian language, Georgian history, and the defense of historical monuments, incorporating many of the Georgian nationalists' expressed concerns.[21] When this failed, it tried intimidation, forcefully breaking up public demonstrations or denying them permission to meet. Finally, it tried to maintain its power by manipulating the republican elections in March 1990 for the Congress of People's Deputies. Eighty-four percent of those elected were Communist party members (although not all were orthodox *apparatchiks*), 60 percent of the districts had only one candidate, and the usual 99 percent turnouts were trumpeted. Very few "independents" were elected.[22] However, all three strategies failed to undermine the new sense of "people's power," or the growing authority of the "informal" leaders, many of whom were former political prisoners who embodied the tradition of Georgian national resistance.

THE SECOND STAGE: 9 APRIL 1989

The date 9 April 1989 was a watershed in the battle for political authority in Georgia. A demonstration in Tbilisi numbering 10,000, which was initially directed against an Abkhazian petition in March for secession from the Georgian republic but became a demand for Georgian independence, was bloodily ended by MVD and army troops, leaving 20 dead (mostly young women who were on hunger strike). A Georgian commission investigating the tragedy confirmed the complicity of Georgian Party leaders, the directing role of Moscow and Russian military figures, the use of poisonous gas, and the distorted reporting by the central press and media.[23] The commission blamed the totalitarian system, the Soviet disdain for law, and political and military leaders in Georgia and Moscow, the most prominent of whom were Minister of Defense General Dmitrii Yazov, former KGB chief Victor Chebrikov, former Transcaucasian Military District Commander Colonel-General Igor' Rodionov (later replaced by Colonel-General Valerii Patrikeev), and the former Georgian party first secretary, Jumbar Patiashvili.

The tragedy was a national trauma. Each funeral became a popular demonstration of Georgian solidarity and a platform for nationalist symbols and slogans. The suffering of hundreds of people who were affected by the poisonous gas was shown nightly on television. Mass hysteria led to the hospitalization of thousands of adults and children suffering from what an investigation by Physicians for Human Rights termed "Catastrophe Reaction Syndrome," or a psychological group trauma.[24]

The political impact of the tragedy was threefold. First, it led to a collapse of the already tenuous faith in the Center. The view that coexistence with Moscow was no longer possible was reinforced by military cover-ups of the April events; by the demonstrative support of deputies at the Congress of People's Deputies for Rodionov and the military procurator, Alexander Katusev, both of whom justified the brutal measures taken. The bias of the Russian-language press (especially the organs of the military); and by the lack of successful prosecutions after April 9th were further confirmation of Moscow's insincerity.[25] Anti-military sentiment became one of the major strands of the Georgian national movement. Local military garrisons were picketed, there were demonstrations against the draft and the hazing of Georgian recruits, and there were demands for "alternative service" and the formation of Georgian units that would be obliged to serve only within their republic.

Second, the April tragedy led to the total collapse of political authority in the republic. The Georgian Party, under the new leadership of former Georgian KGB chief Givi Gumbaridze, attempted to regain its authority by following the strategy of the Lithuanian Communist party under Algirdas Brazauskas: adaptation to public opinion, which Lenin called *khvostizm* ("tailism").

The new Georgian Party program published in September 1989, declared that all national wealth--state property, land, and raw materials--should be exclusively Georgian. It called for national sovereignty and the supremacy of republican over All-Union law, promised new laws on Georgian citizenship, immigration, language, and private property; the separation of powers, free multiparty elections; an end to the party's monopoly; and a renegotiation of the republic's relationship with the Center.[26] The invasion of independent Georgia by the Red Army in February 1921, which broke the conditions of the Russo-Georgian Treaty of May 1920, was condemned as illegal.

By the summer of the following year, a great deal of this program had already been enacted by the Communist-dominated Georgian Supreme Soviet. In the last two sessions in June and August 1990, laws were passed on economic sovereignty, alternative service to the draft, the right to form political parties, a system of proportional representation and the right to stand for election after ten years of residence in the republic. A commission was created to work out a judicial mechanism for the restoration of Georgian independence, and direct state-to-state relations with the Baltic republics were approved.[27]

Despite these and other measures, however, such as the disassociation of the Georgian Party from CPSU policies, the wholesale replacement of regional Party cadres (with much of the initiative coming from the grass roots), and the new openness of the party leadership on television and in the press, Gumbaridze failed to fill the political vacuum. The Party was in a no-win situation. In order to maintain support, it undermined its own power base by approving the depoliticization of institutional life and strengthened the opposition by its support of free political activity.

The collapse of the Party's political authority after April 1989 led to a breakdown in civil authority, with the government powerless to disarm independent militias (such as the *mkhedrioni*), evict parties from occupied buildings, prevent the destruction of monuments to Lenin and other Communist heroes, or punish looters and murderers in regions of interethnic strife.[28]

The final result of 9 April was a mushrooming of political parties, clubs, and blocs to over 130 and a vast increase in their influence. They controlled the political agenda through the street and the media. A new phenomenon after 9 April was the breaking away of professional societies and institutions from state and All-Union jurisdiction, leading to the institutionalization of a new independent Georgian civil society. Georgian trade unions, journalists, and jurists, as well as the former youth section of the Georgian Communist party (now renamed the Free Georgian Youth League) and even the Georgian football league all severed their links with All-Union bodies.

THE ISSUES OF GEORGIAN NATIONALISM

Almost every issue in Georgian politics was, nolens volens, interlaced with the national question. Many issues, such as Georgian language and history, were of concern throughout the Soviet period; others, such as the environment and the military draft, became part of the Georgian national agenda relatively recently. These issues, which in most cases were formerly the property of intellectuals, have become the center of an intense political struggle among rival parties and national groups (including non-Georgian minorities). The nature of their resolution became vital, not only to Georgia's future, but to the careers and lives of every person within the republic as well.

THE MINORITIES

The most crucial and most dangerous issue for Georgians is inter-ethnic relations. Despite aggregate figures showing a healthy increase in the Georgian proportion within the republic, Georgians point to demographic weakness on the peripheries: in the South Ossetian Autonomous Region (abolished by the Georgian parliament in December 1990), in the Abkhazian Autonomous Republic, and in the Akhalkalaki, Akhaltzikhe, and Marneuli districts in the south. They also point to their relative decline in Caucasia as a whole compared to Armenians and Azeris.[29] This Georgian insecurity, which has been evident since the 1960s in official and unofficial literature, has become public and alarmist under the conditions of *glasnost'*. There is a fear that in the process of separation from the Union, Georgia's minorities, particularly those like the Azeris and Ossetians, who are part of a larger neighboring ethnic group, will create serious instability in Georgia's strategic border areas that could lead to conflict at an inter-state level, as in the 1918-1921 period of Georgian independence. As a result, almost all Georgian parties, including the Communist party, supplied and financed the attempts of newly formed demographic societies to re-settle Georgians in predominantly non-Georgian areas. The Azeris and Armenians, intimidated by the statements of powerful Georgian parties, official programs of Georgianization, and, in the Azeri case, antagonistic articles in the press (on illegal land seizure), began to leave the republic in increasing numbers. Russians followed suit. Due to their social and economic dispersion in the Georgian labor force, they failed to organize any significant resistance to rising Georgian hegemony.[30]

Georgian and non-Georgian insecurities have fed on each other, opening old cultural disputes and increasing economic and political uncertainty. Bloody interethnic riots have often been the result. The most violent of these occurred in Abkhazia in July 1989, when 22 died and over 500 were wounded in clashes over the opening of a Georgian branch of Tbilisi University in the Abkhazian capital of Sukhumi.[31] Abkhazians, who make up 17.8 percent of the population of the Abkhazian ASSR and who can study in their native language to the fifth grade only, saw this policy as a reversal of the official "Abkhazianization" of the 1970s; Georgians, on the other hand, claimed that as the largest national group in the Abkhazian republic (45.7% in 1989), they had a right to their own educational institution.[32] Underlying this Abkhazian-Georgian conflict, which culminated in an official declaration of independence by the Abkhazian section of the Autonomous Republic's Supreme Soviet in August 1990, are social, economic, educational, and religious differences (many of the Abkhaz are Muslim).

Abkhazian elites fear that the political and cultural privileges guaranteed by Moscow's affirmative action program will be lost.

Similar, though less bloody, clashes have occurred in Georgia's other minority regions. Ossetians, who speak an Iranian language, make up 65 percent of the Ossetian Autonomous Region and, until recently, displayed a pattern of assimilation into Georgian culture.[33] Now, led by the South Ossetian Popular Front, *Adamon Nykhas*, they are demanding union with the much larger body of their coethnics across the Caucasus mountain range in the North Ossetian ASSR. Their demands for autonomous republic status led to an alliance of Georgian parties, including the Georgian Communists, which condemned the Ossetian activities as unconstitutional. In November 1989, there was a tense confrontation in Tskhinvali, the South Ossetian capital, as 400 bus loads of Georgians arrived to demonstrate their anger over Ossetian demands.[34] Georgians claim that the Ossetians are relatively recent arrivals to the area and occupy land that is historically and geographically an integral part of Georgia. Ossetians, who, like the Abkhazians, are concerned about their democratic decline in Georgia, and claim that they have been discriminated against educationally and economically.[35]

Armenian and Azeri minorities in the provinces also see themselves as the victims of social and economic discrimination, but there the most acute issue is land rights and settlement. The Georgian-Azeri dispute, which exploded in June-July 1989 in the Azeri district of Marneuli, was settled by the dispatch of MVD troops. The casus belli was the activity of the Georgian demographic societies, which, along with the Georgian government, were resettling villages and buying up Azeri property. Underlying the conflict was the relative neglect of the district by Tbilisi, a clamp-down on the Azeris' illegal purchase of land, which had been going on for years, and a reshuffling of the local leadership.[36] More broadly underpinning the conflict were differences between the Georgian Christian and Azeri Muslim cultures. Georgia was a frontline Christian state and was frequently invaded by Muslim armies. Although religion was rarely the issue, Muslims, whether Persian, Turk, or Daghestani, have entered the national mythology as Georgia's most threatening enemies. Many Georgians feel that Muslim groups have no right to reside on Georgian territory. A similar conglomeration of factors led to a confrontation over land between Muslim Avars and native Georgians in the southeastern district of Qvareli in August 1990.[37]

There have been similar problems between Armenians and Georgians in Akhalkalaki and Akhaltsikhe. Armed conflict was barely avoided over the Georgian purchase of land in Bogdanovka district after villages were vacated by the Russian Dukhobors in the summer of 1990. The more radical Georgian nationalists briefly blockaded the railway into Armenia in protest at local Armenian resistance. The Armenian-Georgian conflict is long-standing, being culturally rooted in the Armenians' economic dominance of Georgia in the nineteenth century.[38]

Georgian nationalist concerns go beyond their own borders. Taking up a Georgian dissident theme of the 1970s, all Georgian parties publicly champion the Ingilos, a small enclave of Georgians in the Kaspii district of western Azerbaijan who have been the victims of Azeri discrimination.[39] Contrariwise, the mostly Muslim Mesketians' attempt to return to southern Georgia, from which they were expelled in 1944, is universally opposed. Their return, it is argued, would displace Georgians, strain the economy, and strengthen Islam at a strategically vital border area.[40] Recent articles in the press have raised questions about the isolation of Georgians in Iran (estimated to number 50,000) and in the former Georgian territories of Turkey (estimated at over 1 million) from their native culture.[41] The latter, as well as the Georgian Muslims in Adzharia on Georgia's southwestern border, could become a serious issue in Georgian-Turkish relations.

THE ENVIRONMENT

The environmental question is a major plank in the programs of all Georgian parties. There are two aspects to the question for Georgians. First, damage to the environment which, according to Georgian press accounts has been catastrophic, is blamed on the anti-national policies of the Georgian Communist Party and on the careless projects pressed on the republic by Moscow. Second, Soviet policies of industrialization and growth have endangered the Georgian nation's biological health. Pollution of rivers and the cities' air, the careless use of chemicals in workplaces and on the land, and the nuclear power program, have all been tied in with Georgians' increased mortality rate and health problems in the 1980s.[42] There have been campaigns against grandiose hydroelectric schemes which, it has been suggested, are behind a series of floods and landslides that have destroyed villages and killed many people over the last three years. Environmental politics in Georgia, as elsewhere, have also taken on an anti-militaristic tone with calls for the demilitarization and denu-clearization of Caucasia.[43] A campaign has been mounted aimed at the removal of a military base adjacent to Mtskheta, the ancient capital of Georgia. The long-festering question of a now-removed army firing range near the ancient monastery of Davith Gareji continues to be a focus of Georgian nationalist politics.[44]

LANGUAGE AND HISTORY

Language and history are perhaps the most important foci of Georgian identity. Throughout the Soviet period, and in particular since the 1960s, the defense of the Georgian language had been at the center of official and unofficial nationalism. Calls for the purity of the Georgian language, demonstrations and petitions against Russification measures, the glorification of the language in the media and literature, and official measures to promote Georgian characterized the 1970s and 1980s.[45]

In the new context of ethnic conflict, the politics of language has taken on a new intensity. An official policy of linguistic Georgianization is being pursued in schools and government institutions following the publication of a Georgian-state language program by the Georgian Communist party in November 1988. During discussion of the new electoral law in August 1990, the more radical Georgian parties insisted that candidates needed to know Georgian to be elected. The law that was finally passed rejected this proposition, but, as a compromise, the Supreme Soviet Presidium decreed Georgian the Supreme Soviet's "working language."[46] The June 1991 law on Georgian citizenship was also more liberal than anticipated. The radical nationalists' demand that knowledge of the Georgian language be a pre-requisite was dropped for all those currently living in Georgia, although any new petitioner for citizenship would have to know the language. Despite such moderation, the pressure from Georgian parties to intensify Georgian language teaching throughout the republic succeeded in alarming Georgia's minorities.

A common and revered past is an essential element of nationalism. Georgians have little need to invent their past. They have a long history of independence and are justifiably proud of their cultural and political longevity. The glories of Georgian history, which have long been a focus in Georgian literature and the media, constantly confront Georgians in their daily lives--in school, on the street (historical monuments), and around the dinner table, where the Georgian tradition of toasting always touches on the achievements of ancestors. The orthodox Soviet interpretations of Georgian history, which place Georgian national formation in the nineteenth century and stress the Russians' progressive role, were never taken seriously by Georgians.

Glasnost' intensified Georgians' interest in their past, particularly in the twentieth century, previously considered a "dead zone." The period of Georgian independence (1918-1921), led by the Mensheviks; the national revolt of 1924 against Bolshevik rule; the resistance of the Georgian "national deviationists" against Moscow's centralization; the rehabilitations of those purged in the 1930s and deported in the 1940s; the 1956 riots; and the history of Georgian anti-Bolshevik emigration filled the pages of the Georgian press. Traitors were transformed into heroes and their works have been published.[47] Significant dates in this new history, such as the declaration of independence in May 1918 and its loss in February 1921, are now officially commemorated. The Red Army invasion of Georgia has been investigated by a Georgian Supreme Soviet commission, similar to those of the Baltic republican governments set up to investigate the Red Army annexations in 1940. The 1921 invasion has been declared illegal and, hence, all Soviet claims to jurisdiction in the republic are null and void.[48] In February 1990, a joint commission of historical societies and academic and party institutions drew up a State Program for the Scientific Research, Study and Popularization of Georgian History to extend Georgia's new history beyond the educated elite.

The rediscoveries of the past have already begun to reshape the Georgian landscape. Official monuments to Georgian Bolsheviks have been torn down, Communist-inspired street names have been replaced by those of Georgian historical or popular nationalist figures, and new parties have adopted the names and regalia of former Georgian national parties.[49]

THE CHURCH

The autocephalic Georgian Church is an inextricable part of Georgian national history, having played a prominent role in the preservation and propagation of Georgian language and culture. The Georgian church in this century has been a symbol of national rather than religious loyalty and has never had anything like the spiritual influence of the Armenian church over its flock. From the 1970s onward, under the influence of dissident and human rights activities and the stagnant impersonalism of the Soviet system, there was a renewed interest, primarily among the young, in the church. This was reflected by the emergence of active volunteer groups restoring churches, by increased attendance at religious festivals, and by greater observance of religious marriages and ceremonies.[50] The appointment of the youthful Ilya II (44 years old at the time) as patriarch in 1978 gave the Georgian church a tremendous boost. He reactivated old eparchies and congregations and became president of the World Council of Churches.

However, it is the events of the last three years that have transformed the Georgian church. Restrictions on its income, its activity in charitable and educational work, and its right to reopen new churches and establish congregations have been lifted. As control of the church by the Georgian Council for Religious Affairs and the KGB collapsed, the church's organization grew stronger than it had been for two centuries. In 1988 and 1989, 313 churches and monasteries were opened, a Theological Academy was established, and a new cathedral was commissioned in Tbilisi. The church has also played a prominent role in the national movement. It has participated in national congresses and meetings, opened new churches in non-Georgian areas, and supported the campaigns for the promotion of Georgian language and history. Ilya II personally presided over the funeral of Merab Kostava, the most popular of Georgian national leaders, in October 1989. He was also present at the tragic demonstration on 9 April 1989.[51]

In their programs, many Georgian parties emphasize the special role of the Georgian Orthodox church in national affairs. The National Democratic party calls for a theo-democracy in which the church will play "a leading role in moral questions concerning the nation's life."[52] The Christian

Union party declares the promotion of Christianity a national obligation.[53] Even the Georgian Communist party has joined the bandwagon by funding church activities in non-Georgian areas and by publishing Ilya II's epistles in the party press. Religion and nationalism have reached a new powerful synthesis in Georgia and have transformed the church into a popular and influential actor in Georgian politics.

GEORGIAN NATIONAL MOVEMENT

By the summer of 1990 there were at least 130 parties, blocs, societies, and clubs in Georgia covering a wide political spectrum. Almost all, excepting only the non-Georgian organizations, were committed to Georgian independence, a pluralist democracy (however that may be interpreted), a market economy, and preeminence for ethnic Georgians in political and economic life. The Georgians have demonstrated, however, that a common goal does not necessarily indicate united action or even cooperation. Many of the most prominent Georgian political leaders, such as Gia Dchanturia of the National Democratic party, Irakli Tsereteli of the National Independence party, and Zviad Gamsakhurdia of the Helsinki Union (all former political prisoners) found it difficult to adapt to the new context of legality and shed their vision of politics as one of uncompromising opposition to one's opponents and the Center. They proudly described themselves as "the irreconcilables." Their methods and tactics, such as the denunciation of opponents as KGB agents, the ascription of privilege on the basis of membership of a particular social group (in this case ethnic), the use of emotive terminology ("traitors to the nation"), the tendency toward splitting, and pressure on the press to print or not to print, implied a strain of Bolshevism in their anti-Bolshevism.[54]

The two elections that took place in the fall of 1990 represented a watermark in modern Georgian nationalistic politics. The first took place between 30 September and 14 October for the alternative National Congress. The Congress, dominated by the radical National Independence and National Democratic parties, called for the withdrawal of Soviet occupation troops and immediate negotiations with Moscow for Georgia's independence. The length of the election period was blamed by the National Congress on the failure of provincial Communist party organizations to provide polling stations and sabotage by the opposition Round Table parties led by Zviad Gamsakhurdia. The Round Table parties, which had coalesced around Gamsakhurdia after he split from the National Congress in spring 1990, argued for the proper "parliamentary" path of multiparty elections to the old Supreme Soviet. According to the National Congress Central Electoral Commission, by the third round of elections on October 14, 1,505,547 or 50.88 percent of the republican population had taken part, barely the minimum 50 percent that the National Congress's own electoral law set for a legitimate election.[55] Six electoral blocs, representing about 40 parties, competed for 200 seats on the basis of proportional representation. The two most successful electoral coalitions were Irakli Tsereteli's National Independence Party-National Union which garnered 54 percent of the vote or 71 seats; and Gia Dchanturia's National Democratic Party and Democratic Party bloc which won 33 percent of the vote or 65 seats) both with radical nationalist programs of rapid secession from the USSR. The liberal Democratic Georgia bloc received 37 seats.[56]

After the disappointing turnout, the National Congress downgraded its role from an alternative legislature to that of a coordinating body for the Georgian national liberation movement.[57] It claimed, nevertheless, to represent the will of the Georgian people and described itself as a check on possible authoritarian tendencies in a future Georgian Supreme Soviet. The Congress declared that a democratically elected Georgian Supreme Soviet would be nothing more than a self-administering organ in an occupied country but recognized that body's right (and obligation) to negotiate independence from the USSR. In short, the congress envisaged a form of dual power in which it would act as the people's organ, checking and pushing the new Georgian government.

Official elections to the Georgian Supreme Soviet followed on 28 October. Based on a mixed system of majority and proportional representation, six parties and five electoral coalitions took part. The election was preceded by considerable controversy over the electoral law, which limited candidacies to individuals with ten years residence in the republic, disenfranchised the Soviet military because it was not under Georgian jurisdiction, and refused to register parties "whose activity does not extend over Georgia's entire territory."[58] This excluded separate non-Georgian representation and led to a boycott by *Aidgilara* and *Adamon Nykhas*, the Abkhazian and South Ossetian Popular Front organization. Five other parties, including the conservative Stalin party, were refused registration on technical and constitutional grounds.[59]

The election campaign, which was observed by 40 international monitors, was relatively peaceful. Almost all the party platforms, while differing on tactics, pace, and emphasis, agreed on the need for independence, a multiparty democracy, the sanctity of law, a market economy, national military and security formations, Georgian citizenship, and the declaration of all Georgia's natural resources as national property. The Round Table-Free Georgia bloc, the most radically nationalist coalition, which was led by Zviad Gamsakhurdia, achieved an overwhelming majority, with 54.0 percent of the vote or 155 seats (out of a total of 250). Next came the Georgian Communist party, with 29.6 percent (64 seats), the Popular Front (12 seats), and the Democratic Georgia bloc (4 seats).[60] Those coalitions that most specifically represented middle-class economic interests, such as the Liberation and Economic Renewal bloc (*Ganthavisupleba da economicuri aghodzineba*), or moderate intelligentsia opinion, such as the Freedom bloc (*Tavisupleba*) received 1 and no seats, respectively. The coloration of the new Supreme Soviet was overwhelmingly radical and nationalist.

Gamsakhurdia, who was elected chairman of the Supreme Soviet (president of the republic), appointed the moderate Tengiz Sigua to be prime minister. The new cabinet contained many former government officials and academics, but appointees to parallel posts in the Supreme Soviet, such as chairs of permanent commissions, were more radical.[61] Sigua and Gamsakhurdia initially took a conciliatory approach to other parties and proposed a gradual and negotiated transition to independence. They soon came into confrontations with both domestic opposition and Moscow.[62]

The paramilitary groups who were loyal to Gamsakhurdia and the National Congress continued their armed attacks on one another into the election period. After the failure of conciliation talks in December 1990, the new Supreme Soviet and National Congress painted one another as Kremlin agents. The National Congress, finding itself to be of increasing irrelevance and with restricted access to the media, accused the Supreme Soviet of dictatorship. The armed *mkhedrioni*, who were allied to the Congress and said by its leader, Jaba Ioseliani, to number 5,000, refused to obey a directive by the Supreme Soviet ordering the dismantling of "illegal" paramilitary organizations. Ioseliani warned that he would raise an army of 60,000 against any attempts to disarm his group.[63] The Supreme Soviet meanwhile created a National Guard, whose task was to deal with such paramilitary groups either by confrontation or by incorporation within Georgia's new security system.

The major parliamentary opposition, the Georgian Communist party, has undergone considerable internal turmoil. In December 1990, it announced its withdrawal from the CPSU, changed its leadership, and declared its intention to change its name. Its program is little different from other Georgian parties, but it has taken a more conciliatory attitude toward the national minorities, from whom it draws much of its support. Its departure from the CPSU, however, has angered Abkhazian, Russian, and Ossetian members who have threatened to leave an independent Georgian organization.[64]

The national minorities are the major and most serious source of domestic opposition to the new Government. Tensions resulting from the exclusion of ethnic minority representation in the Supreme Soviet, the lack of non-Georgians in the new cabinet, and a "war of laws" between the Georgian parliament and regionally based Soviets in Abkhazia and South Ossetia, came to a head in December 1990 when the South Ossetian Autonomous Region, after declaring itself the South Ossetian Soviet Democratic Republic and holding elections, was abolished by the Georgian Supreme Soviet. A curfew and state of emergency was declared in the region as civil war erupted. The rival claims of the Georgian militia and Soviet MVD for responsibility to restore order brought Tbilisi and Moscow "eyeball to eyeball." The Georgian government accused the Soviet MVD of collusion with the Ossetians. Fearing that Moscow might declare Presidential power in the region, however, it withdrew its militia from the Ossetian capital of Tskhinvali where the bloodiest fighting had occurred. Talks began, but the Georgian Supreme Soviet's lack of interest in addressing national minority concerns or creating a more tolerant atmosphere for national minorities suggests that such talks can achieve temporary stability at best.[65]

Gamsakhurdia's policies for independence, though conceived within a framework of gradual transition, inevitably intensified conflict with Moscow. The Supreme Soviet removed all references to "socialism" in the Georgian constitution, amended it to ensure the superiority of Georgian law, changed the republic's name (to the Georgian Republic), nationalized the KGB and the Procuracy (official in charge of national revenues), created a National Guard, amended civil and criminal codes, introduced new temporary municipal bodies (until elections, which were set for March 1991), and discussed draft laws on citizenship and the privatization of land. It refused to sign the new Union Treaty and held its own referendum on independence. Moscow instituted an economic blockade and Georgians found themselves in a shortage economy, an unusual situation.

PROSPECTS

Gamsakhurdia's new government faces horrific problems. The economy is in a state of collapse, with declining production (national income fell by 6.5 percent in the first quarter of 1990, compared to the same period the previous year), increasing inflation, colossal pollution problems, a chronic energy shortage, a crumbling urban infrastructure (health and housing), and dependency on deliveries of grain and oil from Russia. There is serious ethnic and social polarization, which is reflected in the continuing disputes between Georgians and their minorities and in the 56,000 person-days lost in strikes in the first quarter of 1990. As the more advantageously positioned Poland and East Germany have shown, a market transition in these conditions can only make things worse before they get better. The affect on the already shaky social and ethnic fabric of Georgian society could be catastrophic.[66]

Quite apart from the explosive domestic situation, Georgians, as always, are extremely vulnerable to their more powerful neighbors. Continued economic ties with the USSR could help prevent the terrible social consequences of a sudden leap into the world market, but political confrontation has already undermined continuing economic cooperation. It remains to be seen what separate agreements with the RSFSR and other republics will bring in real terms.

Although relatively well endowed agriculturally, a market-oriented independent state will face far superior competition internationally.

Georgians, like the Armenians, must also think very carefully about their vulnerability to powerful Muslim neighbors to the south. Georgia has a significant Muslim presence on its borders with Turkey. Some of them, alarmed at the heavy Christian emphasis in the program of the Georgian government, are beginning to establish self-defence organizations which may link up with Turkish nationalists.[67]

Thus Georgia, whether within the Union or without, will go through a traumatic period of economic and political upheaval. Much depends on the skill of the political leadership in coping with rising trade union militancy and strikes, the demands of ethnic minorities, and the opposition. Unfortunately, the experience so far is not good, and the accusation of authoritarianism is well-founded in some cases. There is a strong potential for the exploitation of popular resentment against minorities and unofficial opposition parties. Current ethnic conflict not only invites interference by Moscow and alienates Western support, it threatens to undermine the new democracy itself. If, however, the minorities are invited to participate in the creation of a new political system and force is not used against the vocal but declining National Congress, if the paramilitaries are given some recognized autonomy in recreated Georgian national units, and if Moscow is treated wisely, Georgia may pass, without too much bloodshed, into a stable, multiparty political democracy.

POSTSCRIPT: JANUARY 1991-1992

The concluding lines of this paper, written in January 1991, proved too optimistic. Zviad Gamsakhurdia became President of Georgia in May 1991, winning 87 percent of the vote. His new government, despite its rhetoric, proved incapable of accommodating and coopting opposition interests into the political system. Gamsakhurdia, using the enormous powers he accrued under the new Presidential law of May 1991, became increasingly authoritarian. He alienated the moderate intelligentsia, the parliamentary opposition, and many of his own appointees in the central government and provinces. Alarmed at his abuse of the government's media monopoly, neglect of economic reform, alienation of Western opinion and the increasingly violent suppression of oppositionists, including the shooting of demonstrators and imprisonment of their leaders, many of Gamsakhurdia's former allies abandoned him.

The August 1991 putsch, to which Gamsakhurdia's response was considered inadequate, even complicitous, and the shooting of unarmed anti-government demonstrators in September, galvanized the opposition around Gamsakhurdia's former prime minister, Tengiz Sigua, and commander of the National Guard, Tengiz Kitovani. In December, the opposition felt strong enough to lead an armed struggle against Gamsakhurdia, who had become increasingly dictatorial and had taken direct control of the state security and defence ministries. After almost three weeks of bloody fighting around the central parliament building, where Gamsakhurdia's government took its last stand, the President fled Georgia on January 6, 1992. After a failed attempt to rally support in Western Georgia, where he returned in January, Gamsakhurdia left for Checheniia.

A new government, or Military Council, is now in power. It comprises representatives from all the major opposition groups and is led by Gamsakhurdia's former allies, Tengiz Sigua and Tengiz Kitovani. It is unclear what policies the new government will pursue, although reports suggest it intends to apply for membership in the C.I.S. defense system and initiate new parliamentary elections in the spring of 1992. The potential fissures between parties taking part in the Military Council are manifold. Until recently, many of them had been in opposite camps. We will have to wait until the new elections before we can make any conclusions about the state of political forces in Georgia. Once again, we are left only with the hope that the new leaders will have learned from Gamsakhurdia's failures, and will accommodate all social groups and opposition parties in the attempt to rebuild a Georgian democratic state.

NOTES

1.   Miroslav Hroch, *Social Preconditions of National Revival in Europe: A Comparative Analysis of the Social Composition of Patriotic Groups among the Smaller European Nations*, trans. Ben Fowkes (Cambridge, MA: Cambridge University Press, 1985), pp. 22-24.

2.   For a detailed account of this process, see Stephen F. Jones, "The Establishment of Soviet Power in Transcaucasia: Georgia, 1921-1928" *Soviet Studies* 40, no. 4 (October, 1988): 616-639.

3.   Mikhail Gorbachev, *Perestroika: New Thinking for Our Country and the World* (London: Collins, 1987), p. 119.

4.   For this definition, which attempts to distinguish the ideology of nationalism from national sentiment, see Antony Smith *Theories of Nationalism* (London: Duckworth, 1983), p. 171.

5.   Census figures from 1897 and 1989 are not directly comparable because of different techniques of measurement and territorial changes. However, 1989 does seem to be a demographic landmark of sorts for Georgians. For a more detailed table of changes in the Georgian proportion of the population in historically Georgian territories, see Vakhthang Jaoshvili, *Sakarthvelos mosakhleoba XV111-XX saukuneebshi* (Tbilisi, Georgia, 1984), p. 217.

6.   For an analysis of the 1989 census figures, see *Comunisti*, 13 January 1990, p. 2.

7.   Karl Deutsch in his book *Nationalism and Social Communication* (New York: Wiley, 1953) argued that ethnicity in a competitive economy was "an implied claim to privilege."

8.   According to L. V. Chiuko, a Soviet sociologist who devised a scale for measuring ethnic endogamy preference among non-Russians (with -100 being the highest preference for ethnic exogamy and +100 the highest preference for ethnic endogamy), Georgians scored 80.5, compared to 89.5 for Azeris and 33.4 for Armenians, L. V. Chiuko, *Braki i razvody* (Moscow, 1975), p. 69. See also Brian Silver, "Population Redistribution and the Ethnic Balance in Transcaucasia" in *Transcaucasia: Nationalism and Social Change*, ed. R. G. Suny (Ann Arbor, MI: University of Michigan Press, 1983, p. 386). Within the Georgian republic in 1969, only 6.4 percent of all marriages were mixed; Wesley Fisher, "Ethnic Consciousness and Intermarriage: Correlates of Endogamy among the Major Soviet Nationalities," *Soviet Studies* 29, no. 3 (July 1977): 395-408.

9.   There are some notable exceptions to this. For example, Russians have always dominated military posts in the Transcaucasian Military District, and since 1956, the second party secretary in the Georgian party organization has always been a Russian.

10.   For example, Levan Haindrava, in a TV broadcast on 26 July, 1989, declared that although Abkhazians make up 17.8 percent of the Abkhazian Autonomous Socialist Soviet Republic (AbASSR), they comprise 41 percent of the Abkhazian Supreme Soviet deputies, 67 percent of the republican ministers, and 50 percent of the district and city first-party secretaries. The author of this article has a manuscript of the broadcast.

11.   D. G. Sturua, G. I. Devdariani, et al., *Ocherki istorii kommunisticheskoi partii Gruzii: chast' tret'ia* (Tbilisi, 1985), p. 402. Mary McAuley, "Party Recruitment and the Nationalities in the USSR: A Study in Centre-Republican Relationships," *British Journal of Political Science* 10 (January 1980): 466.

12.   Cited in E. Fuller, "Problems in Higher Education in Georgia," *Radio Liberty Research Bulletin (RL)* 476 (1987): 1-5.

13.   *Narodnoe Khoziaistvo Gruzinskoi SSR v 1985 godu (Nar. Khoz)* (Tbilisi, 1986), p. 250; P. Gugushvili, *Sakarthvelos da amiercavcasiis economicuri ganvitareba XIX-XX ss* 7 (Tbilisi, 1984), p. 272.

14.   See Darrell Slider, "Crisis and Response in Soviet Nationality Policy: The Case of Abkhazia," *Central Asian Survey* 4, no. 4 (1985): 51-68. Most economic indicators suggest relative Abkhazian backwardness. On the backwardness of Marneuli District, see E. Fuller, "Marneuli: Georgia's Potential Nagorno-Karabakh?" *Radio Liberty Research Bulletin (RL)* 477 (1988): 1-5.

15.   Teresa Rakowska-Harmstone, "The Dialectics of Nationalism in the USSR," *Problems of Communism* 23, no. 3 (May-June 1974): 1-22.

16.   For a discussion of this, see E. Fuller, "Manifestations of Nationalism in Current Georgian-Language Literature," *Radio Liberty* 106 (1980): 1-6.

17.   See C. J. Peters (former pseudonym of Stephen F. Jones) and B. Nahaylo, *The Ukrainians and the Georgians Minority Rights Group,*

Report no. 50 (London, 1981), pp. 14-18; R. G. Suny, *The Making of the Georgian Nation* (London: Tauris, 1989), pp. 308-310; E. Fuller, "Expressions of Official and Unofficial Concern over the Future of the Georgian Language," *RL* 149 (1981): 1-4 and E. Fuller, "Georgian Officials Condemn Recent Nationalist Demonstration," *RL* 13 (1982): 1-3.

18.   For a discussion of these themes, see Stephen F. Jones, "Nationalism and Religion in Georgia and Armenia since 1965," in *Religion and Nationalism in the USSR and Eastern Europe*, ed. P. Ramet, 2nd rev. and exp. ed. (Durham, NC: Duke University Press, 1989), pp. 171-195; Stephen F. Jones, "The Transcaucasian Railway Project; An Exercise in Glasnost," *Central Asian Survey* 8, no. 2 (1989): 47-59; E. Fuller, "Disorderly Behaviour at Georgian Sports Events," *RL* 99 (1978): 1-2; E. Fuller, "Nature Conservation in the Georgian SSR," *RL* 443 (1980): 1-7.

19.   Stephen F. Jones, "Nationalism and Religion in Georgia and Armenia since 1965," in *Religion and Nationalism in the USSR and Eastern Europe*, ed. P. Ramet, 2nd rev. and exp. ed. (Durham, NC, 1989), pp. 171-195.

20.   On the rape case, see Zaur Gvazava and Zarya Vostoka, "Georgian Nationalists Accused of Exploiting Rape to Inflame Anti-Azerbaidzhani Feelings", *Current Digest of the Soviet Press* 15, no. 43 (1988): 19 (hereafter *CDSP*). Proposed changes to articles 108 and 119 of the USSR constitution, which would have compromised the republic's right to secession and restricted the republic's control over internal affairs, were seen as particularly threatening.

21.   The Georgian History state program was published in *Comunisti*, 7 February 1989, pp. 2-3; the Georgian Language state program was published in *Comunisti*, 3 March 1988, pp. 2-3.

22.   For the election results and some critical assessments, see *Comunisti*, 30 March 1989, p. 1, 6 May 1989, p. 3, and 2 April 1989, pp. 2-3.

23.   For the report of this commission, see *Comunisti* 28 September 1989, pp. 2-4. Two other commissions also investigated the tragedy: a commission of the USSR Congress of People's Deputies led by Anatolii Sobchak and a commission of the USSR Military Procurator's Office, led by the former Chief USSR Military Prosecutor, Alexander Katusev. The reports of both are in *9 April* (Tbilisi, 1989), pp. 612-636 and pp. 638-648 respectively. The Military Procurator's report was a whitewash which nearly precipitated the resignation of Foreign Minister, Eduard Shevardnadze, in protest. (Julia Wishnevsky, "Shevardnadze Said to Have Threatened to Resign in Dispute over Tbilisi Commission," *Report on the USSR* 2, no. 5 (1990): 1-3.

24.   Physicians for Human Rights, *Bloody Sunday. Trauma in Tbilisi: The Events of April 9, 1989 and Their Aftermath Report of a Medical Mission to Soviet Georgia by Physicians for Human Rights* (Boston: Physicians for Human Rights, February 1990).

25.   Rodionov, who was in charge of the operation, was made head of the Voroshilov Military Academy of the General Staff in Moscow in November 1989. See Sergei Zamashchikov, "A New Job for General Rodionov," *Report* 2, No. 9 (1990): 12-14.

26.   The program is in *Comunisti* 17 September 1989. pp. 1-3.

27.   See *Comunisti* 3 July 1990, pp. 1-2; 5 June 1990, pp. 1-2; 19 August 1990, pp. 1-2; 22 August 1990, p. 1.

28.   The *mkhedrioni* is an independent armed militia that has taken upon itself the preservation of order in ethnic troublespots. Since the summer of 1990, many public buildings have been occupied by Georgian parties, including the Georgian Institute of Marxism-Leninism; *Wall Street Journal*, 28 March 1990, p. A10; and *Moscow News*, no. 14, 8 April 1990. The newspapers are full of reports about the lack of party authority in the provinces and the rising crime rate, and they cite alarming figures; *Samshoblo*, no. 2, January 1990, p. 2; and *Comunisti*, 15 February 1990, p. 4. According to Georgian informants, only one monument to Lenin is left in central Tbilisi and prosecutions for the murderous riots in Abkhazia have been few.

29.   One Georgian demographer recently informed *Comunisti* readers that whereas in Caucasia in 1926, Georgians numbered .25 million more than Armenians and 108,000 more than Azeris, in 1979, they were .5 million and almost 2 million less, respectively; *Comunisti*, 11 January 1990, p. 3.

30.   The most active of these demographic societies is the Merab Kostava Society, which was most recently involved in conflict with Armenians in the Bogdanovka district and Avars in Qvareli over land purchases. See *Moscow News*, no. 33, 25 August-2 September 1990, p. 11. Many individuals in the Russian Dukhobor community in Georgia (to which they were exiled in the 1840s) recently announced their intention to leave the republic; *Moscow News*, no. 28, 22-29 July, 1990, p. 15. No significant Interfront movement has emerged among urban Russians.

31.   For reports of these events, see *CDSP* 16, no. 29 (1989): 14-16.

32.   See Darrell Slider, *CDSP* 16, no. 29 (1989): 61-64; E. Fuller, "Large-Scale Measures to Improve the Teaching of the Georgian Language," *Radio Liberty* 157 (1980): 1-3; and *Kommunisticheskaia partiia Gruzii v rezoliutsiakh i resheniakh s"ezdov, konferentsii i plenumov TsK* (Tbilisi, Georgia, 1980), pp. 795-804.

33.   For a brief Georgian history of Georgian-Ossetian relations, see *Comunisti*, 26 August 1990, p. 4.

34.   For accounts of recent events in Ossetiia, see *Foreign Broadcast Information Services* (hereafter *FBIS-SOV*) 90-036 (22 February 1990): 96-99; *FBIS-SOV* 90-040 (28 February 1990): 95-96; *FBIS-SOV* 90-074 (17 April 1990): 119. See also *Comunisti*, 12 November 1989, p. 1, and *Comunisti*, 14 November 1989, p. 1.

35.   Between 1959 and 1989, the Ossetian proportion of the republican population decreased from 3.5 percent to 3 percent. This, combined with Georgian population gains over and above their natural growth rate (taking into consideration net migration and mortality rates), led B. Anderson and B. Silver to suggest that Georgians assimilated considerable numbers of Ossetians during this period. See B. Anderson and B. Silver, "Estimating Russification of Ethnic Identity among Non-Russians in the USSR," *Demography* 20, no. 4 (November 1983): 461-489. In 1979, 17 percent of Ossetians in Georgia spoke Georgian as their native tongue, *Vestnik statistiki*, no. 10 (1980): 67.

36.   On recent Georgian-Azeri relations, see E. Fuller, "Marneuli: Georgia's Potential Nagorno-Karabakh?" *RL* 477 (1988); *Comunisti*, 30 June 1989, pp. 2-3; *Comunisti*, 7 July 1989, p. 3; *Comunisti*, 6 August 1989, p. 1.

37.   *Moscow News*, no. 33, 26 August-3 September 1990, p. 11.

38.   The conflict in Bogdanovka was barely publicized and most of the information I have has come through Georgian informants. On the background to Armeno-Georgian relations, see R. G. Suny, *The Making of the Georgian Nation* (London: Tauris, 1989), pp. 113-143.

39.   On the Ingilos, see E. Fuller, "The Azeris in Georgia and the Ingilos: Ethnic Minorities in the Limelight," *Central Asian Review* 3, no. 2 (1984): 75-86.

40.   There is an abundance of material on the Meskhetian issue. For background, see *Summary of World Broadcasts* (London) SU/0382B/1-B/2, February 1989; and E. Fuller, "What are the Meskhetians' Chances of Returning to Georgia?" *Report* 1, no. 26 (1990): 17-18.

41.   See, for example, *Comunisti*, 5 August 1990, p. 4.

42.   For a selection of articles on environmental issues in the Georgian press, see *Comunisti*, 5 January 1989, p. 1; *Comunisti*, 15 January 1989, p. 3; *Comunisti*, 29 January 1989, p. 3.

43.   This was a demand of the Georgian Popular Front. See *Gouchagui* (Paris), no. 21 (March 1990): 19.

44.   See, for example, the article on Davith Gareji in *Comunisti*, 29 April 1989, p. 4.

45.   For background to the Georgian language issue, see G. Hewitt, "Georgian: A Noble Past, a Secure Future," in *Sociolinguistic Perspectives on Soviet National Languages: Their Past, Present and Future*, ed. I. Kreindler (Berlin, 1985), pp. 163-182. See also Peters and Nahaylo.

46.   *Comunisti*, 25 August 1990, p. 1.

47.   It would be pointless enumerating specific articles, as there are so many. For an assessment of changes on some of these issues, see E. Fuller, "Georgian Historians Reassess 1918 Declaration of Georgian Independence," *Radio Liberty* 251 (1988): 1-5, and E. Fuller, "Filling in the 'Blank Spots' in Georgian History: Noe Zhordania and Josef Stalin," *Report* 1, No. 12, (30 March 1989): 19-22.

48. *CDSP* 17, no. 10 (1990): 8-9.

49. For example, Lenin Street and Plekahnov Street, both major thoroughfares in Tbilisi, have been renamed after the modern Georgian heroes Mereb Kostava and David Aghmashenebeli, respectively.

50. For a history of the Georgian church in the Soviet period, see C. J. Peters (former pseudonym of Stephen F. Jones), "The Georgian Orthodox Church," in *Eastern Christianity and Politics in the Twentieth Century*, ed. P. Ramet (Durham, NC: Duke University Press, 1988), pp. 286-308; and Jones.

51. For the most recent assessment of the Georgian church's progress under *glasnost'*, see Stephen F. Jones, "Soviet Religious Policy and the Georgian Orthodox Apostolic Church: From Khrushchev to Gorbachev," *Religion in Communist Lands*, 17 (Winter 1989-1990: 292-312.

52. *Gouchagui*, no. 18 (February 1918): 33-37.

53. *Gouchagui*, no. 20 (November, 1989): 45-49.

54. The materials on these groups are abundant. G. Tseretheli, the editor of *Gouchagui*, has published a series of articles on the groups and their programs. See *Gouchagui*, no. 20 (November 1989): 25-49; *Gouchagui*, no. 21 (March 1990): 14-41; and *Gouchagui*, no. 22 (June 1990): 10-41. For information on the disputes between the various parties, see *FBIS-SOV* 90-087 (1990): 109-111; *FBIS-SOV* 90-085 (1990): 118, *Samshoblo*, no. 6, March 1990, pp. 2-3; *Sakhartvelo*, 23 March 1990, p. 1; *Karthuli Philmi*, 21 March 1990, p. 2; *Karthuli Philmi*, 30 May 1990, p. 2; *Comunisti*, 24 May 1990, p. 3; and *Comunisti*, 27 May 1990, p. 3.

55. *Samshoblo*, no. 22, November 1990, p. 2; *Comunisti*, 16 November 1990, p. 3. The figure of 50.88 percent is based on a total electorate that is considerably smaller in number than the one given for the Georgian Supreme Soviet elections in October 1990.

56. *FBIS-SOV* 90-207 (1990): 102.

57. G. Dchanturia, in *Sakhalkho ganathleba*, 20 October 1990 (the author has a xerox copy of this article).

58. For the final electoral law, see *Comunisti*, 21 August 1990, p. 1. The most controversial articles were numbers 2 and 8.

59. On the Stalin controversy, see *Samshoblo*, no. 22, November 1990, p. 2.

60. *Akhali Sakarthvelo*, 16 November 1990, p. 3, contains the full election results.

61. For the cabinet appointees, see *Zariia Vostoka*, 23 November 1990, p. 2. The Supreme Soviet commission chairmen are listed in *Akhali Sakarthvelo*, 16 November 1990, pp. 1, 3.

62. Extracts from their opening statements to the Georgian Supreme Soviet are in *Samshoblo*, no. 23, November 1990, p. 5.

63. *FBIS-SOV* 90-237 (1990): 103.

64. *Akhali Sakarthvelo*, 2 December 1990, p. 3 and *FBIS-SOV* 237 (1990), p. 102.

65.   For the most up to date information on the South Ossetian conflict, see *Center for Democracy News Service, Weekly Bulletin* 003 (9 January 1991); *Center for Democracy News Service, Weekly Bulletin* 004 (15 January 1991); *Center for Democracy News Service, Weekly Bulletin* 006 (29 January 1991); and *Center for Democracy News Service, Weekly Bulletin* 007 (5 February 1991).

66.   For alarming economic statistics on Georgia's economic health, see *Comunisti,* 8 May 1990, pp. 2-3.

67.   On concerns of the Adzharians with the policies of the new government, see Elizabeth Fuller, "Zvaid Gamsakhurdia Proposes Abolition of Adzhar Autonomy," *Report on the USSR* 2, no. 48 (1991): 13-14.

6

Armenian Nationalism in a Socialist Century
GORDON BROWN

Modern Armenia has been shaped by the tension and interplay between nationalism and socialism (defined loosely to include socialism and communism). A study of this tension and interplay provides insight into today's Armenian nationalism and illustrates some of the problems currently facing the former Soviet Union.

NATIONALISM AND SOCIALISM: THE DASHNAKS

The Armenian past is a story of control by outside political and religious empires from both east and west. This has not eliminated the Armenians' historic sense of identity. However, it does explain the long existence of an Armenian diaspora. As semi-autonomous Armenia began its decline in the tenth century, Armenians moved into Cilicia under Byzantine sponsorship. Over time, their inability to withstand the power of Turks, Arabs, or Mongols in either Armenia or Cilicia led to large-scale migration throughout the Mongol Empire and to India, Russia, and Europe. Wherever they went, members of the diaspora were particularly noted for trade, and they usually formed an educated, urban minority.

In historic Armenia, Armenians' unique identity led to persecution under the Ottoman Empire. The end of Ottoman rule did not improve the plight of the Armenians. Armenian revolutionaries had been in league with Turkish revolutionaries, the Young Turks. However, once the Young Turks gained control of Turkey in 1908, their goals clashed with those of the Armenian revolutionaries. The Young Turks promoted a pan-Turkism that looked eastward beyond Armenia, and they supported Germany in World War I. Meanwhile, Armenians sought varying degrees of political autonomy, and they were sympathetic to the Entente powers. This led to the greatest tragedy of Armenian history. The Turks forced the exile of

Armenians into the desert, killing between 1 and 2 million in the process and ending the Armenian presence in the western part of historic Armenia. The Armenian experience with the nationalism and socialism of the twentieth century was to be limited to the eastern portion of Armenia, which was controlled by Russia.

At the end of the nineteenth century, Armenia's economic elites were not interested in assuming the role of political leadership. They were scattered throughout the Ottoman and Russian empires, forming significant minorities in such major cities outside historic Armenia as Istanbul, Tiflis (Tbilisi), and Baku. Erevan, the capital of Armenia today, was a small provincial town. The expatriate elites played an important economic role in the Ottoman and Russian empires and were not willing to upset the status quo. This left political leadership to lower, and more easily radicalized, classes of Armenian society.

Those willing to provide political leadership were influenced by the ideals of both nationalism and socialism. Nationalism addressed the political division and repression Armenians had suffered under foreign empires, while it affirmed their long history as a distinct people. Socialism, with its doctrine of modernization and internationalism, could find support among a relatively well educated and Westward-looking people.

Armenia's revolutionary leaders could understandably be attracted to both nationalism and socialism, but these two approaches are not easily reconciled. Nationalism emphasizes the ethnic differences between people, and it looks to the past to find the source of these differences. Socialism undertakes an economically oriented analysis focusing on class differences. It discourages ethnic distinctions, and it looks to the future to build a better, more advanced society. Those who wished to lead Armenians at the end of the eighteenth century had to grapple with the inherent conflict between nationalism and socialism.

The Hunchak party, which was founded in 1887, was the first major Armenian political party. It espoused extremes in both nationalism and socialism,[1] calling for national independence in the short term. In the longer term, the party supported "scientific socialism" which was based on an industrial proletariat, in spite of the fact that Armenians had no such proletariat. Scientific socialism reflected the interests of eastern Armenian socialists from the Russian Empire, who controlled the party. The two extremes could not be reconciled. Splits in the party led to the loss of its leadership position in the mid-1890s. The tension between nationalism and socialism had claimed its first political victim.

The other major party to form in the late 1800s was the Dashnaktsutiun party, or the Dashnaks. The Dashnaks were willing to compromise in order to accommodate both nationalism and socialism. They handled the tension between the two ideologies in several ways.[2] First, they left their socialist ideology vague, second, the party was decentralized; and third, the Dashnaks avoided the extremes of nationalism. The party was willing to compromise in order to achieve at least some of the benefits promised by nationalism and socialism.

When independence came to Armenia in May 1918, it was accepted reluctantly. The Russians' withdrawal from the Transcaucusus after the Russian Revolution led to a power vacuum. At the end of World War I, Russian Armenia was tiny, landlocked, and poor in resources. It lacked any significant infrastructure, it did not include any of the major centres of Transcaucasia, and many Armenians, particularly urban elites, lived outside its boundaries. Armenia was surrounded by hostile armies. The Turks had just destroyed western Armenia, along with its political, cultural, and religious networks. The Russian side was flooded with almost 300,000 refugees.[3] Nevertheless, when the neighboring Georgians and Azeris abandoned a brief federation with the Armenians after a few months, Armenia had no choice but to declare independence.

The Dashnaks had established themselves as the legitimate political leaders of the Armenians, despite their beginnings as a small revolutionary movement. They had done this by mobilizing Armenian protests for the return of church lands expropriated by the tsar in 1903 (and returned in 1905) and by championing the Armenian cause during the Armeno-Azeri conflict from 1905 to 1907. Thus, the party received 90 percent of the vote in the free elections that were held in 1919. While the Dashnaks were never able to reconcile their desire for progressive, democratic government with the authoritative measures the situation required, their administration has been credited with at least some improvement in rural self-administration, the legal system, and education, and with (unsuccessful) attempts at land and labor reform.[4]

The attempts of the Dashnaks to live up to their socialist ideals were cut short. The Turks advanced into Armenia from the east, while the Russians returned to the Transcaucuses in the form of the Red Army. The Armenian government was forced to accept the lesser evil of Soviet control and handed over all authority to the Red Army in December 1920. A fast-developing alliance between the Bolsheviks and the Turks influenced the decision to deny Armenians two Soviet areas that they considered to be part of their historic homeland: Nakhichevan to the west and Nagorno-Karabakh to the east. These areas had a majority of Armenians (at least before the 1915 Armenian slaughter, in the case of Nakhichevan), but were eventually given partial autonomy as part of the Azerbaijan Republic, thus sowing the seeds for future conflict. The Armenians' experiment with indigenous nationalism and socialism had come to an end.

NATIONALISM AND SOCIALISM: THE SOVIET UNION

The Bolsheviks promoted an international, class-based struggle. Before the Russian Revolution, Lenin opposed nationalism as well as any kind of federal accommodation of ethnic differences. The Bolsheviks, however, had to compromise after the revolution in order to extend their revolution to the periphery of the former Russian Empire. The Bolsheviks established geographic republics based on ethnicity as a temporary solution. Lenin believed that with time and education, the old ethnic divisions would disappear. In the meantime, he wanted to win non-Russians over to the socialist struggle.

Lenin adopted a program of *nativization* in order to mobilize the republics for socialism. There were few indigenous Bolsheviks in the republics. Nativization was to generate the leadership and activity necessary for the republics to implement the Bolsheviks' program. Even Stalin had to acquiesce to a limited continuation of this policy after Lenin's illness and death. By the 1960s, in each Transcaucasian republic, nativization had developed a truly national political and cultural character.[5]

Nativization affected several areas, including education, emigration, politics, the economy, and even religion. Nativization allowed Armenians to receive education through to the university level in their own language, while Russian was taught as an additional subject. While many urban Armenians are now bilingual, virtually none have lost their national language.[6] Armenians experienced little ethnic reidentification, a process in which members of one nationality began to claim membership in another.[7]

Soviet policies also had increased the concentration of Armenians in Armenia. The Armenian Republic was the most ethnically homogeneous republic in the Soviet Union. In 1989, 93 percent of its population was Armenian.[8] This was partly because today's Armenia represents only a small area at the heartland of historic Armenia. Armenians are still an extremely dispersed people, with only 67 percent of Soviet Armenians living in Armenia and millions of Armenians living abroad.[9] However, the percentage of Soviet Armenians living in Armenia risen from 56 percent in 1959.[10] This internal migration had been a direct result of the nativization policy. In order to reap the benefits of the Soviet system, members of minority nationalities were attracted to the republic where their nationality makes up the majority, provided they have such a titular republic. Emigration further consolidated the Armenian majority in Armenia. Roughly 150,000 Armenians emigrated to Armenia from the Soviet Union and abroad between 1946 and 1975.[11]

The Soviet Union fostered native political cadres. These cadres were able to wield power, in spite of the heavily centralized Soviet system. Central organizations had to depend on local cadres in order to achieve Union objectives. In turn, the national cadres identified with, and depended on, their own ethnic group. Transcaucasian society placed much greater importance on family and friendship ties than on obedience to the state. This led to particularly pervasive "official nationalism" (and corruption) favoring the dominant nationality.[12] In some parts of the Soviet Union, native political elites had to nurture a "national climate" in order to channel the dominant nationality's dissatisfaction to the elites' benefit.[13] In Armenia, such nurturing was not necessary and such channeling was not always possible. Armenian nationalism already had a life of its own, given Armenia's long history and large, supportive diaspora.[14] Soviet Armenian leaders had to respond to, rather than lead, calls to recognize the 1915 Armenian slaughter as genocide, to protect language rights, and to defend other national interests. Nevertheless, native elites pushed the limits of the centralized Soviet system and allowed Armenian nationalist sentiment some level of legitimate expression.

A major Soviet objective until the 1970s was the equalization of development among the republics. Armenia had fared relatively well in meeting the Soviet call for modernization and industrialization. Starting the Soviet period with virtually no urban working class, Armenia in 1985 was third only to Russia and Estonia in the percentage of workers in industry (29 percent), and fourth in urbanization (68 percent).[15] Armenia placed second only to Georgia in completion of secondary education.[16] Armenia's growth in both national income and industrial production had been well above average over the past three decades and was the highest in the Soviet Union from 1981 to 1985.[17] This growth occurred in spite of per capita investment falling increasingly further below the Union average over the past two decades.[18] The Armenians' greatest economic complaint might be that their economic performance has not been reflected in consumption. Per capita consumption in 1985 was tenth among the 15 union republics, at 84 percent of the Soviet Union average.[19] These latter two statistics may be cause for dissatisfaction, but the Armenian economy has nonetheless been transformed radically from the devastated rural economy that the Soviets took over in the 1920s.

Soviet policy had even given some leeway to religion.[20] There were 40 active churches and 6 monasteries in 1977. Of course, their existence was not the result of simple altruism. The Armenian national church was a useful tool for legitimizing the Soviet system. The Catholicos of all Armenians was the leader of a worldwide church, and the Soviets encouraged him to maintain the allegiance of Armenians abroad. The church leadership received material benefits and privileges.

The effects of nativization highlight the tension between the goals of socialist modernization and the means of nationbuilding that have been used to achieve them.[21] On one hand, Soviet policy left its own unique mark on Armenian attitudes. Religion was less important, male dominance had been partially eroded, and most cultural traditions had been lost.[22] Members of all Soviet nationalities, including Armenians, lived increasingly similar lives. On the other hand, Soviet policy consolidated the Armenian Republic as a national home for Armenians. In spite of all the hardship imposed by the Soviet system, Armenia had been able to maintain its language, increase its population and homogeneity, foster a native political elite, develop an industrial economy, and continue its religious tradition. The Soviet period had been one of accommodating the goal of socialism to nationalist realities. Armenian nationalism, however, might have been nurtured beyond the point of continued accommodation. This possibility is best assessed by first reviewing recent developments.

RENEWED NATIONALISM: THE DEVELOPMENTS

Glasnost' allowed old disputes to resurface in the Soviet Union. For Armenians, these old disputes were primarily with the surrounding Turkic peoples, and not with Russians or even with the Soviet system. A vestige of eighteenth-century Armenian Russophilism still distinguishes Armenian nationalism from Baltic nationalism. The issue for Armenians has not traditionally been how to free Armenia from Russia or from the Communist experiment, but rather how best to protect the Armenian nation in a hostile environment. However, as Moscow failed to respond to Armenian nationalism, Armenians were increasingly willing to take disputes into their own hands and now saw Moscow as an opponent of their rights.

Armenian nationalism did not completely disappear under the Soviet system. Although little open dissent was possible, Armenians were occasionally willing to express such dissent. In 1965, on the 50th anniversary of the 1915 slaughter of Armenian civilians, Armenians rallied in remembrance and successfully pressed for an official memorial to the victims. "Dissident nationalism" developed in the 1970s.[23] It included several secret parties or groups advocating independence or human rights, but the leaders were successfully rounded up. Soviet leadership was effective in suppressing nationalism of the non-official variety until the 1980s.

The main focus of Armenian nationalism today is on the status of the Nagorno-Karabakh Autonomous Oblast, a semi-independent area controlled by Azerbaijan and separated from Armenia by a ribbon of land only a few kilometers wide. Armenians view Nagorno-Karabakh as a part of historic Armenia, but the Russians included it in Muslim-dominated administrative units since the early 1800s.[24] The percentage of Armenians in Nagorno-Karabakh is roughly 75 percent, although the area was approximately 85 percent Armenian as recently as 1959.[25]

Another area that the Armenians claim as part of historic Armenia is Nakhichevan. Nakhichevan is an autonomous republic that is also under the aegis of Azerbaijan, although it is separated from Azerbaijan by Armenia. The proportion of Armenians in the population of Nakhichevan has declined from 80 percent before 1915 to less than half at the start of Soviet rule, and to 2 percent today.[26] Armenians point to their decline in Nakhichevan as being one reason why control over Nagorno-Karabakh is so important. The Armenian leadership, however, is reluctant to admit that claiming Nagorno-Karabakh on the basis of its Armenian majority refutes its claim to Nakhichevan. Nakhichevan itself has voted for annexation by Turkey, and Turkey retains a legal say in any change in status.[27] Nakhichevan today is only a bargaining chip for negotiations and a poignant reminder of the threat to Armenian predominance in Nagorno-Karabakh.

By late 1987 and early 1988, Armenians in Nagorno-Karabakh had begun responding to President Gorbachev's calls for *glasnost'*. A petition to join Armenia gathered 75,000 or more signatures. Meanwhile, Armenians had developed an environmental movement in response to the republic's large chemical industry, its nuclear reactor, and proposals to build a new mercury production factory.[28] In February 1988, when the Karabakh Soviet voted to request a transfer from Azerbaijan to Armenia, minor demonstrations concerning the environment ballooned into massive peaceful demonstrations involving as many as a million people in the streets in Erevan. Thousands also demonstrated in Nagorno-Karabakh. During this period, the environmental movement provided the leadership as the Karabakh Committee. Western commentators have linked the original demonstrations to the spirit of *glasnost'*, noting the placards supporting *glasnost'* and citing the example of a proseparation speaker who was booed down.[29]

Developments in Armenia and Nagorno-Karabakh contributed to an Azeri response. On 28 February 1988, hundreds of Armenians were killed in the Azeri city of Sumgait. Armenian leaders agreed to give President Gorbachev a month free of demonstrations so that he could arrange a solution. In March, however, the Presidium of the Soviet Parliament rejected a transfer and offered an economic and cultural package for Nagorno-Karabakh instead. Erevan was swamped with police and army troops, but protests began again by May. In June 1988 the Armenian Supreme Soviet called for a transfer of Nagorno-Karabakh, while protests grew and strikes paralyzed the district. In July, the Karabakh Soviet declared secession in order to join Armenia as an autonomous region. The Supreme Soviet discussed a transfer in a public debate which included harsh words from Gorbachev, and it rejected any change. By November, troops were called in for a state of emergency and curfew in Erevan and Nagorno-Karabakh.

Armenia was to face its greatest challenge, however, in the earthquake of 7 December 1988, which registered between 7 and 8 on the Richter scale. The official death toll was 55,000. Soviet President Gorbachev rushed back from New York City to deal with the situation and accepted large quantities of foreign aid. The authorities, however, also rounded up members of the Karabakh Committee, who were involved in organizing an independent relief effort. In the same month Azerbaijan began a blockade that has varied in its intensity but that continues to the present. This has had a devastating effect on Armenia, which depends on rail lines through Azerbaijan and on natural gas and oil from that region, Armenia has a sizable chemical industry that is particularly vulnerable to the loss of energy supplies.[30]

For 11 months in 1989, Nagorno-Karabakh was administered by the Special Administration Committee, a form of direct rule from Moscow. This did little to satisfy either side of the dispute. In November 1989, administration of the district was given to a local organizing committee, which was supposed to be comprised of Armenians and Azeris in relation to their population but ended up being controlled by Azeris.[31]

By the beginning of 1990, roughly 600,000 Armenians and Azeris had fled from one republic to the other.[32] The tensions again erupted into violence in January, when 34 Armenians were killed in Baku. A brief period of civil war between Armenia and Azerbaijan followed. Twenty thousand Soviet troops crushed the Azerbaijani Popular Front in what Azeris have called "Black January." In July 1990 the successor of the Karabakh Committee, the Armenian Pan-Nationalist Movement, won a majority in Armenian elections. Voter turnout, however, was low, falling under 50 percent in many of the constituencies.[33] The following month, the new government issued a declaration of independence as "the beginning of a process of affirmation of independent sovereignty."

Armenia continues on its path of self-assertion. Armenia's president, Levon Ter-Petrosian, was interested in economic ties to the Soviet Union, but he rejected the idea of a new Union Treaty as coming too late.[34] Furthermore, his government was concerned that a new Union Treaty could have legitimized Azeri control of Nagorno-Karabakh.[35] This was one reason why Armenia was one of six republics to boycott Gorbachev's referendum of March 1991, deciding instead to hold its own referendum on independence in September 1991. In addition to holding independence votes, the six republics of Estonia, Latvia, Lithuania, Moldavia, Georgia, and Armenia all stayed out of the April 1991 reform agreement between Gorbachev and the other nine Union republics. Meanwhile, violence continued, with Armenia accusing the Soviet government and the Azeris of causing more than 35 Armenian deaths in Azeri border towns during April 1991.[36]

Armenians were bitterly disappointed in Moscow's response to their concerns. Radical nationalists wanted to speed up developments. Paramilitary groups formed in Armenia and stepped up raids on Azeri border villages throughout 1990. They also turned on rival Armenian nationalist groups. After an outbreak of violence in August 1990, the nationalist government felt compelled to declare a state of emergency, impose a curfew, and outlaw the largest paramilitary group, the Armenian National Army.[37] These actions reined in the extreme nationalists only temporarily.

THE NATURE OF RENEWED NATIONALISM
AND ITS FUTURE PROSPECTS

Political problems do not always have a solution, and there is no clear solution in the offing for Armenia. None of the predictions--independence, a crackdown, or the continuation of the status quo--is particularly favorable.

The independence vote in September 1991 was unlikely to lead to any more Soviet response than had the Baltic votes, in spite of the fact that Armenia was the first republic to follow the lengthy process of the 1990 secession law.[38]

Conditions of similar uncertainty and turmoil threatened Armenia's very existence in the past. Admittedly, Turkey may be less of a threat today, given its desire to maintain American backing, its membership in the North Atlantic Treaty Organization (NATO), and its interest in European Community membership. Recent relations between Armenia and Azerbaijan, however, have shown the traditional antipathy of the old dispute with Turkey. While Azerbaijan may have less military advantage than Turkey enjoyed during its conflicts with the Armenians, it may have even more economic leverage through its stranglehold on transportation and energy. Such leverage can make the difference in a conflict. It is perhaps fortunate that independence is a distant possibility.

A crackdown might have been a more likely result, but as the Soviet experience has shown, repression is only a temporary check on nationalist urges. A more effective way for Moscow to have retained at least some control would be to let the explosive ethnic rivalries of the area diffuse the ability of Armenia (and, similarly, Georgia) to establish an effective nation-state. Blockades and violence could have been allowed to continue and even worsen as both Armenian and Azeri nationalism become further radicalized. A policy of limited containment would have maintained a Soviet presence, kept open the supply of resources from Azerbaijan, and focused Azeri nationalism on local concerns. Armenians could not have expected the Soviet Union to respond satisfactorily to their demands.

Why does Armenia not limit its aspirations? Surely there is one more alternative to consider. Armenia could accept the territory and status it has had for the past 70 years. In its present form, Armenia has come back from the brink of destruction. It could have embraced Soviet protection and Soviet reform. Cooperation with its Muslim neighbors could have led to a lift in the blockades, a cessation of most interethnic conflict, and an opportunity to focus on pressing economic, social, and environmental problems. Unfortunately, this scenario was the least likely of all.

It is difficult for others to guess the agony of a people that has been virtually wiped out and supplanted in most of its historic homeland. Armenians are hemmed into a tiny enclave of their traditional territory. They live in a system that has legitimized the borders and political gains of their enemies, the Turks and Azeris. They feel forgotten when they compare the recognition of their situation to the recognition given to the other victims of twentieth-century genocide, the Jews. Certainly, the Armenians were unrealistic in their hopes for what Soviet reform would have offered them in the late 1980s. They were looking for Soviet recognition of their plight and vindication of their position. This was more than Moscow realistically could have offered, given the greater strategic, demographic, and economic importance of the Soviet Union's Muslims. The Armenians' inevitable disappointment, however, prepared their nationalism for a permanent rejection of traditionally accepted federal solutions. Armenia would not accept compromise in order to save itself from the tragedies to come.

Armenia has been a small player in the drama of the Russian and Soviet empires. Life in these empires has not been easy. However, for Armenia, survival itself is an accomplishment. Today, the ties to Russia are weakening. The fact that both the Armenians and the Russians are or were Christians counts for little. The bright promises of socialism have been tried and found wanting, and at the end of the twentieth century, they can offer little support for internationalism. The fraying ties to Russia bring Armenia back to its principal challenge--survival among its immediate neighbors. The natural response to such a challenge is nationalism. However, a political agenda focused on ethnic conflict promises Armenians another difficult chapter in a tragic national history.

NOTES

1.   Gerard J. Libaridain, "Revolution and Liberation in the 1892 and 1907 Programs of the Dashnaktsutiun," in *Transcaucasia: Nationalism and Social Change*, ed. Ronald Grigor Suny (Ann Arbor, MI: University of Michigan Slavic Publications, 1983), pp. 187-188.

2.   Ibid., pp. 186, 190, 194-196.

3.   Richard G. Hovannisian, "Caucasian Armenia between Imperial and Soviet Rule: The Interlude of National Independence," in *Transcaucasia: Nationalism and Social Change*, ed. Ronald Grigor Suny (Ann Arbor, MI: University of Michigan Slavic Publications, 1983), p. 270.

4.   Ibid., pp. 262, 272-275.

5.   Ronald Grigor Suny, "Transcaucasia: Cultural Cohesion and Ethnic Revival in a Multinational Society," in *The Nationalities Factor in Soviet Politics and Society*, ed. Lubomyr Hajda and Mark Beissinger (Boulder, CO: Westview Press, 1990), p. 235.

6.   Ibid., p. 240.

7.   Barbara A. Anderson and Brian D. Silver, "Some Factors in the Linguistic and Ethnic Russification of Soviet Nationalities: Is Everyone Becoming Russian?" in *The Nationalities Factor in Soviet Politics and Society*, ed. Lubomyr Hajda and Mark Beissinger (Boulder, CO: Westview Press, 1990), p. 121.

8.   Suny, p. 237.

9.   Ibid., p. 238.

10.   Ibid.

11.   Anderson and Silver, p. 121.

12.   Ronald Grigor Suny, "The Revenge of the Past: Socialism and Ethnic Conflict in Transcaucasia," *New Left Review*, November/December 1990, p. 25.

13.   Gregory Gleason, *Federalism and Nationalism: The Struggle for*

Republican Rights in the USSR (Boulder, CO: Westview Press, 1990), p. 112.

14.   Ibid.

15.   Gertrude E. Schroeder, "Nationalities and the Soviet Economy" in *The Nationalities Factor in Soviet Politics and Society,* ed. Lubomyr Hajda and Mark Beissinger (Boulder, CO: Westview Press, 1990), p. 48.

16.   Ibid., p. 45.

17.   Ibid., p. 47.

18.   Ibid., p. 53.

19.   Ibid., p. 51.

20.   Bohdan R. Bociurkiw, "Nationalities and Soviet Religious Policies," in *The Nationalities Factor in Soviet Politics and Society,* ed. Lubomyr Hajda and Mark Beissinger (Boulder, CO: Westview Press, 1990), p. 153.

21.   Ronald Grigor Suny, *Armenia in the Twentieth Century* (Chico, CA: Scholars Press, 1983), pp. 77-78, 82.

22.   Suny, "Transcaucasia," p. 249.

23.   Ibid., p. 243.

24.   Christopher J. Walker, "Between Turkey and Russia: Armenia's Predicament," *World Today,* August/September 1988, p. 142.

25.   Suny, "Transcaucasia," p. 245.

26.   Suny, "Revenge," p. 27; "No Surrender," *The Economist,* 18 June 1988, p. 49.

27.   A. Fuat Borovali, "The Transitional Process and Nationalist Re-Structuring in Azerbaijan," in *Nationalism and the Breakup of Empire: Russia and its Periphery,* ed. Miron Rezun (New York: Praeger, 1992).

28.   Walker, p. 143; Suny, "Transcaucasia," p. 245.

29.   Suny, "Transcaucasia," p. 247; Walker, p. 143.

30.   John Tedstrom, "Armenia: An Energy Profile," *Report on the USSR,* 22 February 1991, p. 20.

31.   Elizabeth Fuller, "Democratization Threatened by Interethnic Violence," *Report on the USSR,* 4 January 1991, p. 42; Mark Saroyan, "The 'Karabakh Syndrome' and Azerbaijani Politics," *Problems of Communism* 39, no. 5 (September-October 1990): 27.

32.   "Enter the army," *Economist,* 20 January 1990, p. 47.

33.   Fuller, p. 41.

34.   "When the Juggling Has to Stop," *Economist,* 24 November 1990, p. 48.

35.   "The Referendum Scorecard," *Economist,* 23 March 1991, p. 54.

36.   "Kremlin Seeks War, Armenia Says," in *Globe and Mail,* 2 May 1991, p. A7.

37.   Jeff Sallot, "Trigger-Happy Armies Mark Time," in *Globe and Mail,* 29 September 1990, p. A5.

38.   Ann Sheehy, "Armenia Invokes Law on Mechanics of Secession," *Report on the USSR,* 15 March 1991, p. 21.

Part 4

THE MUSLIM PERIPHERY

The Muslim periphery of the former Soviet Union is composed of five separate Muslim republics: Kazakhstan, Uzbekistan, Turkmenistan, Kirgizia, and Tadzhikistan. The populations are mainly of Turkic stock with the exception of the Tadzhiks, whose culture and language are Iranian. In addition, the Azeris of Azerbaijan, although part of the Caucasian periphery, are also Muslim and of Turkic extraction. The Central Asian republics are comparatively rural and underdeveloped, and the population has increased since the October Revolution to such a point that these former Soviet Muslims now account for approximately 60 million along Russia's southern periphery. This represents almost one-quarter of the whole population.

Kazakhstan is the second largest of the former Union republics and serves as a buffer between China and the Russian Republic. Kazakhs have long taken an interest in using their own language in government and schools and in having the right to their own history, rather than Russian-based history. This idea is also important to the Uzbeks, who are part of a larger community found in Afghanistan, Pakistan, and China. Uzbeks are themselves descendants of nomadic tribes and are concerned, as are all Central Asians, with worsening economic and social conditions in regions republics and with environmental issues.

Turkmenistan is really more of a tribal confederation than a nation. Tribes like the Tekke, Ersay, and Yomud constitute the population. They, consequently, have been slow to press for greater autonomy given their inability to agree on most issues.

Kirgizia is a mountainous region where the vast majority of the population is ethnically Kirgiz. They are part of a larger community that extends into China and Afghanistan. Finally, the Tadzhiks are themselves opposed to separatism, though their territory has been the most vocal favouring a pan-Islamic, Central Asian state.

Islam plays an important role in the lives of the people in this region. However, there has been a problem reconciling Islam (which sees all Muslims as part of a world community) and republican nationalism (which puts the interest of the national group ahead of other considerations). Fundamentalism, rather than democratic parlimentarianism, may become a major force in these republics. Islam has, since the time of the Prophet Mohammed, tended toward empire building. However, the modern idea of nationalism, which is Western, has affected the nationalist revival and consciousness of these peoples, more along the lines of ethnicity than religion. In fact, the dichotomy between Islam and ethnicity has blurred the subject of separatism in these areas and made it far more complex and ambivalent. While these Muslims do seem to opt for sovereignty and want independence, they are not as vocal or strident as is the case in the more highly developed of the other ex-Soviet republics. Paradoxically, even the Georgians and the Armenians of former Soviet Transcaucasia want a complete break with Russia.

An interesting political situation is currently taking shape in these southern regions. As Russian power appears to be on the wane, Iranian and Turkish power is in the ascendant, with Turkey and Iran competing for supremacy in ex-Soviet Azerbaijan and Central Asia. Iran, for example, has been brokering a peace between Azerbaijan and Armenia. But civil strife will likely continue far into the future as Azerbaijan oscillates between Azeri nationalism and communism and struggles to hold on to territories that are now claimed by Armenia such as Nakhichevan and Nagorno-Karabakh. Rumor has it that Iran has purchased nuclear warheads from Kazakhstan and many Turks are appealing to a pan-Turanian (Turkophone) national identity. And there is always the possibility that these former Soviet Muslims are just as innately anti-Western as they are anti-Russian.

When one studies the war between the Azeri Muslims and the Christian Armenians, one is immediately struck by the sympathy in the Muslim world for the Azeris and similar feelings of solidarity in the Christian West for the Armenians. Nagorno-Karabakh, a mainly Christian Armenian region in Muslim Azerbaijan, has been the focus of bitter fighting in which well over 6,000 people, perhaps even more, have been killed to date. In May of 1992, Armenia gained the upper hand in the war, pushing most Azerbaijanis out of Nagorno-Karabakh. That led to popular unrest in Azerbaijan by Azeri nationalists and the resignation of its president, Ayaz Mutalibov, who had been urging peace talks with Armenia and therefore blamed by his people for Azerbaijan's military reverses. Now the new Azeri president, Ebulfez Elcibey, has vowed to take the offensive and recapture all lost territory. While the Azeris strike back, probably supported by the majority of Turks and Iranians, it becomes increasingly difficult to gauge the reaction of Moscow, the wobbling center.

The civil wars and extreme violence in these southern and Central

Asian states is pressing several hundreds of thousands of Russians to migrate back to their homeland--as are the Armenians and Jews. The majority of the Muslims sympathized with and volunteered for Saddam Hussein in his war against the U.S.-led coalition in the Persian Gulf.[1]

NOTE

1.   For a discussion of this development, see my recent book, *Saddam Hussein's Gulf Wars: Ambivalent Stakes in the Middle East* (New York: Praeger, 1992).

7

Azerbaijan:
From Trauma to Transition
FUAT BOROVALI

Ever since Mikhail Gorbachev unleashed the forces of change on an unsuspecting Soviet Union, it has been hard to predict the different responses from the various republics. Let us attempt to place the sometimes traumatic events that have occurred in Azerbaijan in the broader perspective of structural change in the now-defunct Soviet Union.

HISTORICAL LEGACY

The recent interactions between the Azerbaijan Popular Front (APF) and the Communist Party of Azerbaijan (CPA) carry distinct echoes of the relationship between *Musavat* (a party whose platform was based on egalitarianism) and *Hummet* (Muslim Communist party) earlier in this century. Indeed, the APF has not concealed the fact that it is trying to resurrect the ideals and program of the *Musavat* party of Mehmed Emin Rasulzade, the founder and president of the short-lived republic of Azerbaijan (1918-1920).[1]

That party was founded as *Milli Musavat* by Azeri intellectuals in 1911.[2] After the February Revolution of 1917, the party went through a series of changes. During the All-Russia Muslims Congress in Moscow (1-11 May 1917), there were two opposing views aiming at the domination of the party. While Liberal Nationalists aspired to cultural autonomy, Radical (*Inkilapci*) Nationalists promoted the idea of an independent national state to come under a federalist structure encompassing the Turkic peoples of the former Russian Empire.[3]

In 1918, *Milli Musavat* took on the name *Azerbeycan Turk Federalist Musavat Halk Firkasi* (Azerbaijan Turkish Federalist Egalitarian People's party).[4] The party's program, which was ratified in 1919, envisaged a republican state founded primarily on the principles of nationalism, Turkism, democracy, and racism. The program was designed to serve as a draft constitution for the republic, which was founded on 28 May 1918. At the opening session of the parliament in December of that year, *Musavatists* sat in the center, *Ittihadists* to their right, and the *Hummet-*Mensheviks (together with the Muslim Socialist bloc) to their left.[5] Rasulzade delivered an address outlining the updated *Musavat* program.[6] Within a few days, *Hummet* also presented their new platform. It envisaged a Sovietized but culturally and nationally autonomous Azerbaijan within the Soviet Union, suggesting the notion of a national communism. The party adopted the title of Muslim Communist party--*Hummet*. Nariman Narimanov, the party's leader, called for the Sovietization of his homeland with the assistance of Bolshevik Russia. He expected an "independent" Soviet Azerbaijan to be based on the model of a Soviet Ukraine or Byelorussia.[7]

Though *Hummet* was founded in Baku in 1904 by local Social Democrats of Bolshevik persuasion, it never became truly Bolshevik, as it blended socialism with a strong dose of nationalism. Never breaking completely with the national movement, its strongest attacks were directed against tsarist despotism. Even after 1917, the *Hummet* leaders rejected the idea of merging with the Party in Moscow.[8] Vacillating between nationalism and communism, Narimanov appealed to Russian Bolsheviks to grant full independence to Azerbaijan. This strain of independence, which was present within *Hummet* since its beginnings, continued even after the party transformed itself into the Communist Party of Azerbaijan (CPA) in April 1920. Even when Red Army trains were well on their way to Baku, the Central Committee of the CPA proclaimed "full independence of Azerbaijan under the Soviet Socialist Republic of Azerbaijan."

It is evident that much of the recent debates between the CPA and APF, as well as within the APF itself, are grounded in the politics of 1918-1920 and that the CPA and APF can trace their antecedents to *Hummet* and *Musavat*, respectively. The nationalist legacy of the CPA has been manifested over and over again. Most recently, the CPA, the party of Narimanov, has been instrumental in the rehabilitation of Rusulzade, the *Musavat* leader.

THE TRAGIC EVENTS OF 19-20 JANUARY 1990

Tensions between the Azeris and Armenians have deep roots and have increased dramatically since 1987. At the core of the recent confrontations lies the dispute over the Nagorno-Karabakh Autonomous Oblast, an enclave within the Azerbaijani SSR, where some two-thirds of the population are Armenian.

A historical synopsis of the Karabakh question may be helpful. Following the conclusion of the Russo-Persian War of 1826-28 with the Treaty

of Turkmenchai, some 40,000 Armenians living in Iran and 84,000 Ottoman Armenians were settled in the Karabakh (Black Garden) region, in
keeping with Russian imperial practices. A century later, when the Caucasian Soviet Federal Socialist Republic was formed among Armenia,
Georgia, and Azerbaijan in 1922, Karabakh was declared an autonomous
oblast within the Azerbaijani SSR. Upon the dissolution of the Caucasian
Confederation in 1936, the status of Karabakh remained unchanged even
though some borders in Transcaucasia were redrawn; the only change
was nominal, whereby the Russian prefix *nagorno* (mountainous) was
added to the name.[9] Armenians at the time made persistent demands that
Karabakh be integrated into the Armenian SSR, but they were rejected by
the Supreme Soviet of the USSR under Article 78 of the Soviet Constitution.[10] Armenians' demands concerning Nagorno-Karabakh were repeated
during the 1960s and have been voiced intermittently since then.

In February 1988 the Nagorno-Karabakh Soviet passed a resolution
demanding unification with the Armenian SSR. This was promptly reci-
procated by the Supreme Soviet in Erevan, which agreed to work toward
annexation. The issue found its way to the Presidium of the Supreme
Soviet of the USSR, which set up a body to administer the oblast.[11]
However, although this arrangement brought the oblast under direct rule
by Moscow, it failed to produce the desired results.

A remarkable aspect of the Armenian-Azeri confrontation since 1987
has been the nationalistic fervor exhibited by the Communist Party of
Azerbaijan. Indeed, the first secretary of the CPA at the time, Abdurrahman
Vazirov, is known to have rebuked his comrades in Erevan for behaving
unconstitutionally. The Karabakh issue appears to have reinforced the
nationalistic legacy within the CPA.

As the dispute over Karabakh intensified, waves of refugees filled the
roads: Azeris fled from Armenia and Nagorno-Karabakh, while Armenians
fled from Azerbaijan. Since mass migrations started in late 1988, an
estimated 600,000 refugees are thought to have crossed from one republic
into the other, some 200,000 of them Azeris. The ending of Moscow's
direct rule over Nagorno-Karabakh in November 1989 led to a second
wave of migration. Thousands of Azeri refugees came streaming into Baku,
many of them homeless and militant.[12]

The spark that ignited an explosion came during a mass rally in Baku
on 13 January 1990. The rioting that followed spread to Nakhichevan and
later to Nagorno-Karabakh, where sporadic hill fighting in the north turned
into full-scale guerrilla warfare. On 19 January, when Soviet troops and
tank convoys reached the outskirts of Baku, they encountered hundreds
of protestors forming barricades. The commander of the forces issued an
ultimatum for their dispersal. It is interesting to note that the ultimatum was
issued to the APF (Azerbaijani Popular Front) leadership. The protesters
did not move. Finally, the tanks moved into the wall of people and a
carnage ensued and hundreds of Azeris were crushed.[13] It was a traumatic

event that is bound to remain in Azeri collective memory for generations to come.

Some attribute the tragedy to the failure of the APF leadership. Others point to the euphoria generated by momentous events such as the destruction of the Berlin Wall, the dissolution of the Nicolae Ceaucescu regime in Romania, the liberation of Eastern Europe, and the demands for liberation emerging throughout the Soviet Union. A third factor is the internal dynamic of the Azeri-Armenian confrontation, which had reached a crescendo during the preceding months.

The events of 19-20 January ended the political career of Abdurrahman Vezirov, the first secretary of the CPA. He was succeeded by the chairman of the republic's Council of Ministers, Ayaz Muttalibov.[14] These events also had other important consequences. On 20 January, while demonstrations in Baku were still in progress, the Supreme Soviet of the Nakhichevan Autonomous SSR announced its secession from the Soviet Union and issued a demand to be integrated into the Republic of Turkey. The Nakhichevan ASSR is the only part of Azerbaijan that has common borders with Turkey, Iran, and Armenia. Its 1.5 million inhabitants constitute a sizable portion of Azerbaijan's total population of 7 million. Predictably, Moscow declared the Nakhichevan decision unconstitutional, null, and void.[15]

TURKEY'S REACTION

Suddenly finding itself in the midst of a whirlwind of events, Turkey was faced with a series of delicate policy decisions concerning Nakhichevan, Azerbaijan, and, not least, Moscow. The Turkish position was grounded in legal antecedents, specifically the 1921 Kars and Moscow treaties, which contained provisions to the effect that Turkey was to be consulted if Nakchichevan's status was to undergo any revision. Turkey was now faced with a unilateral declaration by Nakhichevan to merge with Turkey.

The foremost consideration for the Turkish government was to avoid getting entangled in constitutional and political wrangles with the Soviet Union. There was visible discomfort in Ankara, as evidenced by a hastily convened meeting between the prime minister, the foreign minister, and the chief of the General Staff. Later, it was announced obscurely that Turkey intended to make full use of its legal rights in any unforeseen eventuality.[16]

Turkey was faced with a similar dilemma regarding Azerbaijan proper. On the one hand, there was public pressure for lending a hand to the Azeri "cousins" in this time of troubles. Public sentiment was echoed by several cabinet ministers. When Ankara indicated to Moscow that it viewed the matter as an internal affair of the Soviet Union, a controversy erupted. Opposition members of the Turkish National Assembly argued that the concept of internal affairs had undergone substantial transformations as a result of the Helsinki Final Act of 1975.[17] Any signatory to the act had to consider that human rights violations on as large a scale as in Azerbaijan could not be considered purely an internal matter.[18]

THE WEST AND AZERBAIJAN

Western views regarding the events in Azerbaijan appeared to have been determined primarily by a concern not to undermine Gorbachev. We must remember that at the beginning of 1990, the status of Eastern Europe had not been fully settled and German unification had not been brought to completion. Most Western commentators portrayed Moscow's decision to send the troops into Azerbaijan as an attempt to stop the ethnic conflict and prevent a massacre. "Mr. Gorbachev had little choice but to send troops into Baku, the Soviet Union's fifth largest city," stated an editorial in the *Economist*. "They were needed not just to stop the increasingly bloody civil war between Azeris and Armenians but also to block a concerted attempt by the anticommunist Azerbaijan Popular Front to seize power in the republic."[19]

In the United States, the White House press spokesperson noted the need to recognize the right of any state to ensure the safety of its citizens. Senator Claiborne Pell, chairman of the Senate Foreign Relations Committee, stated that Karabakh should be given to Armenia. There was also a letter signed by 28 members of the U.S. Congress and addressed to Gorbachev, demanding that the "unjust administrative policy of the Azeris in Nagorno-Karabakh be ended."[20] These and similar episodes led Turkish observers to conclude that Westerners were not prepared to show the same kind of concern for Baku as for Vilnius or even Tbilisi.

MOSCOW AND BAKU

A cloud of doubt and suspicion hung over the way in which Moscow reached its decision to send troops into Baku. Gorbachev reportedly argued against the measure at a meeting of the Presidium of the Supreme Soviet which, nevertheless, resolved to send in the troops. Defense Minister Dmitri Yazov is said to have argued against the use of **regular** forces.[21] Top army officers were reported to have expressed reluctance to use their troops against Soviet citizens. Nevertheless, in the end, some 11,000 regular troops were dispatched to the area to join the 16,700 Interior Ministry troops already stationed in various parts of the country. As it turned out, much of the fighting in Baku was done by the Interior Ministry troops.[22]

Moscow also failed to speak with one voice when asked for an official explanation of the events. Gorbachev blamed "adventurists, black marketeers, and Islamic fundamentalists."[23] According to him, Muslim radicals in Azerbaijan demanded an independent Islamic state without having the support of the people.

Internal splits within the APF had widened over preceding months, and control of the front had increasingly passed to Muslim radicals. We are unlikely to know, however, whether Gorbachev's determined effort to portray the issue in terms of Muslim radicalism and/or Islamic fundamentalism reflected a genuine analysis or was meant merely for Western consumption. He was certainly aware of the U.S. distaste for discovering yet another Ayatollah Khomeini-type regime at Iran's doorstep.

Yazov, on the other hand, seemed to argue that the troops had been sent to Baku to smash the "structures of power" set up by the APF. He made no reference to Muslim radicalism or to Islam. Foreign Minister Eduard Shevardnadze, meanwhile, appeared to be at odds with both Yazov and Gorbachev. He explained that troops had been sent in not for any political purposes connected with dissidence but solely and exclusively to halt the bloodshed.[24]

The contradictory voices coming from Moscow reflected the confusion surrounding the whole issue of nationalism. The events in Baku were bound to exacerbate nationalist conflicts in other republics. The Baku tragedy coincided with a demonstration in Ukraine on 21 January, in which millions of Ukrainians joined hands in a human chain 300 miles long and stretching from Kiev to the western city of Lvov.

THE PARTY AND THE FRONT

Dealings between the CPA and the LPF date back to April 1989, when Vazirov and other Party officials held several (unpublicized) meetings with representatives of the APF to discuss prospects for the front's legislation.[25] The APF had just been formed (March 1989) as a loose collection of intellectuals, journalists, and researchers at the Academy of Sciences in Baku. The main impetus for the formation of the group was the Karabakh issue. However, the APF envisioned a broader program with regard to political, economic, cultural, and environmental issues. In contrast to the popular fronts in the Baltic republics, the APF did not assert even long-term claims for the separation of Azerbaijan from the Soviet Union. It focused instead on enhancing the republic's political and economic autonomy within the framework of the Soviet federal state.[26]

Meanwhile, the influx of refugees into Baku from Armenia and Nagorno-Karabakh was starting to affect the political tone of the country, particularly in and around Baku. As APF leader Ebulfez Aliyev (kin to the notoriously corrupt and better-known Geidar Aliyev) was later to remark, the anti-Armenian riots in Baku turned out to be largely the work of some of those displaced persons whom the APF leadership was unable to control.[27]

Aliyev repeatedly stressed that the Azerbaijani nationalist movement had nothing to do with Muslim radicalism or Islamic fundamentalism. Even a cursory knowledge of Islam, he claimed, was a rarity among the Azeri population.[28] That viewpoint has been echoed by Sheikh-ul Islam Allah-shukur Pashazade, the mufti of the Caucasian Muslims. He has stated that the religious infrastructure of Azerbaijan consists of nothing more than mosques and a couple of prayer houses.[29] Aliyev has pointed out that if an ideological orientation is called for, it could be none other than that of Kemal Ataturk, the founder of the Turkish Republic.

Aliyev has outlined the APF's demands and aspirations and believes that in the short term, Nagorno-Karabakh should be given to Azerbaijan unconditionally. Soviet troops should leave the country, and martial law and all other restrictions should be lifted. Subsequently, while remaining within a Soviet confederation, Azerbaijan should be given economic and political autonomy and constitutional changes should be made to that end. For the establishment of a genuine democracy, multiparty elections should be held as soon as possible. Finally, in the long term, APF aspires to the unification of all Azeris, including the 12 million residing in Iran. Aliyev has conceded that Azeri unification is not imminent and that the process should be gradual. As he put it, "When everyone is talking about German unification, when even Korean unification is on the agenda, why not us Azeris?"[30]

Looking at the CPA's agenda under First Secretary Ayaz Muttalibov during the post-January period, one sees a deliberation effort to co-opt APF policies. As one observer put it, Muttalibov's tactic in attempting to salvage the authority of the Party was to emphasize Azerbaijan's territorial integrity (by rejecting the ceding of Nagorno-Karabakh) while adopting a cautious line on such issues as full economic autonomy and the possibility of secession from the USSR.[31] Muttalibov cultivated business and cultural contacts with Turkey and encouraged Western investment in the republic's oil industry. In October 1990, a business congress in Baku was attended by some 5,000 executives from 43 countries around the world. On the domestic front, Muttalibov restored the dialogue with the APF. In early May 1990 meetings took place between high-level CPA officials and the leadership of the APF, including Aliyev. During the meeting, elections were discussed, among other things.[32]

Measures were taken in quick succession to reinforce CPA's nationalist credentials. In early May, the Supreme Soviet of Azerbaijan took the decision to remove the hammer and sickle from the republic's flag. Instead, it adopted the tricolor flag of the Azerbaijani Republic of 1918-1920.[33] The symbolism of this act was further heightened by the fact that the flag had thus far been used by the APF. Another symbolic measure was the changing of the official founding date of Azerbaijan from 28 April 1920 to 28 May 1918. In an ironic twist, a switch was made from *Hummet's* Narimanov to *Musavat's* Rusulzade.

Some might find in all this an explanation as to why Muttalibov was elected unopposed to the newly established position of the republican president in late May 1990. Others would point out that these actions were consistent with the legacy of nationalism already present within the CPA.

THE ELECTIONS

In late June 1990 the situation was deemed stable enough to set a date for elections to the Republican Supreme Soviet. Within two weeks of the announcement, over 50 political, cultural, and ecological parties formed an election coalition called the Democratic Forum. In late July, under pressure from the minor parties and on grounds that there was not enough time to get properly organized, the election date was moved from 2 to 30 September. Close to 1,200 candidates were registered to contest the 350 seats, an average of 4 candidates per seat. The distribution of candidates was as follows: Democratic Bloc--231; Popular Front--195; Communist party--131; Prime Ministry--110; *Komsomol*--56; KGB, Militia, and Public Prosecutors Offices--56; and informal groups--415. Among the candidates were Geidar Aliyev (former USSR Politburo member and former first secretary of the CPA), Chief Mufti Allahshukur Pashazade, and Abbas Abdullahov, an APF leader. Ebulfez Aliyev declined to be a candidate. Of the potential 4 million voters, approximately 2.5 million turned out.[34]

The first round of voting, under the 50 percent voter-participation rule in any given district, produced outright winners in only 240 of 350 seats.[35] Of those, the CPA won a majority. Only 26 of the APF's candidates were elected. A major surprise of the first round was that Geidar Aliyev was elected in his native Nakhichevan with nearly 95 percent of the vote in his district.[36]

What can be said about the election results? In the first instance, the results can be considered a victory for the CPA and President Muttalibov. Remarkably, in the first relatively free, multiparty elections, voters chose not to oust the CPA. Some have talked about an Ion Iliescu-syndrome (after the Romanian president), where an overwhelming majority of voters chose to stick with the Communist party even after overthrowing Ceaucescu in a bloody revolution. After the traumatic events of January, Azeris would certainly have been justified in their reluctance to leap into the unknown or to entirely trust an inexperienced APF leadership.

The answer probably lies in a different direction. As has been pointed out, in the post-January period leading to the elections (and indeed, up to the final third round), the CPA attempted to co-opt and preempt the APF's program. Added to the measures already mentioned was the serious initiative undertaken to Latinize the alphabet and to restore the traditional names of towns (for example, Kirovabad reverted to its old name, Ganja).[37] Prominent streets in Baku were renamed for Ataturk and Izmir.[38] Just before the third round of voting in December, Muttalibov issued a degree removing the "Soviet Socialist" label from the republic's name; indeed, the Central Committee of the CPA had initially proposed the measure. The Parliament of the Nakhichevan Autonomous Republic had already deleted the "Soviet Socialist" label from its name. The CPA was able to appropriate the mantle of nationalism for itself and left the APF out of the running.

The shifting of the foundation of the state from Bolshevik to national was perhaps the most effective of the initiatives taken by the CPA.[39] The APF could not hope to compete against an established apparatus, with its intricate networks of power, prestige, and patronage.

What of the future? The hope is that after so many traumas and travails, the Azeri people may finally manage a transition to better times.

NOTES

1.   *Musavat* can roughly be translated as egalitarianism. It denotes equality before the law rather than the more socio-political interpretations.

2.   *Mulli Musavat* means "national egalitarianism." For further information concerning the founding of *Milli Musavat*, see Selchuk Alkin, "*Istiklal Doneminde Azerbaycan*" (Azerbaijan during the independence period), *Azerbaycan Degrisi*, no. 264, 1988, p. 29.

3.   For further analysis of the subject, see Ahmet Karaca, "*Azerbaycan Milli Hareketinin Ideolojik Karakteri*" (The ideological character of the Azerbaijani national movement), *Milli Egitim Dergisi*, no. 7, 1980, p. 90.

4.   To avoid a misunderstanding, it should be pointed out that *federalism* here does *not* mean federalism within the Soviet Union but rather federalism among the Turkic peoples of the former empire. In this sense, federalism is viewed as a union of Turkic states with local administrative autonomy.

5.   Mizra Bala, "*Musavat Partisi*," *Istoriia* 3, (1980): 169. The *Ittihadists* fashioned themselves after the Ottoman Union and Progress party, perhaps indicating the extent of Ottoman cultural and political influence on Azerbaijan at the time.

6.   Tadeusz Swietochowski, *Russian Azerbaijan, 1905-21: The Shaping of National Identity in a Muslim Community* (Cambridge: Cambridge University Press, 1985), p. 146.

7.   Ibid., p. 165.

8.   Ibid., p. 182.

9.   See Amer Taheri, *Crescent in a Red Sky: The Future of Islam in the Soviet Union* (London: Hutchinson and Co., 1989), pp. 163-180.

10.   Article 78 stipulated that borders within the Soviet Union could not be changed without the explicit consent of republics involved.

11.   *Report on the USSR* (RFE/RL Research Institute) 2, no. 1 (4 January 1991): 42.

12.   It could be said that ending the arrangement by which Nagorno-Karabakh was run by a Moscow-appointed committee, which was backed up by some 5,000 Interior Ministry troops, triggered the crisis leading to the events of 19-20 January 1990. The USSR Supreme Soviet handed Nagorno-Karabakh back to nominal Azerbaijani sovereignty while granting sub-

stantial autonomy to the enclave, thus satisfying neither the Armenians nor the Azeris.

13.   The actual number of casualties during the events of 19-20 January is a matter of some conjecture. Reported deaths vary from 80 in official figures to between 130 and 160 in the more credible sources and several hundred in some Turkish newspapers.

14.   *Report on the USSR*, p. 42.

15.   *Yeni Forum*, no. 250, March 1990. Nakhichevan has had an interesting history. It was initially established on 28 July 1920 as an SSR (Soviet Socialist Republic). However, when the Nakhichevan Revolutionary Council issued a declaration saying that Nakhichevan was an integral part of Azerbaijan, it was reintegrated into Azerbaijan by the Treaty of Moscow (16 March 1921). On 9 February 1924, following the decision of the Central Committee of the Communist Party of Azerbaijan, Nakhichevan was given its current autonomous status within the Azerbaijan SSR. Given that the whole process entailed a kind of demotion, one wonders why the Nakhichevanis insisted on it. The obvious explanation is that there were justified fears of Armenian designs on the territory and that solidarity with other Azeris bolstered their sense of security.

16.   *Milliyet*, 21 January 1990.

17.   The Helsinki Final Act of 1975 was an agreement signed between European leaders and the Soviet Union which created the Conference on Security and Cooperation in Europe and concerned Western recognition of Soviet preeminence in central and eastern Europe, human rights and economic and technical cooperation.

18.   *Milliyet*, 26 January 1990. Suleyman Demirel, the leader of the lesser opposition party in the National Assembly, was the most vocal on the subject.

19.   [Editorial], *Economist*, 27 January 1990.

20.   *Yeni Dusunce*, 2 February 1990.

21.   *Economist*, 20 January 1990.

22.   *Economist*, 20 January 1990.

23.   *International Herald Tribune*, 19 January 1990.

24.   *International Herald Tribune*, 28 January 1990.

25.   Mark Saroyan, "The Karabakh Syndrome and Azerbaijani Politics," *Problems of Communism* 39, no. 5 (September-October 1990): 23.

26.   Ibid., pp.22-23.

27.   From an interview conducted by Turkish journalist Mehmet Ali Birand, *Milliyet*, 5 February 1990.

28.   *Milliyet*, 5 February 1990.

29.   *Ibid.*

30.   *Ibid.*

31.   Elizabeth Fuller, "Democratization Threatened by Interethnic Violence," *Report on the USSR (RFE/RL Research Institute)* 4, no. 1 (4

January 1991): 42.

32.   *Milliyet*, 15 May 1990; *Tercuman*, 15 May 1990.

33.   The flag is red, blue, and green, with an eight-cornered star. As mentioned to the draft proposed by the Supreme Soviet, red represents independence; blue, the Turkic peoples; and green, Islam. The eight-cornered star represents the eight traditional Turkic tribes of Azerbaijan.

34.   *Yeni Forum* 11, no. 258 (November 1990): 12.

35.   Participation in most areas was below 50 percent, and in the Baku metropolitan area it was even less, around 40 percent. Depending on people's perspectives, this was taken to mean a protest vote, a lack of enthusiasm for the APF and other opposition groups, or a combination of both.

36.   The second round of voting on 14 October produced winners in only half the remaining 110 seats; a third round had to be scheduled for 16 December. Of the 55 seats contested in this final round, 40 were in Baku and the remainder in rural areas; *Cumhuriyet*, 17 December 1990.

37.   It was in Ganja that Rasulzade first declared the republic in 1918, as Baku was still under British (and Armenian) occupation. When Baku was liberated by Ottoman armies (the so-called Caucasian Islamic Army, commanded by Enver Pasha's uncle Halil Pasha and cousin Nuri Pasha) in September 1918, just before the end of World War I, the capital was moved there.

38.   The name Izmir derives from the Agenda port city of Izmir, Baku's sister city (Baku also being a port city along the Caspian). The government of Azerbaijan has also started a formal initiative to open reciprocal consults in Izmir and Baku.

39.   *Gunes*, 2 December 1990.

8

The Muslim Borderlands: Islam and Nationalism in Transition

MIRON REZUN

Given the former Soviet Union's political geography, one area of particular concern to Moscow from the standpoint of the empire's survival is comprised of the Muslim borderlands on the southern periphery: the republics in Central Asia (Kazakhstan, Kirgizia, Uzbekistan, Tajikistan, and Turkmenistan) and Caucasia (Azerbaijan).

This concern stemmed from a combination of demographic, religious, and strategic reasons. The Muslims of the now defunct Soviet Union number approximately 60 million people, or 20 percent of the union's present population. By way of comparison, there are approximately 167 million Great Russians and about 40 million Ukrainians. The Muslims are susceptible to Islamic movements elsewhere, and they are located in strategic areas along the southern tier of the Soviet Union, bordering with Turkey, Iran, Afghanistan, and China.

In view of the Gorbachev reforms, which came to naught, and the diversity of problems to be faced in the proposed transition from a tightly centralized system to a decentralized one, it was important to know what undercurrents were at work in this region. The resolution of problems in a Baltic or Ukrainian setting may not be the same as required in Kirgizia or Turkmenistan. Even within the Turkic world, there are differences, as it is no more monolithic than the Arab world. Moreover, Moscow's endeavor to create new Soviet citizens out of the Central Asian and Azeri peoples was widely regarded as a failure. Thus, as opposition to the Soviet system escalated, how did nationalism and religion interact with each other? Is there an interethnic strife in these borderlands? Are they united by Islamic fundamentalist ideas? Will these Muslims be drawn to the Russian center as a result of an anti-Western bias?

Glasnost' and *perestroika* have emanated from the Center and evoked a nationalist clamor for independence in the Baltic states. This, in turn, reverberated across the Muslim borderlands. Like many Russian politicians, Gorbachev had always been suspicious of Muslims and Muslim political movements. He never agreed with the Kremlin's intervention in Afghanistan. Perhaps as a result of living many years in close proximity to Muslims in the Kuban, he saw Islam as irrational, corrupt, treacherous, and violent. He preferred to keep Russians in top positions at the center of the political hierarchy and the military. One of Gorbachev's earliest changes took place in 1986, when he replaced the Kazakh Communist party first secretary, Dinmukhamed Kunaev, with Gennadi Kolbin, an ethnic Russian. Loud, violent demonstrations occurred in the Kazakh capital of Alma-Ata. Gorbachev was intent on purging the bureaucracies of Central Asia, especially in the Fergana Valley of Uzbekistan, and resorted to wholesale dismissals of party *apparatchiks*, accusing them of xenophobia, nationalism, corruption, and "tolerance for Islam."[1]

Gorbachev's first detailed statement on the nationalities question came at the plenum of the Central Committee of the CPSU on 29 July 1988. The statement was long on self-criticism about past relations between Moscow and the Central Asian republics and the cause of nationalist tensions and ethnic unrest. Unfortunately, it was short on solutions. There was a general neglect of the nationalities. Gorbachev proclaimed that there was active resistance to *perestroika* by corrupt groups to cover up the stagnation of past years. And this he blamed for nationalist unrest in the Soviet Union. Gorbachev believed that the solution to the nationalities problem would become easier when *perestroika* and *glasnost'* laid bare these phenomena, creating the necessary conditions for a democratic solution. That solution could be found by returning to old Leninist norms and principles. Such internationalist ideology was incompatible with chauvinism and nationalism.[2]

Checking the growth of national sentiment and policing the ethnic unrest initially was the responsibility of the Soviet republican governments. The republican authorities attempted to assimilate, or co-opt, the informal nationalist groups within the Party apparatus, thus uniting Party and non-Party political activists who were in support of *glasnost'* and *perestroika*. In Kazakhstan, for example, the state leadership hoped that informal groups would prod the bureaucracies into addressing urgent agricultural, ecological, and cultural problems. This approach served the dual purpose of having the nationalist groups channel their energies in a direction favored by the authorities without causing too many problems. However, this assimilationist strategy was weak and slowly fell apart as a result of the contradiction between democratic *glasnost'* and the necessity of maintaining control over the growth of nationalist sentiment. Informal groups and religious organizations suddenly sprouted and flourished under the impetus and spirit of *glasnost'*. These unleashed criticisms of the republic's political, social, and economic problems struck responsive chords in the population at large.[3]

In 1990, the Islamic Renaissance party (*Islamskaya partiya vozrozh-deniya*) was founded in Tajikistan. Its purpose is to enable Soviet Muslims to live in accord with the Koran and Sunna and to advance the concept of equal rights for all nationalities through constitutional means.[4] The Tajik Communist party (TCP) immediately took steps to outlaw the Islamic Renaissance Party (IRP), whom it perceived as a dangerous political rival. The TCP forced mosques to pledge that they would not join the IRP and passed a law prohibiting the establishment of religious parties, arguing that they were made up of Muslim extremists.[5] However, it was more likely that the IRP was a serious threat to the Communist party's power base.

Similar events took place in Uzbekistan. During the founding congress of the Party, police interrupted the meeting and fined the delegates. The Uzbek Communist party also outlawed religious parties. However, these branches of the Islamic Renaissance party (centered in Daghestan, Chechenia, and Karachaevo-Cherkessia in Tajikistan and in the Fergana Valley in Uzbekistan) stand to gain a large following with their religious and liberal message. The Party is expected to soon found a branch in Turkmenistan and may become a powerful political force in Central Asia before the year 2000.

THE MUSLIMS REVOLT

Nationalist groups in Central Asia (usually in the form of popular fronts) have been seeking a number of different solutions to popular problems. They would all like to see their native languages become official state languages, as has been done in Uzbekistan and Tajikistan. These groups also want a return to the Arabic script. They believe that "one of the Soviet leadership's reasons for switching from the Arabic to the Latin and then to the Cyrillic script for Central Asia was to break with a literary tradition that had a strong Islamic influence and with literary activity in other Islamic countries."[6] Since most young people cannot read Arabic and are uneducated in their own literary traditions, many universities and high schools have sought to introduce courses to remedy the situation (although they make the distinction that they will not teach Islamic ideology along with these subjects).[7] Many of these groups also have sought to have the Koran translated into their respective native tongues so that it is accessible to the common people.

National movements are also concerned with the issue of Central Asians moving away from Central Asia in order to find work or "a better life." They are disturbed that they are losing talented young people who could help the region develop. They also resent the immigration of Russians and Ukrainians into Central Asia. These Slavs often take up the best jobs and the most powerful government positions.[8] They are tired of being treated, as they see it, like children who must be managed. They also seek to rectify the bureaucratic practices of the republic's leadership, to rehabilitate writers and political personalities who were condemned in the 1920s and 1930s, and to fill in the blank spots in their history while rectifying the distortions perpetrated on them.[9]

Moreover, these groups also want to end Russia's economic domination. As they see it, the central government robbed them of their natural resources yet made no major effort to develop the region. They also desire a solution to the ecological horrors that have polluted the region and lowered living standards. The most notorious example is the Aral Sea, which is disappearing. The resultant dust storms carry the salts and the residue of fertilizers and pesticides used on cotton crops from the seabed. These pollutants have caused physical and mental deformities in both animals and humans.[10]

The national movement in Tajikistan is the only one in the region in which at least some of the intelligentsia are definitely Islamic-oriented, ostensibly in view of the fact that they are of Persian, rather than Turkic, stock.[11] Tajikistan has its own popular front, which is called *Rastokhez* (Resurrection) and is led by Bagir Abduljaber. The Tajiks fear that they will be absorbed into a Central Asian, Turkic-dominated, population and hence risk losing their Iranian culture and language. This is the reason why they have sought support from another Persian culture outside the USSR.[12] The bonds between the Tajiks, Iran, and Afghanistan are strengthening as a result of this tension.

The least nationalistic of all the Central Asian republics seems to be Turkmenistan. Turkmenistan is more of a tribal confederation than an actual nation. This nonnationalism has been explained by Annette Bohr as the result of a low level of economic and social development. Most of the population is still rural; the republic itself is geographically separated from areas of active political change, there is no sizable and active intelligentsia, and the Turkmen officials are "almost fearful of *perestroika* and tend to quash any popular initiative in order to retain their fragile ability to govern."[13] Like the rest of Central Asia, Turkmenistan suffers from the distorted development of its economy. The Turkmens have little industrial development and are forced to import their finished goods and export most of their raw materials from Russia.[14] They are thus upset with the Russians and seek to broaden the base of their economy. They also seek to reassess Turkmen history and have been involved in opening a number of new mosques and translating the Koran. As their culture becomes more important, so does Islam. Like many of their Turkophone Central Asian relations, the Turkmens have been involved in interethnic strife, mainly involving clashes in May 1989 with Armenians in Turkmenistan.[15]

The Uzbeks appear to be the most nationalistic of the Central Asians. They believe that they should attain a leadership position in the region, not only because they are the largest indigenous nationality but also because they are the ones whose language and culture are the most identifiable with those of pre-Soviet Turkestan.[16]

The major nationalist group is the Uzbek Popular Front (*Birlik*, or "Unity"), which was formerly led by Abdurrahim Pulatov. It seeks to further Uzbek national interests through various means. In February 1990 Birlik was split and the new splinter group became known as *Erk* ("Independence"). Like its name, Erk sought independence for Uzbekistan within the framework of a renewed Soviet Federation while criticizing Birlik for not taking advantage of the political opportunities created by *perestroika*. Prominent members of Erk include Muhammad Salik and Erkin Wahidov, both prominent activists and poets.[17]

Nationalism has played an important role in the Central Asian identity. Although interethnic conflict has tainted the relations between the different republics, there have been some attempts at reconciliation. On 22-23 June 1990, the three most senior officers of each of the five republics met to sign a regional alliance, the first step in the development of a unified and potentially powerful political bloc within the former USSR.[18] They signed an "Agreement on Economic, Scientific-Technical and Cultural Cooperation" which established equality between the five republics. It established 12 areas on which multilateral accords are to be negotiated, such as economic cooperation, health, and education. It also initiated a mechanism for reaching its goals.[19] This agreement took effect on 1 July 1990. The officials also signed two other accords that indicate policies which the new bloc is likely to pursue in the short term.[20]

With this agreement, it seems that the nationalities of Central Asia may come closer together. What this will mean is unclear. It is possible that they will unify into a cohesive political bloc and challenge Russia through the sheer bulk of their population. If they can modernize their economy, based on their oil wealth, they stand a good chance of becoming economically powerful.

Nationalism became important again in late 1990 and early 1991 with the international furor created by the Gulf War. The central Soviet government became involved in the diplomatic war rather than on the actual battleground. However, not everyone in the Soviet Union was pleased with Moscow's stance. Some commentators felt that if the Soviet Union did actually become actively involved in the war it would lead to civil strife in the Muslim republics. In fact, many Soviet Muslims saw Saddam Hussein as a defender of the faith, in much the same way that they saw the Ayatollah Khomeini.[21] Some Muslim leaders agitated against the United States and the coalition, and this led to demonstrations against George Bush and Zionism in Moscow on January 19, 1991.

The Supreme Soviets of the different Muslim republics could not agree on a uniform policy. The Kirgiz Supreme Soviet wrote official letters to the embassies of the United States, Kuwait, and Saudi Arabia in Moscow asking them to cease hostilities, while Uzbekistan's Supreme Soviet appealed to Gorbachev to stop the conflict. The Supreme Soviet of Azerbaijan said that the war went beyond the United Nations mandate and stated that the liberation of Kuwait was a pretext to protect U.S. oil interests.[22] By the middle of February, the Iraqi embassy in Moscow reported that it had received more than 10,000 letters from Soviet citizens (most of whom were Muslim) volunteering to fight for Iraq.[23]

A CRITIQUE OF SOME RECENT STUDIES ON CENTRAL ASIA

For a long time now this Islamic area has been described as part of the "troublesome crescent," which in modern politico-military parlance is usually designated as the Middle East. The Muslim periphery of the former Soviet empire is and, at the same time, is not a part of the Middle East. The five former Soviet Muslim Republics--Kazakhstan, Uzbekistan, Turkmenistan, Azerbaijan, Tajikistan and Kirgizia--cannot be impervious to political developments in the Arab Middle East. For instance, in William Fierman's edited volume, *Soviet Central Asia: The Failed Transformation* (Boulder, CO: Westview Press, 1991), Kazakhstan does not figure as part of Central Asia proper because the population is only 40 percent Muslim. So we are really speaking about a region that must necessarily be Muslim. However, at the same time, these regions and their ultimate fate are intimately bound up with the fortunes of Russia in the north, and Turkey and Iran in the south. The Great Game of competition that had once been played out over this area by the superpowers has given way to regional political dynamics.

Scholarship about this region has mainly been dominated by a group of European writers. There are the French academics led by the late Alexandre Bennigsen and Hélène Carrère d'Encausse (now of the French Academy). The English specialists congregate around the "Society for Central Asian Studies," whose inkwell produced what I disparagingly call the "Indian old boys" coterie of writers such as Colonel Geoffrey Wheeler, Sir Olaf Caroe, and their latter-day protégés like Enders Wimbush and Marie Broxup. Clearly, two schools of thought emerged in regard to Central Asia and Azerbaijan: one claiming that there will be a Muslim fundamentalist revival that would sweep across the face of Eurasia and the Middle East and the other maintaining that interethnic strife will destroy the economies and the social fabric of the entire region. Neither the French nor the English sit on opposite ends of the fence here. In any one school of thought, there can be both Frenchmen (or Frenchwomen), Englishmen (or Englishwomen). The best among them is a British sociologist named David Lane, who is absolutely isolated from, or ostracized by, the rest. He belongs to no particular school of thought, unless it be a respectable, Western Marxist, group.

The only common thread binding the others is the hackneyed thesis that the Soviets, and the Russians before them, have done irreparable damage to the Central Asian Muslims. A weaker scholarship did emerge

on the North American continent around Kamal Karpat, later improved upon by Martha Brill Olcott and Mary Lubin, but laced with the old Central
Asian faithfuls and mediocrities like Edward Allworth. Indeed, new break-
throughs have been made by women writers like Azade-Ayse Rorlich, Lubin and Olcott. These three, in one sense, have been trailblazers and have
set far more subtle patterns than their predecessors--and there are now
many serious scholars enquiring into the manifold problems of this region.
In a recent article surveying the politics of modern Turkey which appeared
in the *Economist* (December 1991), the author cogently observes there is
"only one large stretch of the world notably liable to produce turmoil and
mayhem on a large scale in the coming 15-20 years: the appropriately
crescent-shaped piece of territory that starts in the steppes of Kazakhstan
and curves south and west through the Gulf . . ."[24]

Of the three books I wish to consider here, Muriel Atkin's *The Subtlest
Battle: Islam in Soviet Tajikistan* (1989) is the worst of the lot. Her
conclusion that "neither the disappearance of Islam nor the disappearance
of Soviet rule in Central Asia is a likely prospect" is too facile a summary,
even if she wrote it in 1989. Touted as an area expert, she should have
known better. One ought not to blow one's horn without speaking to the
issue; nor does one make statements, when it is safer to beg questions.
The worst part about her book is that she offers nothing new. Even her
chapter "Will Muslims Challenge the USSR?" is a recapitulation of what
has already been done in far greater detail by Alexandre Bennigsen *et al*.
This is not a book about a political power struggle--her initial intention--but
about Islamic life in Tajikistan, facts all too well known. She states that
there has always been opposition to the Soviet regime, but then plunges
into a rambling discussion about "folk Islam" and "establishment Islam,"
about Muslim women, Sufism, and so forth. Her style of writing is dis-
jointed, fragmented, and, frankly, boring. The subject of Muslim activism
and influences from Iran and Afghanistan on Central Asia is a garbled
description and so confused in the conclusions she draws that, to me, it
seems the worst piece of writing on Soviet Islam that I have read since
Rosanne Klass's edited volume *Afghanistan: The Great Game Revisited*
(1987). Like the latter, Atkin is so viscerally anti-Soviet that it faithfully
reproduces American scholarship of the 1950s and early 1960s--a Cold
War treatise. She clearly has problems assessing the true value of Soviet
sources (she likes calling them "atheist propagandists") and uses all of
these sources disingenuously, reading into them things which were never
said or meant. Very selectively she reinterprets Russian-language and
Tajik-language materials to fit schemas as if trying to get it all into the
Procrustean bed, moralistically judging what these Soviet writers ought to
have said. She does this with B. G. Ghafurov's *History of the Tajiks* and
she thinks--she is not the only neophyte to the problems of the area--that
T. S. Saidbaev's *Islam i obshchestvo* is one of the best Soviet books on
Soviet Muslims in recent years. Worst of all is her pitiful discussion of the

Basmachi. It is so methodologically and substantively poor as to make it regurgitatively reminiscent of past, Cold War hagiographies. My own views on the subject are in "Basmachism: Banditry, or a Struggle between Turanian, Russian, and English Power?" and appear in my book *Intrigue and War in Southwest Asia: The Struggle for Supremacy from Central Asia to Iraq* (1992). The way I see it the Basmachi in their day were mere bandits. Today's Afghan rebels have likewise been an unruly, fanatical lot.

James Critchlow's book *Nationalism in Uzbekistan: A Soviet Republic's Road to Sovereignty* (1991) is all that Atkin's should have been. He more effectively uses Uzbek and Russian-language sources than Atkin does with her Russian and Tajik. The reason for this is that his conceptualization is better, his premises are not flawed, and it is far better balanced methodologically and stylistically. The author's tone is unassuming. Although studies of the Uzbek people have been done before, the author makes no claim to be doing a definitive study. The second chapter deals with emerging nationalism in the republic which foreshadow the events leading to the 1990 declaration of Uzbek sovereignty. He explains the patrimonial society created after Stalin and how the tranquility brought about by this society created the opportunity for nationalism. The author then claims that, for Moscow, the most important thing in Uzbekistan was cotton production. Due perhaps to the strength of native languages and Islamic customs, the 1960s saw derussification in language, cadres, and history and the resurrection of the pre-Revolutionary past. This happened long before Leonid Brezhnev consolidated his power. Thus, a Soviet Muslim elite was created to press Moscow for greater autonomy.

The author also suggests that Uzbekistan was made more open to outside influence from the Middle East, Eastern Europe, Asia, Africa, and Latin America during this period. The third chapter deals with the post-Brezhnev crackdown when Uzbekistan was singled out as an example of wayward non-Russian nationalists. The elites were particularly targeted since they were at the cutting edge of Uzbek nationalism. After Brezhnev's death, Moscow wanted to tighten central control of cadre policy to root out "negative phenomena" that reached intolerable proportions during Brezhnev's era, especially the corruption over the "cotton" affair (where there were charges that Uzbek officials were defrauding the central government over cotton revenues).

Part two of Critchlow's book is titled "Uzbek Nationalism Today: Selected Themes" and is divided into seven chapters. In a brief introduction, Critchlow states that the elites also used the media to press economic and social issues that went straight to the ethnic sensitivities of their co-nationals. The first chapter deals with the cotton monoculture. He deals with the history of cotton in the republic and its importance in the colonization of the area by the central authorities. Moscow's drive to increase production led to terrible environmental damage, loss of food stuffs (not enough acreage was used to grow food), low per capita earnings (inherent in the industry), and unemployment. High population growth has not helped. The condemnation of the monoculture provided the elites with political and psychological weapons. The second chapter deals with the rape of the environment with cotton as the chief culprit (leading to a loss of water due to irrigation, the shrinkage of the Aral Sea, health problems caused by pesticides, wind erosion, and deforestation). Nuclear contamination is also a problem especially with the nuclear dump located outside of Tashkent.

Uzbeks have rewritten some aspects of their history. The fifth chapter deals with the progressive hardening of their resistance to central authority. After the February 1986 Moscow Party Congress where Gorbachev virtually declared war on Uzbek elites, there have been a number of both direct and indirect examples of Uzbek resistance. Regardless of the central governments' assertiveness, they failed to shake up the Uzbek party and government apparatus. The Uzbeks were themselves able to get rid of MVD General Eduard Didorenko as a symbol of alien authority.

Admittedly, Critchlow's is the most up-to-date book on the Uzbeks I have seen, right up to the latest nationalist tremors that split Uzbekistan's nationalisms into political reformist, not quite Western-style democratic, groupings like *Birlik* and *Erk*. I also agree with his conclusion that "Central Asian strong men of the past have tended to be secular, not religious."[25]

My only problem with Critchlow's book is that, in his chapter on the Islamic factor, he gives us a poor linkage between religion and national identity. There is more to religious influences, especially external religious influences, than Moscow had made it to appear, like Saudi Arabian Wahhabism. Wahhabism certainly came to Central Asia via Afghanistan. The influence of Khomeini's Iran should likewise not be underestimated. Another point that Critchlow fails to notice is that, when there is an increasing pervasiveness of Islamic practices, this could translate into political action. Events in Iran and Afghanistan are more capable of influencing opinion among Soviet Muslims than the other way around, even if the former Soviet Muslims are economically more developed. Thus, Islam may transcend ethnic frontiers, the way a Marxist internationalist, supranational system tried but failed to do. It is true that some analysts have pointed to a pervasive interethnic conflict in Muslim Central Asia and do not see Islam as a major force (Ann Sheehy).

I certainly think religion is a potential apocalyptic force. When the religious identity takes over, the elites in place risk losing control and power. Critchlow speaks at length about Uzbek elites, which is a lot better than Atkin's constant derogatory references to the Soviet elites. For the local elite, the problem of identity is a problem of power; the elite accepts the identity which best corresponds to its interest. Therefore, Islam can be an integrative cultural force, imparting a sense of cohesive identity regardless of elite-mass distinctions. Islam, or religion, can aspire to political power (see Nancy Lubin on Uzbekistan). Furthermore, it is not beyond the realm of possibility that this area could one day be turned into a single Muslim federation or confederation. For instance, there was the Islamic Renaissance Party formed in 1990 in Tajikistan. Critchlow also does not make a distinction between collective identity and ethnic identity.

There is now an increasingly vocal and politically active Turkic element in Central Asia and we must determine whether this Muslim population will seek out a new federalist relationship with Russia (the Center) or whether it will be a sovereign, independent player in Central Asia and Azerbaijan. Given the fact that the Turkic world itself is not a monolith, any more than the Arab world, it becomes essential to any investigation to determine whether or not Russia would differentiate between Azerbaijan and Turkmenistan and how Moscow would perceive the nationality issue when there is interethnic conflict between Uzbek and Tajik or between Meshket and Uzbek, or between Shi'i Azeri and Sunni Turkoman. After all, these Muslims still want to be linked to the center in Moscow, do they not?

Yet nationalism can be a complex phenomenon (for example, German nationalism of World War II was not quite the same as Italian or Japanese nationalism). European nationalism is not the same thing as an Asian-based, Muslim-dominated nationalism. In Central Asia, the problem of nationalism may or may not be viewed as one of collective identity. Alexandre Bennigsen wrote about this in 1984, Kemal Karpat in 1986, M. Nazif Shahrani in 1984, and Enders Wimbush also in 1984. In Central Asia, nationalism can be so complex a phenomenon as to reflect any one of the sub-identities in a given polity. The inference I am drawing here is that there are options with respect to collective identity. The Uzbek identity in particular, given its population and culture, has the potential to emerge as the dominant one, given the right combination of circumstances. Still, the Uzbek collective identity cannot triumph in the political arena without being sustained by preeminent or charismatic individuals and/or some form of organization. In a word, the Uzbeks would need an all-embracing ideology or philosophy. In the political reality of Uzbekistan, that would have to be Islam or something competing with Islam. Now that Marxism is clearly out of the picture, what else could it possibly be if not an Islam driven by external influences? Perhaps even Wahhabism from Saudi Arabia? Shi'i fundamentalism from Iran? Critchlow fails to address this issue.

The good thing about Critchlow's study is the author's definition of the term "elite" which is straightforward and unambiguous. He tells us that he likes Milovan Djilas' view of an elite class as basically one that wields political power.

William Fierman's edited volume *Soviet Central Asia: The Failed Transformation* is one of the best, if not the best, study I have seen in a very long time. It has a stellar group of contributors and Fierman's own writings and analyses are first-rate. It is a pity, however, that Fierman chose Teresa Rakowska-Harmstone to write the foreword. Anyone who reads this blurb will be quick to point out that Rakowska-Harmstone likes absolutely nothing about this real estate we call Central Asia, and dislikes Soviets, Russians, internationalists, and Marxists even more. Rakowska-Harmstone writes in the same vein as Muriel Atkin--scholars who blame everything on Moscow for the past Soviet attempts to change the face of society and the psychology of the Eurasian species.

The other chapters in this book, nevertheless, chronicle the "failed transformation of Central Asia." There is much here about ecological disasters, unemployed youth, poverty, mismanagement, cultural and linguistic cleavages, and ethnic stirrings. There is anarchy here, and potential for war.

The second section is titled "Politics" and contains two chapters. The first, "Power and Politics in Soviet Uzbekistan: From Stalin to Gorbachev" by Donald S. Carlisle, discusses the problems of center-periphery political relations in Central Asia. In doing so, he focuses on the history of the problem using specific instances and personalities beginning with the Stalinist era and its creation of a dual society (for example, Russians versus natives). The second chapter of this section is called "Prelude to "Independence": How the Uzbek Party Apparatus Broke Moscow's Grip on Elite Recruitment" and was written by James Critchlow. It is very much like his own book on Uzbekistan.

Ronald Wixman's "Ethnic Attitudes and Relations in Modern Uzbek Cities" is done especially well. It is a political culture piece based on interviews done in Bukhara, Samarkand, and Tashkent during the summer of 1985. Wixman interviewed different ethnic groups and different social groups in different settings. His chapter is also based on personal observation. He concluded that little socializing took place across traditional cultural lines and that many Russians looked down on Central Asians. He goes on to describe instances of Russians denigrating Central Asians as backward. Many Central Asians are forced to learn Russian but very few Russians learn Central Asian languages. There is also widespread discrimination and competition for positions, jobs, and housing. In his conclusion, Wixman states that the Russians seem unwilling or unable to recognize and respect Central Asia's heritage. The Central Asians feel as if they are hosts and the Russians are poor guests who don't return their hospitality with proper behaviour and respect.

Azade-Ayse Rorlich's "Islam and Atheism: Dynamic Tension in Soviet Central Asia", deals with official and parallel Islam. She states that changes have made it easier for officials at all levels to promote Islam. She also discusses various dimensions of Islam. She examines changes in the promotion of atheism and assertive Islam.

The chapter called "Forging a Soviet People: Ethnolinguistics in Central Asia" was written by Isabelle Kreindler. It examines the importance of language and the imposition of the Russian language on Central Asians. But that is nothing new.

The final section, "Socioeconomic Issues", consists of two chapters.

The first one is "Women and Society in Central Asia" by Martha Brill Olcott. Olcott's main thesis is that Soviet rule has failed to fully integrate women into Central Asian life. Their primary function in this society is still to be a good wife and mother. Women tend to marry young and have many children (an average of two to three times the national average, although the infant mortality rate is 1.5 to 2.5 times the national average, the worst being in the Aral Sea region where the mortality rate is 111 per 1000 births). Women have a low employment rate and minimal role in government but have increased their religious consciousness.

William Fierman's "Central Asian Youth and Migration" deals with out-migration as a response to poor health conditions, poor economic conditions, and unemployment. Although there is definitely an economic crunch in Central Asia, much of the population refuses to move away. Most natives believe that they would be less welcome in other areas of the country despite government programs to entice them to move. Rather than leave in order to attain a higher standard of living, Central Asians were beginning to demand that the Communist party and Soviet government (that is, local Soviet authorities) raise the standards of living in their native region. He concludes by stating: "Any wishes by the Party leadership for a mass migration of Central Asians to other parts of the USSR, and for their contribution thereby to a more socially stable, homogeneous, and prosperous society, seem farther than ever from fulfillment."[26]

What I like most about this book is Fierman's excellent conclusion. He states that one of the central themes of the book is the failure of the Soviet political system to direct political and social change in Central Asia. To prove this, he analyses political development abstracted from a theoretical study called *Crises and Sequences in Political Development*, a book by Leonard Binder, Myron Weiner, Joseph LaPalombara, Lucien Pye, and Sidney Verba. The five areas they discuss are: penetration, identity, distribution, participation, and legitimacy. In the Soviet Union, Moscow's ability to penetrate society and get what it wants from the people has decreased since the end of the political terror practiced under Stalin. Central Asians tend to have many identities--Islamic, Turkic, Central Asian, and local--of which "Soviet" is only one, and not a very important one at that. The participation of Central Asians in getting language laws and other cultural protection laws passed has slowed the center's penetration of their society. Moscow's legitimacy (defined as the basis and degree to which government decisions are accepted by society as to their rightness) was, in the past, considered secondary to Moscow's campaign of terror against the Central Asians and thus, since the end of terror, Moscow's legitimacy has declined. The Party has reduced its activity to create a Soviet people and realize that the Central Asians will remain Muslims. Thus Gorbachev tried to improve local political participation and the economy. The regime's legitimacy among Central Asians relies in part on its ability to raise living standards. However, the Center must be careful: for if the Center's leaders try to improve one of the five areas, they could lose in another (if they try to improve their legitimacy, they may lose their chances at penetration). Although Central Asia did supply the Center with raw materials, Moscow could replace any leader, and Soviet power was successful in curtailing the mass manifestations of Islamic and Turkic identities. Central Asia's development has not proceeded along the lines Moscow wished; the center has never eliminated the cult phenomenon that linked Central Asians to one another and to other Muslims. In effect, the Soviet Center has had only limited success in inculcating Central Asians with a sense of "Sovietness."[27] Gorbachev, himself, first tried to rein in Central Asia. When that didn't work, he tried to salvage the Soviet empire by agreeing to a political system with less ambitious goals, with a limited degree of penetration through legitimacy. Moscow's failure on all of these fronts has been celebrated by Central Asians who feel that they have finally freed themselves of the Russian yoke.

The foregoing analysis by Fierman throws up new ideas that deserve to be explored. That, in itself, makes this a book worth reading.

One of the most striking features of the Central Asian environment is the potential conflict, even outright war, between Uzbeks and non-Uzbeks, between Central Asians and non-Central Asians. Donald Carlisle has even focused on cleavages and friction within the Russian Slavic community in Central Asia. Critchlow reminds us that, ever since the Tsarist occupation of the last century, authority in Central Asia has been wielded by officials sent to govern by the center, "first from Imperial St. Petersburg, later from Soviet Moscow." Now the Central Asians have to go it alone. But are they really capable?

Central Asia must still find a solution to the *priezzhye*, who are non-indigenous officials who had been deployed in recent years to Central Asia from posts outside the region, as part of Moscow's campaign to eliminate corruption; and the *mestnye*, who are local Europeans, born in Central Asia, or had resided there for many years. Then there are the indigenous peoples who were, and still are, loyal to the Soviet system. Finally, there are both indigenous nationalist extremists and moderates who are seeking to reform this region and reaching out to Europe, rather than to Russia, for help. No one--except Hedrick Smith in his monumental *The Russians*--has even come close to analyzing the unique Orientalism (the "*Aziatschina*") that has been characteristic of the area for generations. I do not wish to stereotype the peoples of this region, but it must somehow be said that the Center has had more than its share of troubles and blame for failures that are more than just the result of poor central administration and mismanagement. Studies in anthropology and psychology, in addition to history and modern economics, will be needed in future to formulate typologies on the unique culture and ways of life in the region. One could study the Georgians in a similar way.

CONCLUSION

Which is more important, nationalism or religion? Nationalism and religion together may appear to Russian eyes as a two-edged sword, but so far it is a blunt one as a result of the interethnic infighting that religion finds difficult to moderate. The alleged importance of Islam has, in fact, receded behind the banner of nationhood. If the Muslim area were more developed economically, at least the poverty, which is probably at the root of the internal fighting, would cease. However, this may be wishful thinking.

Two distinct factors appear to be holding the region together and keeping it inside the former empire: the Muslims' fear of other Muslims and the strong presence of Russian forces from the Center, bolstering Russia's southern and southwestern military districts. Moscow, from a military standpoint, is likely to be even less keen on losing these southern, Islamic satraps than it was in losing the Baltic coastline to the secessionist-minded Balts. "Interethnic strife in Central Asia, . . . which [has] pitted Muslim against Muslim," in the words of one perceptive analyst, "has brought the region to the notice of the outside world in a way that press accounts of poverty, social and economic neglect, and environmental degradation failed to do."[28] The Muslim regions of Central Asia and Azerbaijan may thus become a tinderbox of violence in the future if left to themselves. This bleak outlook may explain why the populations of this region proved to be more reluctant to secede from the USSR. In March 1991, in Gorbachev's referendum, Central Asians overwhelmingly voted to stay within the Union. But this reluctance provided only temporary breathing space. The Russian leaders have good reason to be concerned about the "Muslim factor" on the southern periphery.

NOTES

1.   See Yaacov Ro'i, "The Islamic Influence on Nationalism in Soviet Central Asia," *Problems of Communism* 39, no. 4 (July-August 1990): 56.

2.   Ibid.

3.   Bess Brown, "The Islamic Renaissance Party in Central Asia," *Radio Liberty Report on the USSR (Munich)* 3, no. 19 (10 May 1991): 12.

4.   Ibid., p. 13.

5.   *Time*, 15 January 1990, p. 30.

6.   Ro'i, p. 56.

7.   To that end, the Central Committee of the Uzbek Communist party has adopted a set of restrictions on the hiring of labor from outside Uzbekistan in order to train native workers to take over some of the higher government and civilian jobs; James Critchlow, "Uzbeks Demand Halt to Russian In-Migration," *Radio Liberty Report on the USSR (Munich)* 3, no. 9 (2 March 1990): 18.

8. Ibid., p. 57.

9. Shirin Akiner, "Uzbeks," in *The Nationalities Question in the Soviet Union*, ed. Graham Smith (Essex, UK: Longman Group, 1990), p. 221.

10. Ro'i, p. 62.

11. Eden Naby, "Tajiks Reemphasize Iranian Heritage as Ethnic Pressures Mount in Central Asia," *Radio Liberty Report on the USSR (Munich)* 3, no. 6 (16 February 1990): 20.

12. Annette Bohr, "Turkmenistan under Perestroika: An Overview," *Radio Liberty Report on the USSR (Munich)* 3, no. 11 (23 March 1990): 21.

13. Ibid.

14. See Ro'i.

15. Ro'i, p. 56.

16. Ibid., p. 58.

17. Paul Globe, "Central Asians Form Political Bloc," *Radio Liberty Report on the USSR (Munich)* 3, no. 22 (13 July 1990): 18.

18. Ibid.

19. Ibid., p. 19. These documents were entitled "A Declaration of the Leaders of the Republics of Central Asia and Kazakhstan" and "An Appeal to the Peoples of the Republics of Central Asia and Kazakhstan."

20. Bess Brown, *Radio Liberty Reports* 3, no. 29 (20 July 1990).

21. George Stein, "Soviet Muslims Divided on Gulf War" in *Radio Liberty Report on the USSR (Munich)* 3, no. 8 (22 February 1991): 13.

22. Ibid.

23. Ibid.

24. "Star of Islam," *Economist*, 14 December 1991, p. 1.

25. James Critchlow, *Nationalism in Uzbekistan: A Soviet Republic's Road to Sovereignty* (Boulder, CO: Westview Press, 1991), p. 211.

26. William Fierman, "Central Asian Youth and Migration," *Soviet Central Asia: The Failed Transformation*, ed. William Fierman (Boulder, CO: Westview Press, 1991), p. 282.

27. William Fierman, "Conclusion," *Soviet Central Asia: The Failed Transformation*, ed. William Fierman (Boulder, CO: Westview Press, 1991), p. 306.

28. "10,000 Soviet Citizens Want to Serve in the Army of Saddam Hussein," *Novosti*, 5 February 1991.

Part 5

THE INTERNATIONAL DIMENSION

The Soviet Union held the world's attention since its birth. At times considered an "Evil Empire" by the West, this country was perceived as the place from which Communist revolutions would spread to engulf the world. The threat has certainly abated, if not vanished, completely today. Nonetheless, the West monitors developments in the former USSR with as keen and interest as in the past: there are now internal problems that have come to the fore.

Since the late 1980s and the beginnings of nationalist stirrings in the Baltic republics, each of the separate Soviet republics has campaigned for freedom, demanding a separate life away from the Soviet Center, away from a Russian-based empire. This development eventually led to the fragmentation of the USSR as we knew it. One can envision at least 15 distinct nations, and more, with all the attendant problems of nationhood and statehood and security that make the subject of international relations so serious and so fascinating.

The various Soviet republics are watching the unfolding Yugoslav situation to see how another socialist country dealt with separatism. Now that the Slovenes and Croats have been granted their freedom, how can the former Soviet republics legitimately be denied their independence? Baltic separation has itself had profound effects on the countries of Eastern Europe and Europe in general. The Baltic republics could join an economic alliance with Western Europe or join in a union with their less prosperous neighbors, such as Poland, Czechoslovakia, Bulgaria, and Romania, in order to help their struggling economies. Thus, the West can no more dissociate itself from the Russian European periphery than the Islamic countries could from the Soviet Muslim periphery. If the former Soviet Empire completely disintegrates and collapses economically and the ruble becomes valueless because all the republics are bent on establishing their own currency, if the reform experiment ends in a complete failure, it could lead to massive unemployment, penury, and political instability for all. Millions more will be expected to emigrate from the Eurasian heartland. Millions more could be slaughtered in a civil war, already raging between Armenia and Azerbaijan, between Ossetia and Georgia, between Uzbeks and Meshkets, between Tajiks and Uzbeks. Absorption of Ukrainian, Armenian, or Baltic refugees could be internally disruptive for the Western states; it could even jeopardize the cohesion and unity of Western Europe, for it could result in two incompatible and competing European halves. European Russians will need to integrate with the West, and the Muslims will need to integrate with the rest of the Muslim world. However, what if the Muslims do wish to belong to a greater Soviet Empire, supporting the Center from the periphery? These republics were profoundly affected by the last Gulf War, with much of the Soviet Muslim population supporting Saddam Hussein. What will the disintegration of the Soviet Empire mean for China?

China, which is the home of many different nationalities, did not want its large northern neighbor to break apart. Moreover, it did not want its own nationalities to consider independence. Canada, which is itself going through a constitutional and nationality crisis, is currently watching the defunct Soviet Union with trepidation. The ambitious Canadian Prime Minister, Brian Mulroney, was fully aware that a million Canadians claim Ukrainian ancestry when he led Canada as one of the first nations that extended recognition to the newly independent state of Ukraine. Indeed, the breakup of the Soviet Union has had severe repercussions on all federal states, especially countries where separatist sentiment is very strong (such as India).

Thus, in the 1990s, the national and ethnic issue will be the most important one in an otherwise increasingly interdependent economic world.

9

Xinjiang: Ethnic Minorities under Chinese Rule

LAWRENCE SHYU

The problems of ethnic minorities are common to many countries in the world. China, being a close neighbor of the former Soviet Union and the other one of the pair of Communist giants, also shared with the Soviet Union an imperial past and similar problems with national minorities. Of particular concern in China is the region known as Xinjiang (sometimes referred to in Western sources as Chinese Turkestan or Chinese Central Asia), which lies between Russian Central Asia and China proper. Having the status of an autonomous region, which is equivalent to a province, Xinjiang is huge: 1.6 million square kilometers, roughly one-sixth the total area of China. Thanks to its location at the crossroads of East-West commercial and cultural exchange, Xinjiang has evolved into one of the most complex regions in China in terms of the ethnic composition of its population. It is interesting to note that several large minority nationalities in Xinjiang, such as the Uygurs, the Kazaks, the Kirgiz, and the Tajiks, all have kinspeople living across the national boundary in Soviet Central Asia; all of them, plus the Hui, are also Muslim minorities in China. An analysis of their present conditions may provide a comparison with the Soviet Muslim minorities in the neighboring regions and facilitate a better understanding of ethnic/religious minority issues in their global perspective. In China, all ethnic groups that do not belong to the minority Han-Chinese are designated "national minorities." Policies and other matters pertaining to minorities often use the term *nationalities*. A brief summary of the ethnic history of Xinjiang may help explain the current problems of national minorities there.

Xinjiang's Population by Nationality

	1945	1982
Ugyur (Uighur)	3,000,000	6,000,000
Han	222,000	4,800,000
Kazak	439,000	907,000
Hui	100,000	[1]300,000
Kirgiz	70,000	114,000
Mongol	60,000	[1]100,000
Daur (Taranchi)	79,000	[2]94,000
Xibe (Sibo)	10,600	[2]80,000
Tajik	8,200	26,500
Uzbek	10,224	12,500
Tatar	5,600	4,100
Russian	19,000	3,000
Total		
Population	4,023,624	12,441,100

Source: For the 1945 figures, Linda Benson, *The Ili Rebellion*, pg. 30;
           for 1982, *Beijing Review*, no. 21, 23 May 1983. Figures are
           rounded off to four digits.

[1] Population figures are given for the nationality as a whole. Their
     numbers in Xinjiang represent an estimate.

[2] Figures include their population in the northeast.

MAJOR MINORITY NATIONALITIES IN XINJIANG[1]

Hui Nationality

One of the most widespread minority peoples in China, the Hui, number
7.6 million and are the second largest ethnic minority group.[2] The Hui
people are believed to be descended from various ethnic groups such as
Arabs, Persians, and various Central Asians. The establishment of the
Mongol Empire in the thirteenth century marked the beginning of large
migrations of Central Asian people to China. The majority of the migrants
became merchants, but a fair number served as officials for the Mongol-
Y'uan dynasty government. This explains their widespread settlement in
Chinese cities and a particularly heavy concentration in northwestern
China. Before the Mongol conquest of China, some seafarer-merchants
from Arabia, Persia, and India had lived in several large seaports along
China's southern and eastern coasts. They were called *fan-ke* or "bar-
barian-guests," and many took Chinese wives and settled in China per-

manently. The number of these earlier settlers was greatly increased by latecomers in the thirteenth century. Together they came to be called *Hui* or *Hui-min*, largely because of their religious identification as followers of Islam.[3]

The Muslim settlers in China clung tenaciously to their religious traditions and customs despite their long and often isolated existence. Frequent daily contact and intermarriage with the Han majority, however, made them lose their original languages, and they became thoroughly assimilated linguistically and culturally. Even in physical appearance, the Hui are almost the same as the Han, although they prefer to wear white and most male members wear white caps in observation of their religious custom.

The Ugyur Nationality

As the largest single ethnic group in Xinjiang, the Uygur population had reached 6.6 million by 1988, or approximately 50 percent of Xinjiang's population. Although the name *Uygur* appeared during the eighth century when the people became an ally of the Tang Empire, the origins of the Turkic-speaking Uygur people can be traced to as early as the third century B.C. After their defeat by the Jin-ge-si (ancestors of the modern Kirgiz) in the ninth century, the tribes became scattered. The main group migrated westward to Xinjiang. There the Uygurs gradually integrated with various other Turkic-speaking peoples, including some Tibetans and Mongols, to evolve into the largest and most numerous ethnic group in the southern part of Xinjiang. They maintained close cultural and commercial ties with China and withstood several historical invasions.

After the fall of the Mongol Empire, the Uygurs established a more unified khanate with its capital at Kashgar. This, the Uygur Khanate, however, was conquered by Galdan Khan of the Jungar Mongols in 1678. When the Manchu army defeated the Jungars in 1757-1759, Xinjiang was brought under the direct administrative control of the Qing Empire. In the next one and a half centuries, the Uygar, along with other nationalities in Xinjiang, became national minorities within the Manchu Qing imperial boundary.

The Uygurs have become sedentary farmers and are centered in all the oasis settlements surrounding the great Tarim Basin desert. The Uygar language is Turkic. Its written script was based on old Arabic script. A Latinized script, however, has gained popularity since the 1950s.

In earlier times, a number of old religions, such as Buddhism, Manichaeism, Zoroastrianism, and Nestorian Christianity, were brought into Xinjiang because of its strategic location along the great trade route, the Silk Road. They coexisted with each other, with Buddhism exerting greater influence than the rest. The coming of Islam during the late tenth century, however, changed the religious map. After two centuries of sharp competition with Buddhism, Islam won the upper hand in conversions. Virtually all nationalities in Xinjiang, with the exception of the Han and the Mongols, became Muslim. The Uygurs are now numerically the second largest Muslim nationality in China.

The Kazak Nationality

The ancestors of the Kazak people of Xinjiang once inhabited a large area from Mongolia to Lake Balkhash and the Aral Sea. They esta-blished a succession of nomadic kingdoms and formed occasional alli-ances with the Han dynasty in China. In later developments, the Kazaks had close encounters with a number of strong nomadic empires in neigh-boring regions, such as the Rurks, the Khitans, the Uygurs, and the Mongols, resulting in considerable racial amalgamation and cultural blending. When the Manchu armies destroyed the power of the Jungar Mongols in the middle of the eighteenth century, the majority of Kazak people came under the rule of the Manchu Qing Empire. However, a cen-tury later, with the decline of the Qing Empire, tsarist Russia expanded deep into Central Asia. The territories that the Russian empire acquired from the Qing (from Lake Balkhash to the present Chinese border) con-tained large settlements of Kazaks. After the Russian Revolution, the Soviet government created the Kazak SSR over a large part of Central Asia. Those Kazaks living on the Chinese side of the border, now num-bering about 900,000, are found mainly in the extreme northern part of Xinjiang, from the Russian border to Mongolia.

The Kazak people have retained their traditional way of life as animal herders, and many still move with their herds of sheep and cattle in a nomadic life. In the last few decades, however, the discovery and exploita-tion of petroleum, iron ore, and other mineral riches on the land they occupy have transformed many Kazaks into city dwellers and indus-trial workers. The Kazak language is Turkic, which is akin to the Uygur. Its script is based on Arabic but a new Latin alphabet was introduced in the 1950s.

The Kirgiz Nationality

The Kirgiz are a people with a history as old as that of the Uygurs and the Kazaks. The ancestors of the Kirgiz originally occupied a region northwest of Mongolia, along the upper valleys of the river Enisei. They were nomadic tribes and became subordinate to the Turkic Tujue empire during the sixth and seventh centuries. After regaining their independence in the eighth century, a Kirgiz khanate was created. The khanate reached the height of its power after it defeated the Uygurs and extended territorial control over most of Xinjiang in the following centuries. The Kirgiz tribes were subdued by the Mongols and fought many campaigns under Mongol command.

In more recent centuries, the Kirgiz inhabited an area in Central Asia from Frunze to Aksu in the east and Kashgar in the south, on both sides of the Sino-Soviet border. The 1982 Chinese census put the Kirgiz population in China at slightly over 110,000. The Kirgiz in Xinjiang were converted to Islam rather late, probably during the first half of the eighteenth century. However, they belong to the Shi'ite (Shi'a) tradition rather than the Sunni of the neighboring Uygurs. Their language is also Turkic, and is close to Uygur and Kazak.

From this brief historical account we can arrive at a few observations. First, until recently, Xinjiang was a region populated by various non-Chinese ethnic groups, the vast majority being Muslims of Turkic origin (Uygur, Kazak, and Kirgiz) who shared a close linguistic and cultural background. Second, another important minority in Xinjiang, the Hui, probably share greater affinity with their fellow Turkic Muslims than with the Han majority. Third, the remoteness and vast size of the region pose a particular difficulty for the central Chinese authorities, who seek to exercise political and military control over this strategically important region.

XINJIANG'S NATIONALITIES UNDER THE QING EMPIRE, 1753-1911

Chinese control over Central Asia and Turkistan was lost following the collapse of the Mongol Empire and the downfall of the Yuan dynasty in 1368. The Ming (1368-1644) never succeeded in restoring Chinese domination in this region. With the founding of the Manchu Qing dynasty (1644), there was a renewed interest among central authorities concerning Central Asia's strategic importance. However, it took the Manchu court another century to subdue the powerful Jungar Mongols and to establish military control over the region (1731-1760).[4]

Han Chinese farmers from the densely populated provinces in China proper were encouraged to go to northern Xinjiang. As an inducement to move, the new agricultural settlers were given free land from extensive land reclamation projects along the Ili Valley (an average of four and a half acres per family) and loans for seeds, housing, and tools, as well as short-term tax exemptions. Many Chinese merchants were also attracted to Xinjiang by the lucrative frontier markets, the low cost of living, and a favorable tax system. By the end of the eighteenth century, at least 200,000 Han Chinese immigrants had settled in areas from Urumqi to Ili.[5]

In addition to civilian settlers, there were also military colonies. Manchu banner troops and other tribespeople from the northeast and Mongol soldiers from Inner Mongolia were transferred to Xinjiang for garrison duties. When the system of rotating tours of duty was later abandoned, these soldiers and their families remained as permanent colonists.[6]

Perhaps the most curious and controversial part of the Qing colonization policy in Xinjiang was the region's use as a destination for exiles.

Convicts (in most cases serious offenders with various criminal back-grounds) were banished to Xinjiang. They spanned the entire spectrum of Qing society: scholars, bureaucrats, imperial clansmen, soldiers, pirates, merchants, farmers, sectarians, and slaves. They were punished for dif-ferent reasons and were subject to different treatments. In most cases they were allowed to bring their families. Once in Xinjiang, the convicts worked as farmers, miners, transport laborers, and clerks in low-level local gov-ernment positions.

Since the southern two-thirds of Xinjiang was economically more developed and heavily settled by Turkic-speaking Muslims, the Qing court adopted a very different policy there. It restricted Han immigration to prevent potential conflict.[7] It also limited the Manchu military presence for the sake of the sensitivity of the indigenous Turks, while the traditional leaders of the Turkic peoples were given official appointments by the Qing emperor and were encouraged to maintain close ties with the Manchu no-bility. Such a semi-feudal arrangement, however, fell short of winning the allegiance of the Turkic peoples or integrating the region into the Manchu-Chinese political structure.

Once the Manchu military power declined, the tendency by the Turk-ic peoples to seek secession increased. At times the tension between the Turkic peoples and the government was exacerbated by official corruption and oppression or by Han-Muslim disputes. The first serious outbreak of Muslim rebellion in southern Xinjiang occurred in the 1820s, and it took the Qing some years to pacify it. With Russian expansion into Central Asia after the 1840s, the Turkic nationalities in Xinjiang became more restive. By the 1860s, Muslim Hui uprisings broke out in several places in Shaanxi and Gansu. Taking advantage of the general disturbance in northwest China, Muslim Turks in Xinjiang rose in open rebellion. Several Manchu garrisons were sacked, and the Qing authorities faced the imminent dan-ger of total collapse. Under the pretext of restoring order, the Russian army occupied Ili and surrounding areas in 1871. Most observers thought that the Qing had lost Xinjiang for good.[8]

The Qing court's power was miraculously restored, however, by the efforts of General Zuo Zongtang. He led his provincial militia units first to crush the Hui rebellion in Shaanxi and Gansu (1867-1874) and then to de-feat all secessionist Turkic leaders in Xinjiang (1875-1878). Diplomatic negotiations with Russia followed and provided conditions for Russian withdrawal from Ili.[9] In a sudden burst of energy, the Qing government finally officially adopted Xinjiang ("New Territory"). In spite of the growing imperialist interest shown in Xinjiang both by Russians and by the British in India, the Qing government managed to keep control over the region, albeit precariously, to the very end of the dynasty in 1911.

XINJIANG UNDER THE CHINESE REPUBLIC, 1912-1949

The Republican Revolution in China proper created a drastically different political situation. The special ties of the Manchu court with some important national minorities were severed. The Republican government proclaimed equality among "Five Nationalities" (Han, Manchu, Mongol, Hui, and Tibetan), and the revolution rode to its victory on a tide of Han-Chinese nationalism. It is no wonder that the Tibetans and the Mongols of Outer Mongolia immediately wanted separation from the new Chinese Republic. Moreover, the Republican government soon plunged itself into a serious factional struggle that led to a time of military separatism known as the "Warlord period." The power of the central government was so weakened that only a semblance of national unity was maintained.

Xinjiang, however, did not follow the Mongolian and Tibetan examples. Part of the reason was the multiethnic nature of its population, which was not conducive to a cohesive political movement. Also, Xinjiang was made a province with regular and tighter administrative control. On the other hand, the remoteness of this region and the weakness of the central power virtually made Xinjiang a separate satrap of regional warlords during the entire Republican period (1912-1949).

With the Nationalist takeover in 1944, the discontent among the Turkic nationalities became widespread. On 7 November a major rebellion broke out at Ili. Within a few days, the Muslim rebels had seized control of the city. On 12 November they declared the formation of the East Turkestan Republic, with the proclaimed aims of establishing freedom and democracy for all indigenous nationalities and of ousting the Chinese from the ancestral land of the Turks.[10]

The Ili Rebellion (called the Ili Incident in Chinese sources) became the most serious open challenge to Chinese authorities by the Muslim Turkic people of Xinjiang since the 1860s. By the spring of 1945, the rebels controlled a sizable chunk of northern Xinjiang from the Manas river to the Mongolian border. The Nationalist government sent reinforcements and increased its military strength in Xinjiang to about 90,000 troops. The Nationalists were not strong enough, however, to impose a military solution. They turned to negotiations, which led to a truce in 1946.

The Eastern Turkestan Republic existed as a separate political entity until the downfall of the Nationalist government on the Chinese mainland in late 1949. Chinese historiography almost unanimously implicates the Soviet Union in the Ili Rebellion. A recent study by a U.S. scholar has offered a revisionist view, interpreting the rebellion as essentially an aspiration of China's Turkic minorities for freedom and independence without "international" implications.[11]

XINJIANG'S NATIONALITIES UNDER CHINESE COMMUNISM, 1949 TO THE PRESENT

After an intense period of civil war, the Chinese Communist party achieved a final victory on the mainland and founded the People's Republic of China (PRC) on 1 October 1949, with its capital at Beijing. The Communist triumph in China came as a mixed blessing to China's minority nationalities.

A few developments can be accepted as positive to the minorities. First of all, the principle of equality of all nationalities in China was clearly recognized in the state's constitution of 1954, as well as the rights of autonomy for regions with considerable concentration of minorities. By 1989, a total of 141 autonomous units had been created: 5 regions at the provincial level (Inner Mongolia, Ninxia Hui, Xinjiang Uygar, Ghangxi Zhuang, and Tibet), 31 prefectures, and 105 counties. The Autonomy Law of 1984 guaranteed considerable minority rights in social customs and tradition, education, language, and so forth.[12]

Second, the state made a conscientious effort to seek representation of minority nationalities at all levels of People's Congresses and political consultative conferences. The Party recruited and trained minority cadres in increasing numbers. The number of members of minority nationalities serving in high-ranking positions in central and provincial governments, the Party hierarchy, and the military have grown considerably.

Third, since the beginning of China's economic reforms in 1978, minority regions have been given more favorable treatment in terms of state subsidies and revenue allocation. The economically more developed provinces and cities have been made to render technical and other assistance to the underdeveloped minority regions.

Fourth, the state has given increased support to the study of the linguistic and cultural traditions of the various nationalities at various universities and institutes. Minority languages have been promoted in their respective areas, and a new Latin phonetic alphabet was introduced to replace the archaic and cumbersome scripts.[13]

Although Xinjiang benefited from these policies, the minorities of that region became concerned about the application of state and party policies in the areas of political and military control, population, religion, and economics. Unlike the previous Nationalist regime, the central government of the PRC was strong enough to achieve national unity by military means. During the last stage of the civil war, Xinjiang was peacefully "liberated" through the voluntary surrender of the Nationalist garrison forces. People's Liberation Army (PLA) units entered Xinjiang en masse from September to November 1949 and exercised effective military control over the whole of Xinjiang.[14]

With the exception of a few high-ranking officers, the Nationalist army corps, which numbered about 90,000, was not demobilized and dissolved. Instead, it was reorganized into a Colonization Army Corps (*tunken bingtuan*) to work on various land reclamation, development, and transportation projects. The soldier-workers were encouraged to raise families and settle permanently in Xinjiang.

From the 1950s on, the Chinese state has made great efforts to develop the petroleum industry in northern Xinjiang and to exploit other mineral riches in that region. Rapid industrial development in Xinjiang resulted in massive Han migration into the region, and this change has tipped the balance of the ethnic composition.

Since the establishment of the PRC, Beijing has maintained a strong military presence in frontier regions. Xinjiang was one of 11 military regions (recently reduced to 9) in China's garrison system. During the period of the Sino-Soviet rift, China reinforced its defense forces along the Sino-Soviet border. In more recent years, with the improvement of Sino-Soviet relations, China has reduced the size of the military overall; troop strength in Xinjiang has undoubtedly been reduced as well. While the presence of a strong military that is loyal to the central government may not be a guarantee for ethnic peace, it serves at least as a deterrent of major organized ethnic uprisings.

China's population policy is particularly sensitive to the national minorities. Since the late 1970s the Chinese government has systematically pursued an ambitious family-planning policy aimed at a drastic reduction in the population growth rate. The one-child family has been held up as the ideal, yet at the time of its implementation, ethnic minorities in the country were usually exempt from this policy. Among the minorities the desire to have many children is strong and common. A program of birth control promoted by a Han-dominated central government would appear as an attempt at assimilation. Such suspicions are strongest among the Muslim population in the country, particularly in Xinjiang.

State religious policy is likewise highly sensitive to national minorities in China. Although the 1954 constitution of the PRC guaranteed religious freedom for all people, the provision, like others in the same document, remained on paper, with no legal or political authority for enforcement. The source of power is the Party, and the Chinese Communist party is essentially opposed to religion. This antireligious attitude actually comes from two sources. The first is a long Chinese tradition of Confucian agnosticism. Scholars of Confucian persuasion often equated religion with superstition. The other source is Marxism-Leninism, which viewed religion as a tool of the bourgeoisie for the oppression of the working masses, and hence an opiate for the people. The problem for China is that ethnic minorities profess religions other than those of the Han. Therefore, as in Soviet Central Asia, the religious question is intimately linked to the nationality question, especially for the Muslims and the Tibetan Lamaists.

In practice, China's religious policies were discriminatory in the 1950s and extremely repressive during the Cultural Revolution (1966-

1976). Those religious policies, more than any others, were responsible for serious uprisings and rebellions in the recent past.[15] A significant change in the religious policy of Beijing began in 1978-1979.

The vigorous revival of religion in China today has confirmed the experience that religion cannot be simply dismissed. China's official policy now is quite liberal, although several potential areas of trouble with national-religious minorities remain in the areas of education, party membership, and foreign communications.[16] Even with the continued pursuit of a liberal religious policy, there is no assurance that relations between the authorities and the national minorities will remain free of conflict in this area.

A final area of worry to Xinjiang's nationalities is the state's economic policy. In the past, political repression and economic hardship resulting from the rigid collectivization drive were the main reasons why many ethnic minorities fled across the border into Soviet Central Asia. Since 1978, however, China has pursued a policy of major economic reform that has deemphasized collectivization and allowed greater individual freedom in economic activities. Xinjiang's ethnic minorities have benefited from the reform. Nearly every household has acquired modern conveniences; the evidence of relative affluence is visible in the cities of Xinjiang. The region's government is actively promoting trade with its counterpart on the Soviet side. A recent eyewitness report confirms that hotels at Alma Ata, capital of the Kazak Soviet republic, are full of Chinese trade delegations.[17]

The final question to be asked is whether economic development in Xinjiang will help to improve ethnic relations and to minimize tensions between Communist authorities and the region's national minorities. A recent interview elicited a positive response based on more religious freedom, less political restriction, and a better economic life than their kinspeople on the Soviet side.[18]

We know, however, that improvements in economic and religious life could bring higher expectations and a greater consciousness of national and religious identity. Ethnicity and religion, as the Chinese experience in Xinjiang shows, are potent forces that cannot be reined in by limited political and economic concessions. This is a common dilemma facing China and the Soviet Union.

MUSLIM MINORITY NATIONALISM: CHINA AND THE SOVIET UNION COMPARED

Notwithstanding the outward similarities between the vanished Soviet Union and China in their Muslim minority problems, the two countries differed significantly in the actual state of affairs relating to their respective Muslim minorities. The first major difference was the number of Muslim minorities in proportion to the total populations of the Soviet Union and China. While the Muslims constituted a significant portion of the population of the USSR--approximately 50 million, or 19 percent; they number a little less than 15 million, or about 1.5 percent of the total population of China. Furthermore, fully half the Muslim population in China are the Hui, who are widely disseminated in the country and are linguistically and culturally more integrated with the Han majority. Because of their diverse ethnic backgrounds and historical rivalries, China's Muslim population lacks unity and has never developed a religious nationalism to bind them together. Even the fundamentalist religious movements that occurred in the last century failed to appeal to or mobilize large numbers of the Muslim population.

The second major difference was the Muslim minority's historical relations with the central political power that is dominated by the ethnic majority in both the Soviet Union and China. The Soviet Central Asia and the Caucasus, where virtually all the Soviet Union's Muslim population are located, had been politically incorporated into Russia in the recent past. These Muslim territories were first conquered by the Tsarist Russian Empire during the second half of the nineteenth century. After a period of secession following the Russian Revolution, they were incorporated into the Communist state of the USSR during the 1920s and 1930s. China's Muslim minorities, on the other hand, all had very long historical contact with the Han majority. The most important ethnic group in Xinjiang, the Uygurs, have had more than a millennium of relations with the Han-Chinese, while others groups (with the exception of the Tajiks) also had long historical roots in China. The region of Xinjiang was first incorporated into the Chinese Empire as early as the first century B.C. Although China's control of the region was intermittent in later centuries, the Manchu Qing Empire reestablished central political control in the mid-eighteenth century.

A third difference between the Soviet Union and China was the extent of the areas inhabited by their Muslim minorities. In the former Soviet Union, Muslim regions stretch from Kazakstan in Central Asia all the way to Azerbaijan in the Caucasus, covering six nationality republics.[19] In all those republics, Muslims of non-Russian ethnic background constitute a majority of the population, sometimes overwhelmingly so. The threat of secession of the Muslim republics in the Soviet Union was real if the trend of political disintegration continued. In the case of China, on the other hand, there are only two large administrative regions where the Muslims form a majority: Ninxia and Xinjiang. Ninxia, with its majority Hui population, is surrounded by Han on three sides and borders on Mongolia in the north. It is too small and isolated to have any potential for secession. Xinjiang, therefore, is the only region where the Muslim population might have a chance to secede from China, were the nationalist aspiration strong enough. However, there are several inhibiting factors to such a development. First, the ethnic diversity of Xinjiang makes the emergence of nationalism among any of the major Muslim groups extremely unlikely if not impossible. Second, none of the major ethnic groups in Xinjiang has enjoyed political independence for any length of time in recent centuries. Thus, they lack historical experience in this area. Third, the policies adopted by the Chinese Communist government since 1949 to encourage immigration to Xinjiang have increased the Han population to 40 percent of the region's total. In some urban areas the Han have actually become the majority. The last factor is the central government's tight political control and strong military presence in Xinjiang.

In the final analysis, a comparison of the Soviet and Chinese Muslim minority problems lead one to believe that the breakaway of the Muslim republics from a disintegrating Soviet Empire was a distinct possibility, whereas the same is extremely unlikely to happen in China. This is not to say that the Muslim minorities in Xinjiang or elsewhere in China are content with their situation. They will no doubt struggle for equality and religious freedom and aspire after greater autonomy in managing their own political and economic affairs. However, it is unlikely that the Muslim minorities in China would seek open independence even if China's political system goes through a phase of radical change in the foreseeable future.

NOTES

1.   Sources of information for this section are mainly China Nationalities Commission, *Zhongguo Shaoshu Minzu* (China's Minority Nationalities) (Beijing: Renmin, 1981); and various articles in the journal *Xibei Shidi Chubanshe* (History and Geography of the Northwest).

2.   The rounded figure of 7.6 million is given in the *Far Eastern Economic Review* (August 25, 1988, p. 30), as quoted from China's State Statistics Bureau for January 1988.

3.   The Chinese customarily refer to Islam as *Hui-jiao* (the teaching of *Hui*) and Muslims as *Hui* or *Hui-min* (the people of *Hui*).

4.   Damin Sheng, "*Qing dai jinyin Ili ji*" (Qing dynasty's management of Ili) in *Xibei minzu zongjiao shiliao wenzhai: Xinjiang* (Lanzhou, 1985), 1: 389-97.

5.   Joanna Waley-Cohen, "Banishment to Xinjiang in Mid-Qing China, 1758-1820," *Late Imperial China* 10, no. 2 (December 1989): 44-50.

6.   Damin Sheng.

7.   Ibid., p. 48.

8.   Meng Yingyu, "*Ying, E, Ri jiaozhu xia zhi Xinjiang wenti*" (The Xinjiang question under the competition of Britain, Russia, and Japan) in *Xibei minzu zongjiao shiliao Wenzhai: Xinjiang* (Lanzhou, 1985), 1: 470-81.

9.   Ibid.

10.   Linda Benson, *The Ili Rebellion: The Muslim Challenge to Chinese Authority in Xinjiang, 1944-1949* (New York: M. E. Sharpe, 1990), p. 3.

11.   Ibid., pp. 136-84.

12.   Thomas Herberer, *China and its National Minorities: Autonomy or Assimilation* (New York: M. E. Sharpe, 1989), pp. 40-43.

13.   Central Institute of Nationalities, *Collection of Research Papers of Nationalities* (Beijing, 1981).

14.   Benson, pp. 175-6.

15.   These include the Muslim uprisings in Xinjiang in 1958 and 1981; the Tibetan Rebellion of 1959; and, most recently, a Muslim riot in Lanzhou in 1989. The unrest of the Muslim population in western Xinjiang in April 1990 might have been caused by religious issues as well.

16.   Chinese authorities are sensitive to the foreign connections of China's religious and ethnic minorities. They have often accused the exiled Tibetan leader, Dalai Lama, of collusion with foreign powers. After the recent arrest in Xinjiang of two Pakistani nationals, who were alleged to be operatives of Pakistan's intelligence organization, the Chinese accused them of spreading unrest in Xinjiang and protested to the Pakistani government. See *Far Eastern Economic Review*, 16 August 1990, p. 6.

17.   See the article by Ahmad Rashid, "The New Silk Road: Border Republics Strive to Increase Trade Ties," in *Far Eastern Economic Review*, 12 July 1990, pp. 26-27.

18.   Author's interview with Professor Yang Jiancheng, chairman of the History Department, Lanzhou University, Lanzhou, Gansu, China, 18 July 1990.

19.   The six nationality republics with Muslim majorities are Kazakstan, Uzbekistan, Kirgizia, Tajikistan, Turkmenistan, and Azerbaijan.

10

American and French Responses to the Lithuanian Unilateral Declaration of Independence

ALLAN LAINE KAGEDAN

On 11 March 1990, the Lithuanian Soviet Socialist Republic unilaterally declared independence from the Soviet Union. It was the first Soviet republic to take the step, and it plunged the Soviet leadership into a crisis. It also presented a major challenge to Western governments: For sound historical reasons, the West could not ignore Lithuania's bid for sovereignty.

Certain considerations militated against backing the Lithuanians. Gorbachev's historic program of economic and political reform and his "new thinking" in foreign policy had won him legions of Western admirers both inside and outside Western foreign policy communities. Foreign observers noted that, even faced with persistent ethnic strife, Gorbachev had not responded violently to Lithuania's actions. This was uncharacteristic behavior for the Kremlin. Foreigners, concluding that Gorbachev was politically vulnerable to internal conservative criticism that blamed him for the ethnic crisis, were reluctant to fuel that criticism. This chapter seeks to demonstrate how that reluctance prevailed by analyzing the responses of two Western governments--the United States and France--to Lithuania's Unilateral Declaration of Independence.

These countries were chosen because of their global or regional importance, on the one hand, and their historically contrasting policies toward the Soviet Union, on the other. France and the United States, moreover, like Lithuania, were founded through rebellion against authority, and both had ties with the pre-Soviet Lithuanian government.

Like several other Western democracies, France and the United States had refused to recognize the legitimacy of the 1940 Soviet annexation of Lithuania, leaving the door open for the recognition of renewed Lithuanian independence. That republic's Unilateral Declaration of Independence in 1990, therefore, represented a challenge to those countries to live up to their previous indications. Furthermore, it was a democratically elected Lithuanian parliament that had voted for independence. Few in the West could doubt that a majority of the republic's population, which is 80 percent ethnically Lithuanian, supported self-rule. Finally, as one of the most Westernized Soviet republics, with a significant émigré population in North America and Europe, the Lithuanian cause received wide publicity in the West, making support more tempting for Western governments.

Nonetheless, the arguments against support were powerful. Not only was the Kremlin concerned about the potential loss of an economically advanced republic, it also feared the effect of Lithuania's move on other outlying republics, a fear that proved well-founded. By May 1991, five more republics--Latvia, Estonia, Georgia, Armenia, and Moldavia--had, to varying degrees, indicated their commitment to independence and were refusing to participate in discussions regarding a new Union Treaty.[1]

By then, Western "noninterference" (meaning tacit or lukewarm support of fractious republics, including Lithuania) had become tacit policy. As late as the fall of 1991, Moscow was engaging in occasional consultations with Vilnius but was not prepared to negotiate on independence. Indeed, Moscow did not shrink from using strong-arm tactics to intimidate the Lithuanians. On 13 January 1991, Soviet Special-Purpose Police Detachments, known by the Russian acronym OMON, killed 15 civilians in Vilnius in the course of occupying a television tower that they claimed as Soviet property. In January as well, a spokesperson for a group called the National Salvation Committee said that a number of responsible Lithuanian Communist party officials (whom he refused to name) had decided that it was time to take control of the republic's government and accede to Mikhail Gorbachev's wish to retract all Lithuanian laws that were inconsistent with Soviet law. Western governments reacted with sharp rhetoric but little action. In the months that followed, OMON troops attacked Lithuanian officials who were working as customs agents on the republic's borders.[2] Indeed, at the same time that U.S. president George Bush was pleading at the Moscow summit for negotiations to permit Baltic freedom, six Lithuanian customs officials were killed, possibly by their usual antagonists, the OMON.[3] The Balts appeared stymied in their efforts to push the West to support their cause.[4] How did the Lithuanians, the Americans, and the French reach this impasse?

We must examine the period from 11 March 1990, Lithuanian Independence Day, to 29 June 1990, the day the Lithuanian parliament voted to suspend temporarily the effects of its independence declaration, following the commencement of negotiations with Moscow. During these three and a half months, both France and the United States made basic policy decisions regarding nonsupport of Lithuanian independence and, by extension, the independence efforts of all Soviet republics.

POLICY ORIGINS

Since the 1940s, France and the United States have shared a common policy toward the Baltic states. It is based on the international legal concept of the nonrecognition of the results of the forcible seizure of territory, which emerged in the eighteenth and nineteenth centuries.[5] The principle of nonrecognition posited that legal rights shall not arise from wrongdoing. Nonrecognition was bolstered during World War I by the Doctrine of the Self-Determination of Peoples, which was championed by U.S. President Woodrow Wilson. In other words, the doctrine asserted that the occupation of one state by another should be temporary and therefore should receive no sanction from the community of nations.

Until World War II, the Soviet Union, which enjoyed good relations with the independent interwar Baltic states, accepted the nonrecognition doctrine. Thus, in March 1939, the Soviet foreign minister Vyacheslav Molotov refused to recognize the German seizure of Czech and Slovak provinces.[6] As Soviet-German relations warmed, criticism gave way to collaboration. On 23 August 1939, Molotov and Joaquim von Ribbentrop, the German foreign minister, signed a pact that designated spheres of influence for each state. With German acquiescence, the Soviet Union used the pretext of an alleged Baltic military threat to occupy Latvia, Lithuania, and Estonia on 15 June 1940. On 14 and 15 July, pro-Soviet candidates were overwhelmingly "elected" in the Baltic states; in Lithuania, they won 99.1 percent of the votes. On 6 August 1940, according to Soviet sources, Lithuania was admitted into the USSR at its own request.[7]

The United States responded quickly and decisively. The government froze Baltic assets being held in U.S. financial institutions and continued to recognize the non-Soviet Baltic ambassadors in Washington, D.C. France similarly refused to recognize the Soviet annexation of the Baltic countries and left its Lithuanian embassy in non-Soviet Lithuanian hands until 1944. France also accepted Baltic assets for safekeeping, including 200 tons of Lithuanian gold bullion.[8]

After the 1940s, such nonrecognition retained profound symbolic significance for the Baltic peoples, who never relinquished their quest for independence. For Western states, however, nonrecognition gradually became more a useful rhetorical platform to criticize the USSR than an active policy measure. Practically speaking, in addition to keeping open certain Baltic embassies, the policy facilitated limited Western support for anti-Soviet guerrilla groups that were active after World War II in the Baltic region and enabled the U.S. agency that was responsible for commenting on internal Soviet affairs to broadcast via Radio Liberty to the Baltics in their local languages.[9]

In theory, the standing of nonrecognition in the postwar period was enhanced by the rising global acceptance of norms of human rights. Agreements such as the Universal Declaration of Human Rights of 1948 and the Commission on Security and Cooperation in Europe's Helsinki Final Act (an agreement signed between European leaders and the Soviet Union which created the Conference on Security and Cooperation in Europe which concerned Western recognition of Soviet hegemony in central and eastern Europe, economic and technical cooperation, and human rights) in 1975 recognize certain inalienable human rights, including the freedom of association and expression. These rights strengthen the doctrine of nonrecognition since the coercion inherent in forcible seizure of territory necessarily undermines the rights of a people to freely choose how they wish to be governed.[10] In 1974, the United States adopted the Jackson-Vanik Amendment, which linked the granting of Most Favored Nation (MFN) status to the adoption of free emigration policies by Communist countries: one of the rare instances when a human rights issue has directly influenced the foreign policy of any Western country.[11]

However, a contrary tendency, which is rooted in the Western acceptance of the (now-defunct) USSR as a superpower with legitimate interests, weakened support for the nonrecognition of Moscow's control of the Baltics. Particularly since the 1960s, when the U.S. and European governments first perceived the Soviets as potential negotiating partners, human rights considerations have often collided with arms control agreements and East-West trade in the fashioning of policy regarding the former USSR. Supporters of improved ties with the former USSR have argued that the West should not imagine altering the Soviet system. It was, they claimed, a dangerous fantasy that could fire up the arms race. Instead, the USSR should be treated as a bargaining partner which might be influenced positively on concerns like human rights as collateral issues in negotiations. This view, identified as détente, won strong support in France, which developed close ties with Moscow, but received less consistent backing in the United States.

The Helsinki Final Act of 1975, which embraced both traditional human rights and newer aspects of Western policy concerning détente, captured the ambiguity in Western policy toward the USSR. The act included chapters on "the inviolability of frontiers," the "territorial integrity of states," and "nonintervention in internal affairs," along with a section on "respect for human rights and fundamental freedoms."[12]

In 1985 Gorbachev came to power, the apparent embodiment of détente. By liberalizing cultural and economic life and changing the direction of Soviet foreign policy, he turned Western discussions of human rights in the USSR upside down. Gorbachev offered, on paper and also somewhat in practice, individual human rights to Soviet citizens. However, minority nationalities in the USSR, led by Lithuania, demanded the right to leave the Soviet Union and determine their own future. Just as freedom within the USSR seemed possible, certain people were demanding freedom from the Soviet Union and thereby, seemingly, imperiling plans for reform.

INDEPENDENCE ASSERTED

A painful choice, therefore, faced the West when, on 11 March 1990 the Lithuanian Supreme Soviet issued a declaration of independence and elected Vytautas Landsbergis as president. At first, the Soviets fired a rhetorical volley. On 12 March Gorbachev called the Lithuanian proclamation "alarming." The next day he termed the move "illegitimate and invalid." The Congress of People's Deputies endorsed Gorbachev's statement on 15 March.[13] Rebuffed by Moscow, on 17 March Landsbergis appealed for international recognition of independent Lithuania.[14] He called for an explicit statement from foreign countries that recognized the Republic of Lithuania as an independent state and moved toward the establishment of normal diplomatic relations.

Moscow quickly tightened its vise. On 18 March Soviet helicopters and jets buzzed the Lithuanian capital and Soviet technicians disrupted communications contacts with the West. Military convoys rolled through the capital, Vilnius, on 22 and 24 March. On 27 March, Landsbergis again appealed for Western support. On 3 April a Lithuanian delegation met with Gorbachev's advisor Alexander Yakovlev seeking grounds for negotiation.[15] On 9 April Gorbachev rejected a negotiation proposal forwarded by Landsbergis and announced that economic sanctions would be initiated, including an economic blockade of oil supplies, beginning on 18 April.[16] The deadlock seemed unbreakable: the Lithuanians refused to revoke their independence declaration and Moscow refused to negotiate until they did so. Meanwhile, Western support for Lithuania was not forthcoming.

During May and June, Lithuanian and Soviet leaders attempted to reach the bargaining table. The central issue was how to amend the declaration of independence: whether to revoke, suspend, or freeze it. Moscow's objective was to ensure that the Lithuanian declaration did not stand and that it remain a statement of intent rather than an operative legal document. Finally, on 29 June, the Lithuanian parliament softened its stand. After serious debate, it declared that once negotiations over independence began, it would decree a 100-day moratorium on the legal actions stemming from the 11 March declaration.[17] This compromise was made on the tacit assumption that it would lead to an end of the Soviet economic blockade.

Effectively, the Lithuanians had agreed to suspend--though by no means abandon--their drive for independence. This position was satisfactory from a Soviet point of view; the other side had "blinked" and thus had provided Gorbachev with the breathing space he craved. It allowed Moscow to lift the economic blockade, and this in turn removed Lithuania from the East-West agenda. Lithuania's inability to achieve independence unilaterally not only reinforced the diplomatic notion that such matters were internal Soviet matters but also served Moscow as a useful example for other fractious republics.

U.S. POLICY

From March to June, U.S. policymakers had struggled to balance sympathy for the Lithuanians with support for Gorbachev. To Lithuania's chagrin, the U.S. administration chose what amounted to a hands-off approach toward Baltic independence. The United States would continue to refuse to recognize Soviet annexation of the Baltic republics, but how the Balts achieved independence to be was their own affair.

As Lithuanian independence drew nearer, in January 1990, an unnamed U.S. State Department official allowed that the United States favored "peaceful movement toward self-determination." U.S. policy had become centered on the Soviet leader; there was little room left for other considerations.

Faced with the 11 March independence declaration, U.S. policymakers responded in three phases: quiet diplomacy (12 March to 4 April), public diplomacy under pressure (5 April to 28 April), and a return to quiet diplomacy (until 29 June, when Lithuania compromised).

From 11 March to 4 April, the U.S. administration avoided making extensive comments on Lithuania. Moscow, meanwhile, was firmly rejecting the Lithuanian declaration. Pushing from below, the U.S. Senate had asked the president to "consider" Lithuania's 17 March appeal for foreign recognition; the House of Representatives on 4 April urged the president to formulate a recognition plan.[18] The Soviets were comfortable with the U.S. position. On 10 April, President Bush expressed satisfaction with Gorbachev's handling of the Lithuanian crisis.

Unhappily for the U.S. administration, Moscow intensified its punitive sanctions against Lithuania. Despite the increasing pressure, Washington still refused to act. In mid-April, the administration repeated its vague warning that commercial agreements with the USSR could be affected by Soviet behavior.

The assumption that Soviet foreign and domestic policy, let alone prodemocratic national and social movements, might be undermined by Western recognition of Lithuania was dubious. It underestimated the internal pressures for change in the Soviet Union, regardless of Western action.

It was in late April, after Soviet sanctions had peaked and the United States had refrained from reacting, that tempers flared. Lithuanian president Vytautas Landsbergis compared Western actions to those taken by Neville Chamberlain in Munich (when the British Prime Minister gave in to Hitler's demands and left Czechoslovakia defenseless). President Bush replied angrily, "The policies and decisions I have taken have had strong support from the American people, and that's who I work for." Being unwilling to argue on principle, political tactics, or any other policy basis, the president's heated statement may have suggested personal discomfort with his administration's Lithuanian policy.[19]

Tensions mounted as the U.S. administration planned for a super-power summit in late May and early June. One of the centerpieces of the meeting was to be a U.S.-Soviet trade agreement, including the granting of MFN status to the USSR, which had been denied since the 1974 Jackson-Vanik Amendment. To Congress, however, it was one thing for the administration to refuse to recognize Lithuanian independence; it was another, however, to ask Congress to approve a trade deal, which was seen to be in the Soviet interest, at a time when that government was implementing punitive sanctions against Lithuania. On 27 April, nine Republican Senators criticized the administration and called on it to withdraw the trade agreement.

The U.S. administration became more comfortable with the Lithuanian independence issue when Lithuania responded favorably to, and the Soviet government endorsed, a 27 April French-German letter suggesting the Lithuanians soften their stand. On 3 May President Bush received Lithuanian prime minister Kazimiera Prunskiene but was careful to treat her as a private citizen rather than as a visiting head of state.[20] On 19 May U.S. secretary of state James Baker openly urged the Lithuanian prime minister to suspend the declaration of independence, a step the U.S. administration had been unwilling to take a month earlier.[21]

Although the Lithuanians' grudging acceptance of the Western notion of suspending their declaration disarmed the U.S. administration's critics, the projected trade treaty with the USSR continued to irritate Congress. The Bush administration cleared this hurdle by assuring it that no trade deal would be concluded as long as Lithuania was blockaded. It also informed Moscow that a precondition for congressional approval of the trade agreement was Soviet passage of a liberal emigration law (which the administration knew was not imminent). Ultimately, the president did sign the trade agreement during his early June summit meeting with Gorbachev, but he indicated that he would not forward it to Congress for approval.[22]

On 29 June the U.S. Administration breathed a collective sigh of relief when Lithuania accepted the temporary suspension of its declaration of independence. President Bush said he was "very encouraged" to see this occur. American-Soviet relations could thus progress less burdened by the Lithuanian issue.[23]

FRENCH POLICY

France's response to Lithuania's declaration of independence reflected both its long-standing policy of nonrecognition of the Soviet annexation of the republic and its determination to further its ideal of a united Europe by improving relations with the USSR. France was less reticent than the United States in articulating a policy of nonrecognition of Lithuanian independence.

Before 11 March 1990, French president François Mitterand had indicated his disinclination to address internal Soviet affairs. Early in 1990,
the French leader floated the notion of a European confederation uniting
both East and West. Mitterand suggested that the new entity would establish common rules for the protection of ethnic minorities. This system, he
believed, could satisfy Soviet and Eastern European nationalities without
altering any borders.

Thus it was not surprising that France received news of the Lithuanian declaration of independence coolly. The initial response seemed more
promising than Washington's, but the tide soon turned. While the United
States refused to recognize Lithuania on the ground that this would be
contrary to U.S. foreign policy interests, France took matters one step
further by publicly questioning the feasibility and advisability of Lithuania's
decision to become independent. The French foreign minister Roland
Dumas argued against independence; in fact, he echoed Moscow's stated
concerns for the Russian, Polish, and German communities in Lithuania
and commented on the extensive economic, administrative, and historical
links between Vilnius and Moscow. France opposed the issuing of a statement on Lithuania by NATO foreign ministers, ambiguously proposing
instead that a committee of experts be established "to assess the damage
which could be caused to Lithuania by the breaking of relations with the
Soviet Union." At the same time, France refused to return the 2.2 tons of
Lithuanian gold that it had been given for safekeeping in 1939 until, in
France's view, Lithuania had achieved independence.[24]

While the United States hesitated, at least publicly, to advise the
Lithuanians to back down, France and Germany together issued a letter
to the president of Lithuania. The letter recognized that the Lithuanian
people craved sovereignty but also pointed out that historical ties with the
Soviet Union made the achievement of sovereignty (not independence)
complicated and required dialogue. To permit these discussions to proceed, Lithuania should temporarily suspend the effects of its decision.[25]
The document was addressed solely to Lithuania, clearly indicating that it
was the Lithuanian and not the Soviet stand that should be compromised.

The letter drew praise from the Soviet Union and the United States.
Lithuanians denounced the letter in street demonstrations, but the
Lithuanian leadership, which sensed that its quest for recognition in the
West had failed, looked for a silver lining. It claimed that the letter was not
wholly bad since at least it demonstrated international concern for the
Lithuanian issue.[26]

The letter raised a storm of right-wing criticism within France. These
attacks prompted the Foreign Ministry to issue a clarification of the letter,
stating that it did not call on Lithuania to retract its independence
declaration. However, the message from Paris to Vilnius was clear:
compromise.

CONCLUSIONS

In light of past differences between France's quieter approach to human rights in the USSR and the more proactive U.S. policy, the similarity of the two nation's responses to the Lithuanian independence pronouncement was odd. Both governments refused to recognize Lithuania's action. Both were criticized from the right of their respective political spectrums, but to little effect, since Western public opinion was firmly on Gorbachev's side.

The U.S. and French positions represented a fundamental change in policy, since before 11 March 1990 both countries had refused to recognize Soviet control over Lithuania. Despite the sympathy that both the U.S. and French administrations expressed for the Lithuanians, and despite the U.S.'s warnings to Moscow against taking violent action to quell the independence drive, the failure of both countries to reconfirm this policy by supporting the demonstrated decision of the people of Lithuania amounted to a tacit recognition of the central Soviet government's decision-making role regarding Lithuania's future. The reason for this policy change was the strong desire of the United States and France to avoid harming either their own relations with the then-USSR or the political position of the Soviet president within the USSR. Furthermore, France believed that independence was not in Lithuania's best interests.

The reluctance of the United States and France to rock the boat of East-West relations is understandable, especially in light of the intense negotiations that were underway in the spring of 1990 between the United States and the USSR over arms control and German reunification. As a long-term measure, which the policy became, however, it raised several objections. First, it ignored the legitimacy of Lithuanian claims of illegal conquest, which have long been held by in the West. Second, the Western democratic tradition ought, in principle, to have left a decision about independence to the democratic process.

As for the argument that Western pro-Baltic action would have strengthened authoritarian forces in the USSR, it might have been argued with equal force that only world attention kept Gorbachev from giving in to those authoritarian forces over the Baltic question. Others replied that, in the light of the events in the Baltics in January 1991, Gorbachev joined those forces as far as the issue of independence for the republics was concerned.

The U.S. and French responses to Lithuanian independence probably assisted Gorbachev as they were intended to do: They temporarily defused an internal political problem and represented a foreign policy victory for him. They signaled that Gorbachev would have a relatively free hand in dealing with the Balts. At the same time, those responses shocked and angered the Lithuanians. Nonrecognition of Soviet control failed to translate into the recognition of Lithuanian independence. Without Western support, the Lithuanians had little choice but to compromise.

Perhaps in the context of a broader political rearrangement of the Soviet Union and a renegotiation of the terms of the Union, Moscow would have considered serious negotiation over Baltic independence. The hurdles that had to be cleared, which lie principally in the areas of dividing economic assets, negotiating Soviet troop withdrawal, and making security arrangements, guaranteed a lengthy and difficult negotiation. The Baltic leaders understood the need for Western support. More quietly since 11 March 1990, they are attempting to build economic and political ties with the Nordic countries, their neighbors and natural allies within the European community.[27] The Balts have sought and received Czechoslovakian support for their admission to the Commission on Security and Cooperation in Europe (CSCE).[28] However, as of mid-1991, these associations have not been enough to push negotiations with Moscow forward. On the internal front, the election to the Russian presidency of Boris Yeltsin, whose republic formally recognized Lithuanian sovereignty in July 1991, had provided them with a valuable internal ally.[239] Nevertheless, the Balts' timetable for rejoining Europe--and the possibility of doing so with a minimum of rancor--would be much enhanced by the creative diplomatic efforts of a broad cross section of CSCE members.

Throughout their quest for independence, the Balts have insisted that their achievement of independence represented a reassertion of sovereignty rather than the collapse of several pillars of the Soviet empire. However, in their dogged determination to gain independence, they are setting an example that will lead to an imperial unraveling beyond their own nations. Moscow understood this, as do the other republican leaders, and, in private, the Balts.

NOTES

1. *New York Times*, April 25, 1991, pp. A1, A6.

2. Salius Giurnius, "Lithuania's National Salvation Committee," *Report on the USSR* 3, no. 4 (25 January 1991): 6-8 and Salius Giurnius, "Conflicts with Soviet Troops in Lithuania," *Report on the USSR* 3, no. 20 (17 May 1991): 27-30.

3. "Gorbachev and Bush Transcripts: Dealing with a Rapidly Changing World," *New York Times*, 30 July 1991, p. A10; and Bill Keller, "Gunmen Kill 6 Lithuanian Border Guards," *New York Times*, 1 August 1991, p. A8.

4. *New York Times*, 9 May 1991, pp. A1, A12. Interviews with Andrejs Krastins, Vice-President, Latvian Supreme Council, on 18 December 1990 (Riga) and 29 April 1991 (Ottawa). Krastins has been a participant in Latvian-Soviet meetings.

5. U.S. Congress, *Hearing before the Commission on Security and*

Cooperation in Europe, The Baltic Question, Comments of William J. Hough, III, 101st Cong., 1st sess., 19 October 1989, p. 43.

6.   Ibid.

7.   Bohdan Nahaylo and Victor Swoboda, *Soviet Disunion: A History of the Nationalities Problem in the USSR* (New York: Free Press, 1990), pp. 82-87.

8.   France, "Lithuania, Reply by M. Roland Dumas, Ministre d'Etat, Minister of Foreign Affairs, To a Parliamentary Question (National Assembly, 4 April 1990), in *Speeches and Statements*, Ambassade de France a Londres, Sp.St/LON.55.90.

9.   Alexander Motyl, "Helping Gorbachev or Helping the Republics? The Unreformable Soviet Federation and the West," in *Ethnicity and the Soviet Future*, ed. Allan L. Kagedan (Ottawa: Carleton University, Norman Paterson School of International Affairs, 1991), pp. 136-37.

10.   United Nations, Universal Declaration of Human Rights, Article 21(3) in *Human Rights: A Compilation of International Instruments* (New York: United Nations, 1978), p. 2.

11.   Allan L. Kagedan, "Jackson-Vanik and Its Critics," *Freedom at Issue*, no. 97 (July/August 1987): 31-32.

12.   "Conference on Security and Cooperation in Europe: Final Act," in *Current International Treaties*, ed. T. B. Millar (New York: New York University Press, 1984), pp. 250-59.

13.   *New York Times*, 12 March 1991, pp. A1, A10. See also S. Paul Zumbakis, *Lithuanian Independence: The Re-Establishment of the Rule of Law*, Ethnic Community Services document 12 (Chicago: Ethnic Community Services, 1990), p. 70.

14.   *New York Times*, 18 March 1991, p. 5.

15.   *New York Times*, 5 April 1991, pp. A1, A16.

16.   *New York Times*, 19 April 1991, pp. A1, A10.

17.   *New York Times*, 30 June 1990, p. A5.

18.   *New York Times*, 5 April 1991, p. A16.

19.   *New York Times*, 19 April 1991.

20.   *New York Times*, 26 April 1991, p. 12.

21.   *New York Times*, 20 May 1991, p. 16.

22.   *New York Times*, 1 June 1991, p. A1.

23.   *New York Times*, 1 July 1991, p. A1.

24.   *Le Monde*, 21 March 1990, p. 4.

25.   *Le Monde*, 20 April 1990, p. 2.

26.   *Le Monde*, 28 April 1990, p. 4.

27.   Interview with Andrejs Krastins, Vice-President, Latvian Supreme Council, Ottawa, 29 April 1991.

28.   Jan Arveds Trapans, "Baltic Foreign Policy in 1990," *Report on the USSR* 3, no. 2 (11 January 1991): 15-18.

29.   R. W. Apple, "Summit Meeting May Focus on the Mideast," *New York Times*, 30 July 1990, pp. A1, A6.

11

Constitutional Crises in Two Countries: The Soviet Perception of Federal-Provincial Relations in Canada

LARRY BLACK

Outward similarities between movements for independence in Lithuania and Quebec have not gone unnoticed in the Canadian press. As Gorbachev prepared to visit Canada in May 1990, on his way to a summit meeting with George Bush in Washington, Canadian newspapers were filled with cartoons poking fun at the troubles faced by both the Canadian and Soviet governments.[1] The fact that Gorbachev's rest stop in Ottawa was preceded by a visit from Kazimiera Prunskiene, Prime Minister of Lithuania, made this point even better than the caricatures. However, a headline in the Toronto *Globe and Mail*, "Canada Offers Lithuania Constitutional Expertise," probably caused more hilarity than reflection among its readers. More to the point, perhaps, were simultaneous cover stories in the U.S. magazine *Time* and Canada's *Maclean's* on 12 March 1990: "Soviet Disunion" (*Time*) and "Canadian Crisis" (*Maclean's*). Both carried dramatic depictions of crumbling structures, in *Time's* case, a giant red star, and in *Maclean's* case, a large map of Canada.

Neither scholarly nor facetious comparisons were normal practice for the Soviet press for a variety of reasons, not least their traditional reluctance to appear to be sinking in the same boat as a government from a "different social system." Nevertheless, a study of Soviet writing about the federal-provincial relationship in Canada and its "nationality crisis" (phenomena that the Soviets see as interchangeable) might reveal certain interesting patterns and initiative preferences that the Soviet observers could not help but apply to their own situation.

We shall examine here the way in which Soviet scholars and journalists perceived the situation in Canada, in particular the federal-provincial relationship.

Soviet writers were drawn to the question of "separatism" in Canada since 1926, when an important Soviet journal of international affairs carried a long article on the subject.[2] Movements for autonomy on the part of Quebec and also of the Western provinces, the potential for interference by both the United States and France, and the likelihood of the disintegration of the British Empire (and an imperialist war to protect it) were pondered at length. The author suggested that many French-Canadian leaders preferred to remain within the British Empire in order to be protected from the Anglo-Canadians and the Americans by British legislation. His main theme, however, was the inevitability of a U.S. "economic conquest of Canada" unless various progressive forces in the latter country acted soon in their country's defense.

In the period following World War II, Stalinist views of world affairs assumed the intensification of a "crisis in capitalism" generally and a U.S. drive for world hegemony in particular. In world affairs, Canada was deemed to be little more than a U.S. satellite.[3] All domestic issues in Canada, not least federal-provincial relations, were seen to be shaped by pressures from the United States or as issues of a class struggle until the 1960s, when direct U.S. military expansion into Canada seemed less likely and Soviet-Canadian relations were normalized. It was in the early 1960s that Soviet writers began to examine the French-English dialogue as a serious threat to Canadian unity and therefore as a relationship that might help undermine Canada's resistance to U.S. economic and political expansion. In November 1964 a lead article in *Izvestiia* asked whether Canada would soon disintegrate. Its author said that Canada was no longer a confederation, that all the provinces were going their own way, that separatism was very strong in Quebec, and that a number of immigrant groups were opposed to both "Anglo-Saxon and French" domination. If Quebec separated, the author said, the United States would pick up the pieces, with the Maritime provinces the first casualty.[4] If there was any anxiety in the USSR about this trend, the potential for U.S. gain was its sole cause. The only element in Canada that seemed to be opposed to this trend, according to many Soviet writers of the time, was the Communist Party of Canada (CPC), whose role and influence were vastly exaggerated. Indeed, up to that time, most of the publications on Canada in the USSR were translations of works by CPC members. Moreover, the 1964 viewpoint did not differ much from the message presented in 1926.

In 1968, however, Soviet scholars, journalists, and officials discovered a non-Communist "white knight" on the Canadian political scene, Pierre Elliot Trudeau. From that time until this day, Soviet writing-- especially in journalism--about federal-provincial relations in general and English-French relations in particular can, in many ways, be termed "Trudeau-watching."

The year 1968 was doubly important to Soviet Canadianists because that was the year that Rene Levesque broke with the Liberals and formed his own political party in support of "sovereignty-association." Thus, there appeared in the Quebec political arena a "mass party of the middle class, with a programme similar to the European social-democrats," whom Marxist-Leninists long had regarded as their chief political opponents. The *Mouvement Souverainete-Association*--later the *Parti Quebecois* (PQ)--was deemed, therefore, to be a "petty-bourgeois, reformist" group that threatened the perceived leadership role of the CPC among Quebec's workers.[5]

Trudeau's appeal to Soviet officialdom and theoreticians during the 1970s was a consequence of his Canadianization and "Third Option" policies, both of which delighted Soviets with their anti-American side effects. The crisis of 1970, marked by the imposition of War Measures Act, saw Soviet writers searching for explanations.[6] The Soviet press deplored acts of terrorism perpetuated by the FLQ and followed the CPC line in insisting that the solution to Canada's dilemma lay in strengthening Canadian unity and tempering it by alleviating the social and economic conditions of Franco-Canadians.[7]

Trudeau and the Quebec government were congratulated for their behavior in "Canada's time of crisis" and blame for the 1970 events was cast on U.S. and Canadian monopoly capital. Trudeau's much-publicized state visit to the USSR in 1971, which Soviet writers saw as a break in the bloc solidarity of the West, helped assure that his policies at home would be given the benefit of the ideological doubt in Soviet writing.[8] From the Soviet perspective at the time, the merits of Canadian unity, which came to be personified in Trudeau, were summed up as follows: "The struggle for Canadian unity will provide the best conditions for a successful struggle on behalf of Canadian independence and against Canadian and American monopoly imperialism. This can be made possible only be means of a unified working class."[9]

Although the perceived injustices faced by Francophones in Canada were discussed from time to time, the PQ usually was depicted as a political exploiter of the situation rather than an advocate of change for "progressive" reasons.[10] Nevertheless, Soviet scholars noted seeds of economic disintegration in Canadian confederation during the latter quarter of the decade. The growth of separatist tendencies in western Canada also attracted their attention.

In the late 1970s, when Trudeau established a Committee for National Unity and Levesque prepared a referendum on sovereignty-association, the "crisis in Canadian confederation" was treated in part as a battle between two personalities. This was an unusual approach for Marxist-Leninist writers. The "No" vote in the Quebec Referendum of 1980 was described as a great "Trudeau victory." The sources of the general crisis, however, were found almost entirely in economic conditions, and Levesque's loss was attributed mainly to "Canada's big business leaders," who did not want to see the "French-Canadian bourgeoisie strengthened."[11] Thus, the ideological framework tended to emerge supreme even as late as 1985, when an essay on the repatriation of Canada's constitution (1980-1982) again featured Trudeau prominently, but found its explanation for events mainly in a CPC statement.[12]

When Trudeau lost an election for the second time, in 1984, S. F. Molochkov wrote his political epitaph. Trudeau was a warrior against internal division and foreign encroachment. The mark of his success was the fact that Quebec had not separated and Canada had not split into a number of pieces "doomed to be devoured by the United States." Molochkov warned, however, that although separatism had declined, the conditions that generated it might have worsened. It was Trudeau's policy of Canadianization and his willingness to associate with the USSR, rather than his federalist policies, that generated Molochkov's closing observation to the effect that Trudeau was "one of the greatest figures in Canadian history."

A much more detailed study on Canada's internal policies, under Molochkov's general editorship, appeared in 1986. In a chapter entitled "The Franco-Canadian Problem and Canadian Federation," N. B. Bantsekhin concluded, "The fact that the federal government was not able . . . to solve the economic, political, and social causes of the crisis . . . gives cause to assume that a new outbreak of the Franco-Canadian problem will erupt again very soon."[13] In summarizing the book itself, Molochkov wrote that Canada's "ruling circles" had constantly to direct their attention to three separate but linked conflicts: labor and capital, nationality issues, and federal-provincial relations.[14] These were long-standing conflicts, he said, but each seemed to have reached some kind of watershed by the mid-1980s.

The labor movement, which had been making slow but steady gains in its struggle for decision-making roles in the social and economic affairs of Canada, was now faced by a new government headed by a prime minister who was experienced as a negotiator on the side of business. Moreover, in the Soviet view, Brian Mulroney was a proponent of "tripartism," a "smokescreen" through which government could pretend to allow labor to participate.

The second conflict was over the question of Canada's future as a unified country. Molochkov described the growth of national feeling among "Franco-Canadians" as a movement of social-democracy against the "bourgeois ruling circles," that is, the "Anglo Canadians." However, the victory of a separatist party in Quebec in 1976 had, for the Marxist-Leninists, the inevitable result. The "petty-bourgeois" Pequistes moved to the right and separatism declined when an economic downturn made them aware of the "benefits of federalism." Nevertheless, Molochkov predicted that the Mulroney government would, in all likelihood, soon alienate the "Anglo-Canadian bourgeoisie" by making "further concessions" to Quebec, thereby reestablishing an atmosphere conductive to the reemergence of Quebec separatism.

The third conflict in Molochkov's scheme of things was a struggle for economic power among three elements of the bourgeois class: the federal government; Ontario, the stronghold of the "old" bourgeois economic power, which controlled federal policy-making; and members of the bourgeoisie from the western provinces, who were attempting to control their own natural resources. While Trudeau's Liberals were in power, the central powers had been weakened somewhat, but Mulroney's sweeping Conservative victory of 1984 and the dominance of Conservative governments in the provinces had created such an imbalance of forces that all the "preconditions" for a further deterioration of federal powers were deemed to be in place. The overall strength of the Conservatives, a party "not naturally committed" to a strong central government, and with much of its strength in the West, would be bitterly opposed to any special rights and privileges for Quebec.[15] The implication was that Mulroney would lose control of the course of events.

Most of Molochkov's predictions proved to be accurate, despite the fact that most Canadian historians would not have accepted his ideological premises. Similar predictions had been offered already in 1978 by V. A. Kachenov, one of the USSR's most prolific writers on Canadian federalism. However, Kachenov focused on regional disparities as the most pressing problems of Canadian federalism.[16] These two writers have described Canada's situation as typical of bourgeois, capitalist societies, but with characteristics unique to Canada. In contrast to other federated states, Canada's problems were exacerbated by the proximity of an economically aggressive United States. In fact, before 1989 no Soviet scholar or journalist suggested seriously that Canada's problems might be endemic to large, multicultural states in which the relationship between Center and components was not clearly defined.

Let us turn now to a sampling of Soviet press versions of the Canadian situation. In October 1989 a professor of juridical sciences in Moscow ruled Canada out as a useful model for a renewed Union Treaty in the USSR. She insisted in *Pravda* that the Soviet republics already "enjoy broader rights" than any Canadian province, including "the right to withdraw from the Soviet federation."[17] She was contradicted a few weeks later by Leon Bagramov, head of the Canadian Section of the Institute of the USA and Canada, who said in an interview for a Canadian paper that the Canadian example was "important" to the USSR.[18] Bagramov noted that "all disputes on ethnic problems [in Canada] are handled in a polite manner." Although the Soviet press failed to draw direct parallels between the situations in Canada and the USSR, there were many newspaper reports on Canada in 1989 and 1990 that could be taken as Aesopian commentary on the interethnic situation in the USSR.

As the situation changed in 1990, the All-Union Soviet press regularly noted the increased support for separatism in Quebec and no longer spoke of the Canadian situation in such glowing terms.[19] Moreover, in late June, Shal'nev wrote that Quebec would have a very difficult time surviving economically without the good will of both the United States and Ontario, a remark that certainly would be applicable to many Soviet republics if they moved to independence status.[20]

In one area of federal-provincial relations, however, Soviet observers were surprisingly consistent; that is, on the question of the rights and claims of native peoples against the federal government. Protests by native peoples in Canada were catalogued by Soviet journalists, who wrote about the terrible conditions in which many of the former lived. Still, the issue tended to be treated as an economic, rather than a constitutional, problem, and the question of native traffic in drugs, cigarettes, alcohol, and gambling tended to receive pride of place.[21] In short, the traditional outpouring of sympathy for Canada's native peoples as victims of bourgeois imperialism had diminished considerably.

While the All-Union Soviet press was regularly describing the ongoing confrontation between government agencies and Canadian native peoples, commentators in some important regional papers turned to Canada as a model. In a recent piece for the *Tyumenskaia Pravda*, for example, Y. Konev (Regional Executive Committee) and A. Ushakov (Head of Section for Northern Peoples), lauded the Canadian system for allowing the native peoples "eternal" use of certain land, including the right to develop it for their own use as long as environmental protection and the reservation system generally are assured.[22] The article was part of a major debate underway in Tyumen (Northwest Siberia) over control of local natural resources. As economic power devolved to regions in the RSFSR, the inhabitants of the vast Tyumen region, which produced a large percentage of Soviet oil, wished to claim a more favorable share of the income from their resources. However, the rights of native peoples in this regard remained unclear.

Aside from the journalists who wrote on specific events related to nationality issues in Canada, and aside from the Soviet scholars who took a specific interest in Trudeau, there were a number of Soviet researchers who studied federal-provincial relations in Canada. These individuals tended to look at broader issues and drew rather disparate conclusions. Let us conclude our search for patterns in Soviet writings about federal-provincial relations by turning to two specific Soviet works on the subject, one written at the beginning of Gorbachev's era and the other in 1990.

In a monograph on Canadian federalism and international relations printed during Gorbachev's first year as CPSU general secretary, V. E. Shilo characterized the "current stage" of world development as a "deepening general crisis of capitalism."[23] The crisis in Canadian federalism was interpreted almost entirely in terms of long-standing Marxist-Leninist positions: the increased economic integration of Canada and the United States, and a concomitant weakening of internal trade and economic links, had led to demands for provincial autonomy and a move toward decentralization in Canada. Mulroney's election in 1984 was seen as a watershed in a process of decentralization that had already begun when the provinces began to play autonomous roles in international trade.

In a fairly recent Soviet scholarly article on nationality relations in Canada, however, L. V. Pozdeeva and V. A. Koleneko presented quite a different perspective on federal-provincial relations.[24] They ignore the United States altogether and pay only slight lip service to long-standing ideological preferences. Instead, the authors provide readers with a detailed history of the French-English relationship in Canada, describe the political structures of Canada and the individual provinces, and divide the problem rather rigidly into a conflict between proponents of the "diametrically opposed positions" of centralism and decentralization. In their introduction, they point out that the growth of "ethnic groups" (namely; other than French or English) complicate the issue since they have come to comprise nearly one-third of the population. However, Pozdeeva and Koleneko drop the issue. In their conclusion, they insist that "the future of the country depends on the official recognition of its two-nation character."[25]

The Liberals, according to these Soviet writers, are centralists, and the Conservatives are decentralizers. However, in contrast to earlier scholarly or journalistic Soviet commentary, Pozdeeva and Kolenko credit the Conservatives with a "more positive and realistic position in relation to the Quebec problem."[26] In contrast to Soviet observers in the 1960s, they see "sovereignty association" as it was presented by Rene Levesque in 1976 as a means to provide a stronger union between the "two Canadian nations" and "not a plan for separation [from Canada]" (sovereignty association proposed political sovereignty with economic association). Moreover, Brian Mulroney was awarded indirect praise by these two writers for speaking against "the political ridgity of centralization" during his 1982 campaign. Writing before the collapse of the Meech Lake Agreement in the spring of 1990, they described the 1987 proposal as a victory for the "decentralizers."[27]

Pozdeeva and Koleneko drew no comparisons whatsoever to similarities--or even differences--between the Canadian and Soviet situations. However, they made it clear that they support decentralization, and they repeated verbatim Shilo's argument of 1985 to the effect that "strong bureaucratic centralization and attempts by a government in the center to subordinate fully the components of federation inevitability lead to crisis in bourgeois federalism."[28] At the same time, they warned against extremism and noted the irony of a Francophone minority that fights for its own language and other rights in Canada but opposes such rights for minorities within its own midst.

What can one conclude from this survey of Soviet discussions of Canada's federal-provincial situation? In the first place, certain interesting patterns remain consistent. Rarely would one see a comparative observation from Soviet writers, unless the comparison could clearly be drawn as a sign of the superiority of the "socialist system." It seemed that ideology mitigated against such analogies.

U.S. involvement in Canadian affairs was no longer featured in Soviet deliberations about federal-provincial relations in Canada, perhaps because the "Free Trade" debate exhausted the issue or perhaps because Soviet economic thinking swung naturally in favor of regional integration. Nevertheless, Russian preferences--and the individuals noted here were Russians--for strong central government and interethnic and interrepublic calm and cooperation rang clear throughout. The tradition of the press as an educating forum might have been undermined by the recent trends of *glasnost*, but the pedantry of Soviet observations about Canada was still plain to see.

EPILOGUE

The relationships between the Center and the republics in the former USSR have changed dramatically since this chapter was prepared in October 1990, and the Soviet vision of federal/provincial relations in Canada has shifted accordingly. More data has been forthcoming on the impulses for separation in Quebec, and most Canadian polls on the growing percentage of Quebecers who support independence were reported. Direct comparisons with the USSR remained rare, however, unless Soviet writers were reacting to negative Canadian statements about the situation in the USSR. Moreover, every Soviet piece on Canada's federal-provincial relations stressed the acceptance, even by separatists, of the principle of economic interdependence. This pattern remained consistent as increasing numbers of Soviet writers cited the example of Canada as a country faced with internal division but coping because of increased economic and "modernizing" pressures for integration.

The first detailed item in the press to compare the Canadian and Soviet crises in federalism directly came only in May 1991, when the RSFSR Communist party paper, *Sovetskaia Rossiia*, attributed the apparent casualness toward the possibility of Quebec separating on the part of Anglophones to the fact that Canada was a "nation of immigrants." This was a starting point for the author's contention that Canadians were incapable of understanding the Soviet stress on unity. He drew many parallels between Quebec and the Baltic states and used every Canadian argument to the effect that Quebec should not separate as justification for opposing Baltic separation. After listening to a representative of Canada's Department of External Affairs explain his department's official position on the USSR, the Soviet journalist wrote, "If I replaced the words 'Soviet Union' with 'Canada,' and 'Baltic states' with 'Quebec,' then Quebec certainly would be free."[29]

Amid the cacophony of calls for and against sovereignty and independence in the USSR, the widespread interethnic violence, and the ups and downs of the debate over a new Union Treaty, Soviet writers who sought foreign examples from which to draw helpful analogies could turn only to Canada. Canada is the second largest country in the world. It is multicultural, with nationality problems of its own and a federal/provincial relationship that has been debated hotly for more than a century. However, the mirror image can be unsettling as it loses focus. Proponents of a renewed federation in the USSR who pushed Canada to the forefront in the late 1980s as an encouraging model for their own country to emulate might have seen events in Canada as an ill omen for unity at home.

NOTES

1. See, for example, *Windsor Star* (24 May 1990); Ottawa *Citizen* (29 May 1990); Toronto *Globe and Mail* (17 May 1990).
2. Yu. Konitsyn, "*Proiskhozhdenie i formy kanadskogo separatizma*," *Mezhdunarodnaya zhizn'*, no. 8 (1926): 30-41.
3. On this subject, see J. L. Black, "The Stalinist Image of Canada: The Cominform and Soviet Press, 1947-1955," *Labour/Le Travail* 21 (Spring 1988): 153-72.
4. "*Raspadiotsia li Kanada?*" *Izvestiia*, 19 November 1964. Premier Buchanan (now senator) of Nova Scotia was quoted as saying the same thing this summer.
5. See, for example, O. S. Soroko-Tsiupa, "*Iz istorii franko-kanadskogo natsional'nogo voprosa*," in *Natsional'nye problemy Kanady*, Ys. P. Averkieva, ed. (Moscow, 1972), pp. 126-227.
6. See, for example, *Sel'skaia zhizn'*, 20 October 1970; *Komsomol'skaya pravda*, 28 October 1970; *Pravda*, 29 October 1970; and *Literaturnaya gazeta*, no. 45, 4 November 1970. An essay by Sam Walsh, the head of the CPC in Quebec, was printed in several Soviet newspapers; see *Pravda Ukrainy*, 25 October 1970; and *Leningradskaya pravda*, 25 October 1970.
7. In 1970, the *Front de Libération du Québec* (FLQ) kidnapped British Trade Commissioner James Cross and the Federal Minister of Labour and Immigration, Pierre Laporte (who was subsequently found murdered). Pierre Trudeau's federal Liberal government imposed the War Measures Act which enacted martial law throughout the country.
8. On this visit, see David Farr, "Prime Minister Trudeau's Opening to the Soviet Union, 1971," in *Nearly Neighbours: Canada and the Soviet Union from Cold War to Detente and Beyond*, J. L. Black and Norman Hillmer, ed. (Kingston, Ontario: R. P. Frye, 1989), p. 102-115.
9. *Canadian Tribune*, 6 February 1971, quoted in Soroko-Tsiupa, p. 131; see also *Canadian Tribune*, 14 October 1970.
10. See, for example, V. E. Shilo, "*Bor'ba za sokhranenie kanadskoi konfederatsii: Poiski kompromissa*," *SShS* 5 (1979): 54-65.

11.   See, for example, N. V. Bogacheva, V. V. Popov, "*Eknonmiche-skie osnovy krizisa kanadskoi konfederatsii*," *SShA*, 6 (1980): 52-56.

12.   N. I. Kochegarova, "*Velikbritaniya i novaia kanadskaya konstitutsiya (1980-1982 gg)*," in *Velkobritaniya, Frantsiya i SShA mezhdunarodnykh otnosheniyakh novogo i noiveishego vremeni* (Moscow, 1985), pp. 84-105.

13.   S. F. Molochkov, ed. *Sovremennaya vnutrennyaya politika Kanady* (Moscow, 1986), p. 149.

14.   Molochkov, pp. 216-218. Molochkov is the head of the History Section of the Canadian branch of the institute.

15.   Molochkov, pp. 5-6.

16.   V. A. Kachenov, "*Federalism v Kanade*," in *Sovremennyi burzhuaznyi federalizm* (Moscow, 1978), pp. 125, 127. See also V. A. Kachenov, *Kanada: Aktual'nye problemy* (Moscow, 1973).

17.   N. Mikhaleva, "*Eto plenuma: Sud'ba nashei federatsii*," *Pravda*, 18 October 1989.

18.   Ottawa *Citizen*, 5 December 1989.

19.   *Izvestiia*, 4 May 1990; *Izvestiia*, 18 May 1990; *Sovetskaia Rossiia*, 27 June 1990.

20.   Shal'nev, "*Konstitutsionny krizis v Kanade. Vyzhivet li kvebek?*" *Izvestiia* (25 June 1990).

21.   See, for example, *Pravda*, 12 May 1990; *Pravda*, 16 May 1990; *Pravda*, 24 May 1990; *Pravda*, 5 July 1990; *Izvestiia*, 20 July 1990; *Sovetskaia Rossiia*, 22 July 1990.

22.   Yu. Konev and A. Ushakov, "*Avtonomiia: Mify i realnost*," *Tymenskaia pravda*, 1 September 1990.

23.   V. E. Shilo, *Kanadskii federalizm i mezhdunarodnye otnosheniia* (Moscow: Nauka, 1985), p. 3.

24.   L. V. Pozdeeva and V. A. Koleneko, "*Mezhnatsional'nye onosheniia v Kanade*," *Novaia i noveishaia istoriia*, no. 1 (1990): 35-47.

25.   Ibid., p. 47.

26.   Ibid., p. 44.

27.   Since Quebec had not signed the 1982 Constitution Act, the Meech Lake Accord, proposed by the Mulroney government, included amendments to secure Quebec's assent to the Constitution. Quebec's premier, Robert Bourassa, proposed a number of federal powers be transferred to the provinces and asked for Quebec to be recognized as a distinct society. A number of provinces severely criticized what they perceived as the federal governments capitulation to Quebec's demands. Newfoundland, Manitoba, and (until the last minute) New Brunswick refused to sign the Accord and, after the deadline had passed for its recognition on 24 June 1990, the Accord was scrapped.

28.   L. V. Pozdeeva and V. A. Koleneko, p. 43; Shilo, p. 14.

29.   S. Dukhanov, "*A kak tam v Kvebeke! Kanadskii podkhod k suverenitetu u nas i u sebia doma*," *Sovetskaia Rossiia*, 31 May 1991.

Suggested Reading

Alexeyeva, Ludmilla. *Soviet Dissent: Contemporary Movements for National, Religious and Human Rights*. Trans. Carol Pearch and John Glad. Middletown, CT: Wesleyan University Press, 1987.

Allworth, Edward. "A Theory of Soviet Nationality Policies." In *Soviet Nationality Policies--Ruling Ethnic Groups in the USSR*, ed. H. R. Huttenbach. London: Mansell, 1990.

Amel'chenko, V. V. *Shkola zhizni*. Moscow: DOSAAF, 1978.

Ammosov, A. A. "*O Yakutskoi natsional'noishkole i ee vupusknikakh*." *Voenno-istoricheskii zhurnal*, no. 1 (1986).

Bergmann, H., J. Smilga, and L. Trotskii. *Die russische sozialistische Rote Armee*. Zurich, 1920.

Black, J. L., ed. *Soviet Perception of Canada 1917-1987. An Annotated Bibliographic Guide*. Vol. 1. Kingston: R. F. Frye, 1989.

Black, J. L. "The Stalinist Image of Canada: The Cominform and Soviet Press, 1947-1955." *Labour/Le Travail* 21 (Spring 1988).

Bociurkiw, Bohdan R. "Nationalities and Soviet Religious Policies." In *The Nationalities Factor in Soviet Politics and Society*, ed. Lubomyr Hajda and Mark Beissinger. Boulder, CO: Westview Press, 1990.

Bushnell, John. "Peasants in Uniform: The Tsarist Army as a Peasant Society." *Journal of Social History* 13 (1980).

Chan, F. Gilbert. "Regionalism and Central Power: Sheng Shih-ts'ai in Sinkiang, 1933-1944." In *China at the Crossroads: Nationalists and Communists, 1927-1949*, ed. Gilbert Chan. Boulder, CO: Westview Press, 1980.

Chengzhi, Chen. "*Xinjiang de Mianji he jenkou*." In *Xibei minzu zongjiao shiliao wenzhai: Xinjiang*. Vol. 1. Lanzhou, China; 1985.

"*Chitaite Konstitutsiiu SSSR!*" *Baltiiskoe Vremia*, 5 March 1991.

Chiuko, L. V. *Braki i razvody*. Moscow, 1975.

Curran, Susan L., and Dmitry Ponomareff. *Managing the Ethnic Factor in*

the Russian and Soviet Armed Forces. An Historical Overview. Rand
    R-2640/1. Santa Monica, CA: Rand Corporation, July 1982.

d'Encausse, Hélène Carrère. *Decline of an Empire: The Soviet Socialist
    Republics in Revolt.* New York: Newsweek, 1979.

Dreifelds, Juris. "Latvian National Demands and Group Consciousness
    since 1959." In *Nationalism in the USSR and Eastern Europe in the
    Era of Brezhnev and Kosygin,* ed. George W. Simmonds. Detroit,
    MI: University of Detroit Press, 1977.

Erzunov, M. M. *Praporshchiki i michmany.* Moscow: Voenizdat, 1973.

France. "Lithuania." Communique Issued by the Ministry of Foreign Affairs,
    12 March 1990. In *Speeches and Statements,* Ambasade de France
    à Londres, Sp.St/LON/41/90.

France. "Lithuania." Reply by M. Roland Dumas, Ministre d'Etat, Minister
    of Foreign Affairs, To a Parliamentary Question (National Assembly,
    4 April 1990). In *Speeches and Statements,* Ambassade de France
    à Londres, Sp. St/LON.55.90.

Frunze, M. V. *Izbrannye proizvedeniia.* Moscow: Voenizdat, 1977.

Gleason, Gregory. *Federalism and Nationalism: The Struggle for Repub-
    lican Rights in the USSR.* Boulder, CO: Westview Press, 1990.

Goble, Paul. "Central Asians Form Political Bloc." *Radio Liberty Report on
    the USSR,* 14 July 1990.

Goble, Paul. "Ethnic Politics in the USSR." *Problems of Communism* (July-
    August 1989).

Gorbachev, Mikhail. *Perestroika: New Thinking for Our Country and the
    World.* London: Collins, 1987.

Heberer, Thomas. *China and Its National Minorities: Autonomy or Assi-
    milation?* New York: M. E. Sharpe, 1989.

Henze, Paul B. "The Spectre and Implications of Internal Nationalist Dis-
    sent: Historical and Functional Comparisons." In *Soviet Nationalities
    in Strategic Perspective,* ed. S. Enders Wimbush. London: Croom
    Helm, 1985.

Hovannisian, Richard G. "Caucasian Armenia between Imperial and Soviet
    Rule: The Interlude of National Independence." In *Transcaucasia:
    Nationalism and Social Change,* ed. Ronald Grigor Suny. Ann Arbor,
    MI: University of Michigan Slavic Publications, 1983.

Jones, David R. "The Soviet Defence Burden Through the Prism of His-
    tory." *The Soviet Defence Enigma: Estimating Costs and Burdens,*
    ed. C. G. Jacobsen. Oxford: SIPRI/Oxford University Press, 1988.

Jones, David R. "The Two Faces of Soviet Military Power." *Current History*
    86 (October 1987).

Jones, Ellen. *Red Army and Society. A Sociology of the Soviet Military.*
    Boston: Allen and Unwin.

Jones, Stephen F. "Nationalism and Religion in Georgia and Armenia since
    1965." In *Religion and Nationalism in the USSR and Eastern Eur-
    ope,* ed. P. Ramet. 2nd rev. and exp. ed. Durham, NC: Duke Uni-

versity Press, 1989.

Jones, Stephen F. "Soviet Religious Policy and the Georgian Orthodox Apostolic Church: From Khrushchev to Gorbachev." *Religion in Communist Lands* (Winter 1989/90).

Kachenov, V. A. "Federalism v Kanade." In *Sovremennyi Burzhuaznyi federalizm*. Moscow, 1978.

Kachenov, V. A. *Kanada: Aktual'nye problemy*. Moscow, 1973.

Kagedan, Allan L. "Jackson-Vanik and Its Critics." *Freedom at Issue*, no. 97 (July/August 1987).

Karaca, Ahmet. "*Azerbaycan Milli Hareketinin Ideolojik Karakteri*." *Milli Egitim Dergisi*, no. 7 (1980).

Karasik, Theodore, and Brenda Horrigan. "Gorbachev's Presidential Council." RAND Publication-7665. Santa Monica, CA: RAND Corporation, August 1990.

Khaturin, F., and A. Shchelokov. "Lieutenants: Sociological Portrait." *Soviet Military Review*, no. 7 (1969).

Khomenok, F. A. *Pravovye voprosy sluzhby v Sovetskie Vooruzhennykh Silakh*. Moscow: DOSAAF, 1977.

Kipp, Jacob W., and W. Bruce. "Autocracy and Reform: Bureaucratic Absolutism and Political Modernization in Nineteenth Century Russia." *Russian History* 1, no. 2 (1979).

Kochegarova, N. I. "*Velikobritaniia i novaia kanadskaya konstitutsiya 1980-1982 gg.)*." In *Velikobritaniya, Frantsiya i SShA v mezhdunarodnykh otnosheniyakh novogo i noiveishego vremeni*. Moscow, 1985.

Konitsyn, Yu. "*Proiskhozhdenie i formy kanadskogo separatizma*." *Mezhdunarodnaya zhizn'*, no. 8 (1926).

Lang, David Marshall. *The Armenians: A People in Exile*. London: George Allen and Unwin, 1981.

Libaridian, Gerard J. "Revolution and Liberation in the 1892 and 1907 Programs of the Dashnaktsutiun." In *Transcaucasia: Nationalism and Social Change*, ed. Ronald Grigor Suny. Ann Arbor, MI: University of Michigan Slavic Publications, 1983.

McAuley, Mary. "Party Recruitment and the Nationalities in the USSR: A Study in Centre-Republican Relationships." *British Journal of Political Science* 10 (January 1980).

Matuszewski, Daniel C. "Nationalities in the Soviet Future: Trends under Gorbachev." In *Gorbachev and the Soviet Future*, ed. L. W. Lerner and D. W. Threadgold. Boulder, CO: Westview Press, 1989.

Motyl, Alexander. "Policing Perestroika: The Indispensable KGB." *Harriman Institute Forum* (August 1989).

Motyl, Alexander J. "The Sobering of Gorbachev: Nationality, Restructuring and the West." In *Politics, Society and Nationalism inside Gorbachev's Russia*, ed. Seweryn Bialer. Boulder, CO: Westview Press, 1989.

Motyl, Alexander J. *Will the Non-Russians Rebel? State, Ethnicity, and*

Stability in the USSR. Ithaca, NY: Cornell University Press, 1987.

Naby, Eden. "Tajiks Reemphasize Iranian Heritage as Ethnic Pressures Mount in Central Asia." *Radio Liberty Report on the USSR,* 16 February 1990.

Nahaylo, Bohdan. "Nationalities." In *The Soviet Union under Gorbachev,* ed. Martin McCauly. New York: St. Martin's Press, 1987.

Nahaylo, Bohdan, and Victor Swoboda. *Soviet Disunion: A History of the Nationalities Problem in the USSR.* New York: Free Press, 1990.

Peters, C. J. "The Georgian Orthodox Church." *Eastern Christianity and Politics in the Twentieth Century,* ed. P. Ramet. Durham, N.C.: Duke University Press, 1988.

Peters, C. J., and B. Nahaylo. *The Ukrainians and the Georgians.* Minority Rights Group; Report No. 50. London: Minority Rights Group, 1981.

Pozdeeva, L. V., and V. A. Koleneko. "*Mezhnatsional'nye otnosheniia v Kanade.*" *Novaia i noveishaia istoriia,* no. 1 (1990).

"*Priem v Kremle v cheste vypushnikov voennykh akademii.*" *Krasnaia zvezda,* 2 July 1974.

Rakowska-Harmstone, Teresa. "Dialectics of Nationalism in the USSR." *Problems of Communism* (May-June 1974).

Rakowska-Harmstone, Teresa. "The Soviet Army as the Instrument of National Integration." In *Soviet Military Power and Performance,* ed. John Erickson and F. J. Feuchtwanger. New York: Archon, 1979.

Rashid, Ahmad. "The New Silk Road: Border Republics Strive to Increase Trade Ties." *Far Eastern Economic Review,* 12 July 1990.

"The Referendum Scorecard," *The Economist,* 23 March 1991.

Ro'i, Yaacov. "Islamic Influence on Nationalism in Soviet Central Asia." *Problems of Communism* (July-August 1990).

Rtischev, P. "*Leninskaia natsional'naia politika i stroitel'stvo Sovetskikh Vooruzhennykh sil.*" *Voennoistoricheskii zhurnal,* no. 6 (1974).

Saroyan, Mark. "The 'Karabakh Syndrome' and Azerbaijani Politics." *Problems of Communism* (September-October 1990).

Schroeder, Gertrude E. "Nationalities and the Soviet Economy." In *The Nationalities Factor in Soviet Politics and Society,* ed. Lubomyr Hajda and Mark Beissinger. Boulder, CO: Westview Press, 1990.

Shanidze, Nino Candelaci. "*Godebis cedeli marti 1956.*" *Mamuli,* no. 1 (June 1989).

Sheehy, Ann. "Armenia Invokes Law on Mechanics of Secession." *Report on the USSR,* RFE/RL, 15 March 1991.

Sheng, Damin. "*Qing dai jinyin Ili ji.*" In *Xibei minzu zongjiao shiliao wenghai: Xinjiang.* Vol. 1. Lanzhou, China; 1985.

Shilo, V. E. "*Bor'ba za sokhranenie kanadskoi konfederatsii: poiski kompromissa.*" *SShA* 5 (1979).

Simon, Gerhard, ed. *Nationalism and Policy toward the Nationalities in the Soviet Union: From Totalitarian Dictatorship to Post-Stalinist Society.* Trans. Karen Forster and Oswald Forster. Boulder, CO: Westview

Press, 1991.

Smith, Graham, ed. *The Nationalities Question in the Soviet Union*. New York: Longman, 1990.

Solchanyk, Roman. "Beginnings of the Ukrainian Popular Front: An Interview with Pavlo Movchan." *Report on the USSR*, RFE/RL, 28 July 1989.

Soroko-Tsiupa, O. S. "*Iz istorii franko-kanadskogo natsional'nogo voprosa.*" In *Natsional'nye problemy Kanady*, ed. Yu. P. Averkieva. Moscow, 1972.

Sporzuk, R. "Dilemmas of Russian Nationalism." *Problems of Communism* (July-August 1989).

Strong, Anna Louise. *Peoples of the USSR*. New York: Macmillan, 1944.

Swietochowski, Tadeusz. *Russian Azerbaijan 1905-20--The Shaping of National Identity in a Muslim Community*. Cambridge: Cambridge University Press, 1985.

Taheri, Amir. *Crescent in a Red Sky: The Future of Islam in the Soviet Union*. London: Hutchinson and Co., 1989.

Trapans, Jan Arveds. "The Sources of Latvia's Popular Movement." In *Toward Independence: The Baltic Popular Movements*, ed. Jan Arveds Trapans. Boulder, CO: Westview Press, 1991.

Tsypkin, Mikhail. "The Conscripts." In *The Soviet Union Today: An Interpretative Guide*, ed. James Cracraft. Chicago: Bulletin of the Atomic Scientists, 1983.

United Nations. "Universal Declaration of Human Rights." Article 21(3) in *Human Rights: A Compilation of International Instruments*. New York: United Nations, 1978.

U.S. Congress. *Hearing before the Commission on Security and Cooperation in Europe. The Baltic Question. Comments of William J. Hough, III*. 101st Cong., 1st sess., 19 October 1989.

Waley-Cohen, Joanna. "Banishment to Xinjiang in Mid-Qing China, 1758-1820." *Late Imperial China* 10, no. 2 (December 1989).

Walker, Christopher J. *Armenia: The Survival of a Nation*. New York: St. Martin's Press, 1980.

Walker, Christopher J. "Between Turkey and Russia: Armenia's Predicament." *The World Today* (August September 1988).

Wimbush, S. Enders. "The Ethnic Costs of Empire." In *Soviet Nationalities in Strategic Perspective*, ed. S. Enders Wimbush. London: Croom Helm, 1985.

Zakharov, I. Z. "*Sovetskie Vooruzhennye Sily na zashchite natsional'nykh i internatsionnal'nykh interesov narodov SSSR.*" In *Uchenye zapiski kafedr obshchestvennykh nauk vuzov Leningrada: Istoriia SSSR*, 13.

Zenkovsky, Serge A. *Pan-Turkism and Islam in Russia*. Cambridge, MA: Harvard University Press, 1967.

Zumbakis, S. Paul. *Lithuanian Independence: The Re-Establishment of the Rule of Law*. Chicago: Ethnic Community Services, 1990.

Index

About the Editor and Contributors

MIRON REZUN, born in Israel, is Professor in the Department of Political Science at the University of New Brunswick in Canada. He has published widely on the Soviet Union and the Middle East. His articles have appeared in *Etudes Internationales, International Journal, Queen's Quarterly*, and *Problems of Communism*. He has also written for *Agora* and *Le Monde* and he has published articles for the Centre Québécois des Relations Internationales in Quebec City. His *The Soviet Union and Iran* has been called the definitive study of Soviet-Iranian relations during the Reza Shah period. In addition, he has edited *Iran at the Crossroads: Global Relations in a Turbulent Decade* (1990). In 1992, both *Intrigue and War in Southwest Asia* and a highly controversial book called *Saddam Hussein's Gulf Wars: Ambivalent Stakes in the Middle East* came out with Praeger Publishers in Westport, Connecticut.

LARRY BLACK is a Professor of History at Carleton University and has written or edited 12 books on Russian and Soviet historiography, education, foreign policy, and Canadian-Soviet relations. The most recent of these are *Nearly Neighbours: Canada and the Soviet Union from Cold War to Detente and Beyond* (1989); *G.-F. Muller in Siberia, 1733-43* (1989); and *Soviet Perception of Canada, 1917-1987* (1990). He is currently working on an encyclopedia of Soviet nationalities. Formerly Director of Carleton University's Institute of Soviet and East European Studies in Ottawa (1982-1990), he is now Director of Carleton's Centre for Canadian-Soviet Studies.

FUAT BOROVALI, a Turkish Muslim, has published several articles in Canadian and U.S. journals, including *The Iranian Journal of International Affairs*. He wrote a chapter for *Iran at the Crossroads* (1990), and teaches at Bilkent University in Ankara, Turkey. He is a world expert on the Kurds in Iran, Turkey and Iraq.

GORDON BROWN, born in Montreal, is a staff auditor in the Office of the Auditor General in Canada.

JURIS DREIFELDS, born in Latvia, is currently Associate Professor at Brock University in St. Catharines, Ontario. He has published several articles in journals and a number of chapters in books, including articles in *Problems of Communism, Baltic Forum,* and *The Journal of Baltic Studies.*

KURT NESBY HANSEN is a Major in the Canadian Armed Forces. He is currently completing his graduate work in political studies at the University of New Brunswick in Canada.

BOHDAN HARASYMIW, of Ukrainian descent, is Professor of Political Science at the University of Calgary in Alberta. He has published on the subject of elite recruitment in the Soviet Union, as well as on ethnic representation in the Communist party. Harasymiw has worked under contract for the Canadian Security Intelligence Service (CSIS) in Ottawa, Ontario. He is working on a manuscript dealing with the roles of Communist party officials and is a member of the ongoing workshop on Soviet nationalities at the Center for East-West Trade at Duke University in North Carolina.

DAVID JONES is Professor of History at Acadia University in Nova Scotia, Canada and Director of the Russian Micro-Project at Dalhousie University, Nova Scotia, Canada. A scholar of Russian and Soviet military history, he is editor of *Soviet Armed Forces Review Annual* and the *Soviet Military Encyclopedia.* He received his doctorate from Dalhousie University and is a visiting scholar at the U.S. Naval War College.

STEPHEN JONES is presently Assistant Professor in the Program of Russian and Soviet Studies at Mount Holyoke College, Massachusetts. He is the author of numerous articles on Georgia and on nationality politics in the USSR. His dissertation on the independent Georgian Democratic Republic from 1918-1921 will shortly be published in book form. Currently, he is completing a book entitled *Twentieth Century Caucasia,* due to be published in 1992.

ALLAN LAINE KAGEDAN serves as Adjunct Professor in the Institute of Soviet and East European Studies at Carleton University, Ottawa. In 1990-1991, he was the Post-Doctoral fellow at Carleton's Norman Paterson School of International Affairs and an Associate of the Centre for Canadian-Soviet Studies. He has coedited *The Status of Minorities under*

International Law (1988) and contributed a chapter on Soviet federalism to *Soviet Nationality Policies* (1990). Kagedan, who has been a policy advisor to the Canadian government, is currently engaged in research on linguistic politics in multiethnic societies.

LAWRENCE SHYU is Professor of History at the University of New Brunswick in Canada. He previously taught in Hong Kong and New York. He has published widely in the area of Chinese history, most recently with articles in *China Insight, East Asia Insight,* and *Proceedings of the Conference on Overseas Chinese.*